WOOD

FOR WOODTURNERS

WOOD

FOR WOODTURNERS

REVISED EDITION

MARK BAKER

First published 2016 by
Guild of Master Craftsman Publications Ltd
Castle Place, 166 High Street
Lewes, East Sussex, BN7 1XU

Text © Mark Baker, 2004 and 2016
Copyright in the Work © GMC Publications Ltd, 2016

ISBN: 978-1-78494-126-0

First published in 2004; reprinted 2006
ISBN: 978-1-86108-324-6

Publisher Jonathan Bailey
Production Manager Jim Bulley
Senior Project Editor Sara Harper
Editor Stephen Haynes
Managing Art Editor Gilda Pacitti
Designer Chloë Alexander
Photographer Anthony Bailey, except as listed on page 184
Illustrator Simon Rodway

Set in MankSans, Interstate and Adobe Caslon
Colour origination by GMC Reprographics
Printed and bound in China

CONTENTS

ABOVE
Vase in masur birch
(Betula alba) *by*
Mark Baker

Introduction

We turners love exploring shapes and forms and using timbers that allow us to show everything off to its fullest potential. Wood, for many people, has a warmth, a vibrancy and a certain quality that no other material can mimic. Have you noticed that people can rarely resist touching a wooden article?

Timber always amazes me and I love the fact that no two pieces are truly the same. The amazing variety of colours and figuring that wood exhibits – burr, crotch, ripple, spalting, quilting, roe, wavy – all intrigue me; and let's not forget that we can also explore (with care) timber with natural bark edges, bark inclusions, splits and wormholes. All this provides ample variety to keep me exploring for the rest of my turning career.

This book is by no means a treatise of turning techniques – there are many fine books available to provide help with that. Nor can a reasonably sized book possibly cover every type of wood available and detail every aspect of working it. It does, however, provide a practical guide to over 150 woods from around the world, to help take out some of the guesswork should you have the pleasure of working with those listed.

Practical experience and observations

I have included a wide variety of species that are available from specialist importers and retailers, and some trees you are likely to encounter from friendly tree surgeons or from your friends' and neighbours' gardens when they want to clear some space. All the woods listed are ones that I have had the pleasure of turning. I must admit that it has been a pleasure to turn many different timbers, but some turn more easily than others, and in some cases I loved the end result but did not much enjoy the process of getting there – especially with the dusty timbers. But I always

love exploring something new. I would point out that turners are experimenting ever more with their work and a lot has changed since I wrote the first edition of this book. People are now regularly doing other things to their work, both on and off the lathe.

This includes colouring the wood, carving, texturing, piercing, routing and so on. I have included the carving, staining, dyeing and routing characteristics of the timbers where applicable, to give a little more rounded information for you should you wish to explore such options in your work.

A lot of technical data has been published elsewhere, but this is mostly confined to the more readily available timbers, and the information is chiefly aimed at those involved in the construction industry, where considerations of load bearing and shock resistance are important. Much of this information is irrelevant to turners, which is why this book came about.

I do not profess to be a scientist: like you, I am a turner. I have tried to give information about each wood that is important to turners, such as its name, weight, size and any specific known health risks. Working with wood poses some health implications due to potential toxins within the timber, lichen on the bark, fungal infections and, of course, fine particle dust inhalation. I have tried to list the known and verified information available for each timber, and precautions must be taken to minimize personal risk as far as possible.

Some timbers list the possible health risks as 'not known'. This means nothing else is verifiably known, apart from the risks associated with dust. *All dust produced from*

BELOW
Befriend your local tree surgeon. This eucalyptus is bound to supply pieces of interest to a turner

working with timber is potentially hazardous to health, and all means should be employed to minimize exposure to and inhalation of it. That typically means dust extraction at source, to get rid of the dust as close as possible to where it is generated, as well as personal protective equipment (PPE) such as suitably rated dust masks or respirators. Chips, dust and potentially a piece of wood coming off the lathe are also hazards, so think about protecting your eyes and face, too.

I have added my own observations on what the wood feels like to turn. The book's editor, Stephen Haynes, mentioned when reading the descriptions of wood that the terms used reminded him of a journalist describing wine: 'This spalted piece is precocious, bordering on petulant.' This made me laugh, and I realized that his comments were very close to the truth. When describing the colours, I have tried to use terms that will strike a chord with most people, but who is to say that we all view colour in the same way? Some of my comments are bound to be subjective, but hopefully they will serve to indicate what you are likely to encounter in your own wood turning ventures.

Wood classification

I have listed the common names of each wood, but these vary a lot from place to place and can cause confusion, so I have also included the scientific or Linnaean name, which is

ABOVE
A respirator with full face protection makes turning safer and more enjoyable

usually in Latin or Greek. The advantage of this is that these terms are standardized worldwide so as to identify unambiguously each type of tree, and types that are closely related are placed in family groupings. Most of us do not need to know the full botanical classification, so this book gives only the two most important categories: genus and species. The genus denotes a particular group within the family, and the species is the individual type within the group. Walnut, for instance, is given the generic name of *Juglans*, but the species name will identify exactly what kind of walnut we are talking about: for example, European walnut is *Juglans regia* (genus and species names are always written in italics), while American black walnut is *Juglans nigra*. The wood lists in this book are in alphabetical order according to the Linnaean names, which makes it easier to see which woods are closely related to one another.

Appearance of timber

The pictures in this book show, as far as possible, typical examples of the woods concerned. That said, every piece of wood is different, even when they come from the same tree, and colouration, grain and figuring will all vary. Woods darken or mellow with age and exposure to light, and will change again with the application of a finish – sometimes to a spectacular degree – so when you go and buy a piece of wood it may be quite a bit darker or lighter than the specimen shown. A little tip is to buy a small piece and apply the finish of your choice to it to see how it will look once finished. It can save you a lot of money if the colour change is not what you wanted.

There will also be colour variations due to the printing and photographic processes used in the book – sadly, there is no way that technology can match the diversity of rich, subtle variations that nature creates. The pictures, though, will provide a good indication of what you are likely to find.

Using timber responsibly

There are timbers in this book from various countries and regions around the world, including tropical rainforests. Sustainability is a key issue nowadays: we must consider how the extraction of threatened species can be properly managed, monitored and certified as legal. The carbon footprint of transporting timber is also important. No matter where you live, it is worth considering carefully what timber you use and where it comes from. Even if it is from your own area or country, it could still be threatened as a species, and may be illegal to cut down and use. And even woods that are not officially listed as endangered should be avoided if there is any suspicion that they may have been obtained from old-growth or otherwise unsustainable sources.

The symbols below right used in the Woods in Brief section of the book (see page 118) give a rough-and-ready indication of which species should be avoided, but there are two international organizations that can give you much more detailed and up-to-date advice. One is CITES (the Convention on International Trade in Endangered Species of Wild Fauna and Flora). Its website (www. cites.org) lists endangered species under three categories, and the difference between these is explained on the page 'The CITES Appendices'. The other organization you

ABOVE
Small pieces like these can be made from timbers that are not usually regarded as commercial, perhaps even garden species. The ones shown have been made from both commercial and non-commercial timbers

RIGHT
Trees and bluebells in a local woodland. Provided wood is harvested responsibly, our descendants can continue to enjoy scenes like this

should be aware of is the International Union for the Conservation of Nature, which publishes a 'Red List' of species under threat (www.iucnredlist.org). Both these sites allow you to search for any species by name, and both are updated frequently, so the information published there may well supersede the indications in this book.

The laws applied in various countries concerning the import and export of timber, and the international awareness of sustainability issues, have changed immensely since the first edition of this book appeared, and the subject is far too complex to be considered in detail here. Various international organizations are working with governments to help them use their timber resources responsibly. Some, such as the Forest Stewardship Council (FSC), will certify timber that has been managed and harvested in accordance with best working practice and international guidelines. If you plan to make wooden objects for export, you will need to find out what form of certification is required by the importing country. That country's customs service may be a good place to start.

When you read inspirational books and admire things made from lovely timbers from faraway places, I encourage you to be aware of what you are using, of the potential impact on the environment, and to fully explore the timbers that are native to your locality. I bet you have not tried them all yet. Learn how to use these to their fullest potential before trying species from further afield, most of which will carry a price premium.

I hope that the information in this book is helpful, and wish you well in the wonderful journey that is woodturning.

Key to symbols

| no info | not at risk | slight concern | concern | vulnerable | threatened | endangered |

Buying and seasoning wood

Timber varies in its growing habits, working qualities, appearance and price. This is especially true of figured pieces such as burrs (burls), crotches and rare timbers from far-flung places, which can be expensive.

Selecting and buying wood is, for many, a daunting but fascinating experience. There are so many ways in which the unwary can be caught out and make expensive mistakes: by buying the wrong timber or sizes for the job they want to do, failing to prepare or season it properly, or simply being lured by the lovely looks of some pricey piece of wood when they are just starting out and do not yet have the skills to get the best from the timber.

What to bear in mind

The primary considerations when buying timber are to work out what you want to make, what the item is for, what size it will be and what other techniques, if any, you are going to use on the piece. If you want to carve, colour, pierce or rout, the wood needs to be able to be worked in such a manner. If you are creating a piece in order to show off its form and shape to the fullest, you might want a

BELOW
A selection of turned work by Mark Baker

bland-looking timber so there are no visual or tactile extras to distract from the clean look. If you want to use a highly figured piece of wood for your work, consider how much fine detail you want to have – will there be clashes visually between the high figuring and the detail? If an item is totally sculptural and solely to be looked at, then select a timber that has the working qualities you need to create the desired shape, detail, appearance and feel.

If the finished piece is to hold edible items, then the choice of timber is very important, as is the finish selected. You want a strong timber that does not splinter or fracture easily on the edges, so it can withstand the rough and tumble of use, and which does not have pores or fissures in which the food can play peek-a-boo (nor will you want to place unnecessary details such as beads or coves in areas that will become food traps). You also need to choose both a wood and a finish that are not harmful, will not taint the edible items placed inside, are easy to clean and withstand staining.

You need to ask yourself a lot of questions when planning to make something, and they all have a bearing on what wood you eventually select.

Sources of wood

Woodyards and specialist timber suppliers offer a wide selection of timber, as do local park and forestry authorities. Check the Internet for suppliers near you – there are many excellent suppliers around the world.

Friendships with tree surgeons are also well worth cultivating. It is worth noting that many tree surgeons have to pay to dump or dispose of the timber they cut down. If they know that you want timber, then they may be willing to let you know what they have, and even transport it to you instead of the tip. Some of my tree surgeon friends will also cut pieces to a more manageable size for customers. This is a must for me, as I simply don't have the space for a whole tree in my

front garden and I certainly don't have the equipment to break down a tree properly. Instead, I arrange an amicable payment for the wood and the time taken to cut it and get it to me.

As in most things, it is vital to get to know the people we are doing business with – many friendships develop over the years, to mutual benefit. I trust implicitly the timber suppliers I use and their knowledge is invaluable. The wood suppliers I buy from will give me a call when they get something special in. Like many woodworkers, I will happily travel many miles for something 'special' – especially when I get the call to say that the wood I have been hunting for has finally arrived.

Experience is the only way to learn how to spot faults and potential problems – just as practice is the only way to get better at turning, fishing, golf or any other activity. If we don't practise, we don't learn and develop. It is imperative that we take the time to understand what a piece of wood is truly worth – not only monetarily, but as the raw material of our craft – and how the asking price of the wood relates to the potential value of the finished product.

BELOW
Tree surgeon cutting a tree trunk into manageable sections

How to buy

There are numerous ways to buy timber, but the first things to consider are: what do you need in order to make what you intend to make, and how frequently do you turn? There is no point in buying a tree if you only turn five projects a year – no matter how little the wood cost you.

Buying a felled tree or part of a trunk

Without doubt the least expensive way to buy wood is as a log or trunk – sometimes it is even free. But there are a number of problems when buying wood in this way, beginning with the cost and time factors involved in transporting it. You need space, too. And once you have it, you need access to the appropriate machinery to cut it to the required size, and the knowledge of how to convert it and season it. You also have to have the equipment, workers and strength to move potentially large sections of wood around safely, and storage space for the resulting cut wood.

What you want from your timber is going to dictate how it is sectioned up. So, are you doing mostly bowls and platters (often termed

ABOVE
Spindle work timber sections and turnings

BELOW
Blanks for bowl/ faceplate work, and some finished articles

'faceplate work') and, if so, how thick and wide will they be? Or are you mainly doing goblets, boxes, vases, chair and table legs, table lamps or similar ('spindle' or 'between centres' work?). For this work, you have to decide how thick and how long these will be.

Conversion

The process of sawing trees or logs into smaller sections is called 'conversion'. Things to consider before you cut the wood are not only what you are going to be turning, but your strategy for making use of the wood: will you go for maximum yield, opt for the best cuts to yield the most stable timber, or will you cut the wood to show off any figuring to its maximum potential? Of course, all these considerations must be balanced against the need to minimize wastage – though wastage during conversion is never entirely predictable. The most common configurations for converting whole logs are illustrated in the Glossary of terms on page 23.

You must also learn how to spot potential faults and figuring so you can work out what is the best route to take. You will want to avoid splits, shakes, rot and so on, which may not be evident from the outside. You also want to recognize areas that may have attractive figuring, and to judge how extensive they are likely to be.

Then, once you have cut your tree into sections – usually into boards – you need to season them and minimize any degrade while doing so. It is a huge learning curve and a

ABOVE
A section of a tree trunk ready for milling

BELOW
A log being sawn into boards

potentially costly one at the outset, in terms of both equipment and timber wastage. But if you turn a lot and possibly want to sell timber too, then this route provides you with a lot of options. It gives you total control over how the wood is cut, and there is a massive cost saving – once you have learnt the ropes and acquired the equipment – over buying converted and seasoned timber.

Having said all that, I know of only about 30 turners who do this on a regular basis. Most turners do not do enough work or have enough time or space to justify this approach.

Buying boards

The next cheapest method is to buy sawn boards, which are available in various widths and thicknesses, depending on the species and how the board is cut. Through-and-through-cut boards are the cheapest – this is where a tree is sliced horizontally through its length. The most expensive option is planed, predimensioned boards of specific widths, lengths and thicknesses. Either kind can be bought partially seasoned or kiln-dried, and wastage is reduced compared to buying a tree and converting it yourself.

The downside for the turner is that because the tree has been transported, stored and then worked on at the woodyard, there is a price premium to cover the supplier's time and other costs. And because the board's surface is fully visible, the dealer will be fully aware of the extent of any special figuring and will charge you a premium accordingly.

Typically, boards are available in thicknesses of 1–4in (25–100mm), but larger sections may be cut to special order.

ABOVE
Boards stacked and ready for inspection

ABOVE RIGHT
Racks of prepared blanks for turners and carvers

RIGHT
Boxwood (**Buxus sempervirens**) *and yew* (**Taxus Baccata**) *sold as sections of branch or small trunks. The left-hand boxwood section has split*

Many professional and hobby turners buy wood this way. Some go direct to timber suppliers and ask for boards to be cut to a given size when a tree becomes available, while others will buy a thickness of board that will suit a wide variety of projects. When you buy a whole board, make sure you like the timber and are prepared to work with it on

ABOVE
Boards racked and
ready for purchase

a number of projects. Buying boards gives you maximum flexibility in how the wood is cut. Boards are also simple to store, but unless the wood is kiln-dried, further drying will be necessary once you get it home.

Buying predimensioned blanks

The most expensive way of buying wood is as predimensioned blanks or sections, which are available in a large array of sizes, either partially seasoned or kiln-dried. These are ideally suited for the amateur who requires only a few pieces in a year, or for those who are after a small piece of something special – a burr, perhaps – for a one-off project. The plus points to buying wood this way are that the pieces are usually planed and sealed so that you can see exactly what you are buying, faults and all. Blanks can also be bought at a size that is close to your requirements, so that storage is easier and takes little space – depending, of course, on how many blanks you keep in stock. Blanks are the most expensive option because the woodyard has converted and dimensioned the tree trunks (thereby incurring wastage), sanded the surface and possibly also seasoned the wood. But this will save you the time and cost of doing it yourself.

Some timbers may be sold as small branches. These can be useful, but be careful of the splits that can occur during drying.

Drying wood

There is not space here for more than a brief outline of the problems involved in choosing wood and preparing it for use. For comprehensive explanations and theory, I particularly recommend *Wood and How to Dry It*, by the editors of *Fine Woodworking* magazine (Taunton Press, 1986), and R. Bruce Hoadley's *Understanding Wood* (2nd edition, Taunton Press, 2000).

Wood moves, and this is caused by various factors, but typically, 'movement' is a general descriptive term for the various ways in which wood shrinks and distorts as it seasons, due to moisture loss or the relief of inherent stresses within the wood. As we shall see, this is more important for some projects than others.

Seasoning is the process by which 'stable' timber is created. It reduces the moisture content, but also relieves the inherent stresses in the wood so as to minimize the likelihood of movement when it is placed in the environment in which it is to be used. Dry wood is more dimensionally stable than wet (green) timber. When seasoned, a wood's strength, hardness and stiffness increase by 50% compared to green wood.

Wood can be obtained in one of three states: wet, partially seasoned or kiln-dried.

Wet wood

Wood from trees that have been freshly cut has a very high moisture content and is said to be wet or 'green'. (The term 'green' does not refer to the colour of the wood; it just means that it is wet.)

Partially seasoned wood

This is wood that is not fully dried. More often than not this refers to timber that has been air-dried rather than kiln-dried, but it may apply to wood that has not been seasoned or dried to the moisture content required for the place in which it will eventually be situated. In the UK, for example, air-dried wood often has a moisture content of 15% or higher, depending on how long it has been cut and stored, whereas the average moisture content in a centrally heated room is 8–12%. When the moisture content in a piece of wood exceeds that of its immediate environment, it is deemed to be partially seasoned, and is liable to show further movement.

ABOVE

Turning wet wood is great fun. Note the distinctive ribbon-like shavings

Air-drying or air-seasoning is a process in which felled timber – usually after conversion to specific sizes – is placed to dry in the open air, relying on a combination of airflow, atmospheric humidity and the ambient temperature of the surroundings to reduce the moisture content of the wood slowly. Usually the wood is protected from direct sunlight and rain by some form of cover over the top, but the sides are left open to allow the air to pass through unhindered. The pieces are stacked on top of each other, and uniformly sized sticks or 'stickers' are placed between them at regular intervals to create gaps through which the air can pass; this stickering is essential to make sure all the wood is exposed to the drying air. Air-drying can only reduce the moisture content to a limited extent: in the UK, for example, the equilibrium moisture content of air-dried timber is deemed to be about 15–20%, depending on the local climate and humidity level.

LEFT
When wet-turned items dry, distortion and movement will happen to varying degrees. This goblet decided to twist and warp, and lean over

Turning wet and partially seasoned wood

The methods I use for turning and stabilizing wood have been used successfully by turners around the world – with tweaks to suit their local environment – for many years. These will hopefully give you the basis for working out what you need to do. I typically buy boards and predimensioned blanks, but also have sections of logs and branches.

Working with wet wood

Wet or 'green' turning is the process of turning freshly cut or unseasoned wood. Wet timber is very enjoyable to turn – large shavings and a lot of water are produced instead of chippings and dust – but, to reduce the likelihood of splitting, the item should be turned to a thin, even wall thickness. Excessive or uneven thickness will cause differential drying rates across the work, and the resulting tension and stress is likely to cause splits. Make sure that the water spraying from the work does not come into contact with any electrics; water on steel is not good either. Sometimes I have ended up wearing a showerproof jacket, such was the water content of the wood.

You can stabilize wet wood by rough-turning, as described below. But you can, if you prefer, turn wet wood from start to finish (taking it down to a thin, even wall thickness as mentioned above), then sand it while wet and let it dry as it will. If you choose this method you will have to be prepared for the wood to move unpredictably – sometimes a lot, sometimes not much at all and, occasionally massively, in an organic, uncontrollable way. Provided the wood thickness is nice and even and drying occurs at an even rate, the wood will move without splitting. Once dry, sand with very fine abrasive and apply a finish of your choice.

Kiln-dried wood

Kiln-drying is a process that uses a heated chamber, operated by gas, electric or solar power, to dry the wood to a predetermined moisture content. Some woods need to be air-dried before they are kilned, to prevent degrade; others can be kilned immediately after conversion from the log. The best results are obtained when the pieces in the kiln are of a uniform size or thickness; otherwise each piece will respond differently and dry at different rates. Each species of wood requires a specific drying regime in order to produce stable timber that does not degrade during drying. Kiln-dried wood can vary in its moisture content, but it is usually taken down to 10% by this process. However, if the wood sits around for a long while after being taken out of the kiln, it will suck moisture back in from the atmosphere in which it is sitting.

Rough-turning

When work is turned from solid timber, whether wet, partially seasoned or kiln-dried, movement occurs for two reasons: moisture loss and tension release. The removal of the central core will release some of the stresses inherent in the wood, which is likely to twist a little – or a lot, depending on the species. Rough-turning, also called twice-turned work, is a technique used to ensure that wood is fully seasoned and as dimensionally stable as possible before final turning, so any movement in the finished piece will be minimal.

When rough-turning, decide on the wall thickness you want on your finished piece and then add 10–15% of the overall blank diameter. Some woods which have a higher shrinkage rate may need a greater percentage (up to 20%) of the overall blank diameter to be added.

First turn the external profile of the work piece to approximately the required shape of the finished item. Then reverse the work and hold it on a chuck or faceplate while turning the inside to mimic the external shape, leaving the appropriate thickness needed while creating an even wall profile. Be warned that if the external and internal wall shapes are uneven, the differential moisture loss, uneven shrinkage rates and different tensions that occur mean there is a highly increased likelihood of the wood splitting and cracking.

Moisture is lost fastest through the endgrain, and if you live in a hot or arid environment you may find the wood drying out too fast, in which case coating the rough-turned piece with PVA adhesive will help to retard and even out the drying process. (The late Bert Marsh first introduced me to this highly effective technique.) With some woods it is sufficient to only coat the endgrain surfaces. An alternative approach is to seal the rough-turned piece in a plastic bag. Every two or three days, take the piece out, turn the bag inside out, and reseal. This creates a very controlled humidity level and ensures slow, even drying.

Once the rough-turned piece is dry, remount it on the lathe and turn the outside, sand and finish as appropriate, then mount it in a chuck, finish-turn the inside, and sand and finish that. If all goes well, you should have a nicely dry and stable turning.

This technique is especially important when you are making boxes or other items

BELOW
Rough-turning allows the wood to dry evenly and distort as it does so. Providing you have left enough thickness, you should be able to get something from it when it is finally dried out and turned to finished size

with close-fitting lids, where movement may prevent the lid from fitting properly; and in segmented work, where the tensions may cause glue joints to break.

I am able to rough-turn most of the woods I work (depending on the intended result) and then let them season in my workshop, weighing the wood regularly to monitor the drying process; once the weight has stabilized, it is ready to be finish-turned. However, much depends on the climate where you live. An arid climate will suck the moisture from wood very quickly, probably causing splits. Conversely, those working in areas of high humidity will need to find a way of drying the timber to suit the environment in which it will be used. Please bear in mind when reading this book that I cannot know all the conditions you are likely to encounter, and can only speak of my own situation and the techniques that work for me.

Drying wood in a workshop is OK, provided there is enough air movement to remove humidity and moisture in the air.

Remember also that some workshops are very cold and damp, and have a different climate from a house, which probably has central heating. My workshop has some

heating but usually sits at about 46–54°F (8–12°C); it has two air vents to provide some circulation. Some turners I know, having dried their rough-turned blanks in the workshop until they lose no more weight, then place them in a cool room in the house for a while to try and stabilize them further.

Storage and handling
Please do not be tempted to lift anything that is very heavy on your own – it's surprising how much even small pieces of timber can weigh when wet. It gets even trickier if you are trying to cut it to size or mount it on the lathe on your own. Always seek help to hold or lift (or use specialist lifting or holding equipment) when dealing with awkwardly shaped or heavy pieces of timber.

If the wood is damp or wet, always ensure that there are gaps between the pieces being stored; this will permit airflow and reduce the likelihood of fungal staining and decay. It is best to do that with drier wood, too.

If you have to store pieces on the floor, make sure that it is not damp. If you are unsure about this, place a few wooden stickers on the floor and lay the pieces on this; it is best practice to do this anyway.

BELOW

A rough-turned bowl (left) and one that has been re-turned on the outside after drying. Note the difference in wall thickness, which highlights the amount of movement that has occurred during the seasoning process

A glossary of woodturning terms

Every art, craft or profession uses special words to describe processes, concepts and techniques specific to their own work. These can be confusing to anyone just starting out and may act as a barrier to better understanding. In this book, technical or descriptive terms are explained in down-to-earth words and, where necessary, pictures. Hopefully, you will these find helpful.

ANNUAL RINGS or **GROWTH RINGS** The concentric rings of wood added yearly to the growing tree; in wood from temperate zones these are visibly distinct.

BEVEL-RUBBING TOOLS Tools in which the bevel of the blade is kept in contact with the wood during the cutting process, and serves as a primary control point of cutting. The main examples are gouges and skew chisels, but parting tools or beading-and-parting tools may also be included, depending on the cutting technique used.

BIRD'S-EYE FIGURE Figure on the sawn surface of wood that shows many small, rounded, lustrous areas resembling birds' eyes; common in hard or rock maple *(Acer saccharum, A. nigrum)*. This is caused by localized grain irregularity, probably due to damage to the **cambial layer**.

BLACKHEART Abnormal brown or black discoloration of the heartwood, which is not necessarily decayed. Ash *(Fraxinus* spp.) can be prone to this.

BLEACHING The process of lightening the colour of a timber by the application of chemicals. There are various products available, most of which use a two-part process: one solution is used to lighten the wood, the other to neutralize the bleaching agent.

BELOW
Blister figure in English elm (Ulmus procera)

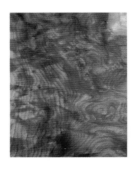

RIGHT
Bowl by Mark Baker, showing quilted figure in soft maple (Acer saccharinum)

BELOW
Vessel in bleached boxelder (Acer negundo) *by John Jordan*

BLISTER FIGURE Figuring, caused by irregularities in grain direction, which resembles billowing clouds, or sometimes bubble-like forms. If the bubble is ovoid in shape, the term used is **quilting**.

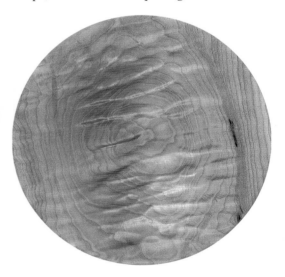

BOTANICAL NOMENCLATURE We usually refer to woods by their common or local names, such as walnut, ash or jarrah. Much of the time this is adequate, but the names for various types of wood can vary considerably from place to place, and the same name may be used for quite unrelated species. We can avoid confusion by using the system of nomenclature devised by the Swedish botanist Carl Linnaeus. The science of classification, for both plants and animals, is called taxonomy. The full classification for a plant is quite long, but there are usually only two categories that a woodworker need be concerned with: **genus** (plural **genera**) and **species**. The names used are usually in Latin or Greek, but are not that difficult to memorize with a little practice. European walnut, for example, is termed *Juglans regia*, whereas American black walnut is *Juglans nigra*; the first element of the name is the same because both these species belong to the same genus *(Juglans)*.

BREAKOUT A term used to describe a section of wood breaking away from the surrounding timber; typically experienced when cutting beads, coves, threads and similar detail.

BRITTLEHEART Heartwood that snaps easily across the grain as a result of compression failure in fibres during growth.

BURR (also called **BURL**, especially in the USA) A lumpy, carbuncle-like growth resulting from parasitic attack or damage to the tree, which causes numerous small shoots to develop in that location as the tree grows over the damaged area. The grain orientation in burrs is extremely erratic, yielding some fantastic figuring which varies enormously from piece to piece. Variants include loose, dotted arrangements of small **pippy** (pip-like) knots amongst contorted, swirling grain; tight, swirling, cloud-like groupings of larger knots; and more tightly packed groupings or clusters of small pippy knots.

RIGHT
Section of a tree trunk showing the various layers

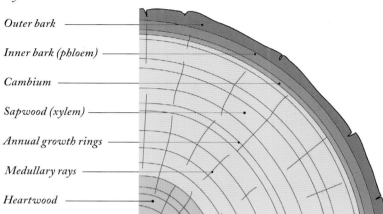

Outer bark
Inner bark (phloem)
Cambium
Sapwood (xylem)
Annual growth rings
Medullary rays
Heartwood

CAMBIUM or **CAMBIAL LAYER** The layer between the **sapwood** and the inner bark, where new wood is created.

RIGHT
A tree with burr clusters on the main trunk and branches

ABOVE
Irregular figure in English elm (Ulmus procera) burr

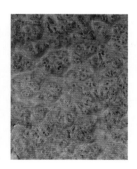

ABOVE
Tightly packed figuring in amboyna (Pterocarpus indicus) burr

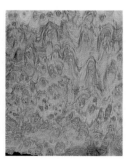

ABOVE
Swirling grain and pippy knots in York gum (Eucalyptus loxophleba) burr

CARVING The process of shaping wood in relief, using either hand or power tools, to create a three-dimensional pattern, texture or shape. Techniques may include cutting with chisels, knives and gouges, or abrading with files, rifflers and dental burrs. Carving can be done on or off the lathe.

CASE HARDENING A defect caused by excessively fast kiln-drying. The surface of the wood dries faster than the core, causing permanent stresses that are released when the wood is cut, resulting in severe distortion.

CHATTERWORK A form of decoration, usually applied to the endgrain, made by placing a specially made cutter against the rotating work. Because the blade is quite thin, it vibrates and makes an intermittent cut on the surface. The pattern is affected by the speed of rotation, the pressure of the cutter against the work and the amount of flex there is in the cutter.

CHECKS or **CHECKING** Cracks running along the grain, caused by uneven or too-rapid drying, which creates stresses within the wood that are greater than the latent strength of the wood. In most cases they are not very deep – hence the term **surface checking**.

ABOVE
Carving a piece of work on the lathe

CLOSE-GRAINED Having narrow growth rings. This usually indicates that the wood is slow-growing and therefore relatively dense and heavy. Conversely, if the wood is faster-growing the rings will be wider apart and the wood can be described as **open-grained** or **coarse-grained**.

COLLAPSE A situation in which the outer layers of the wood dry at a faster rate than the inner parts, creating tension which compresses and distorts the cells of the inner wood. Collapse reveals itself as a corrugated surface on the outside of the wood.

BELOW
Corrugations on the surface are a symptom of cell collapse

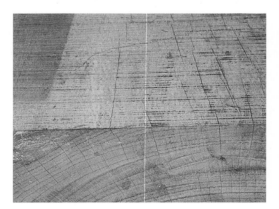

ABOVE
Shallow checks in the end of a sawn board

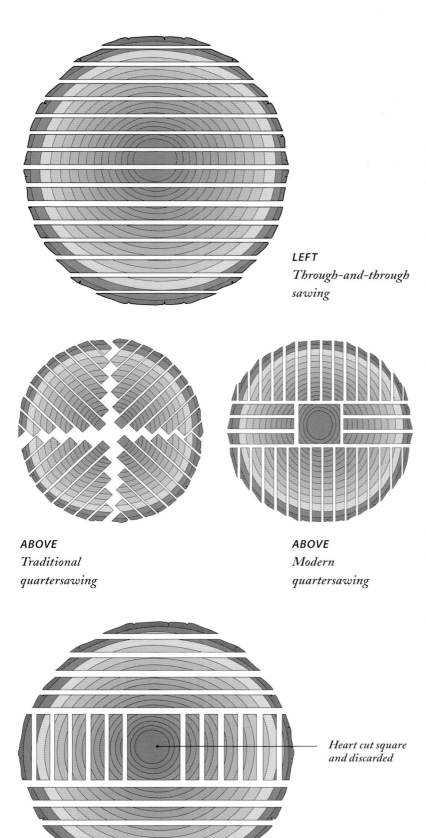

LEFT
Through-and-through
sawing

ABOVE
Traditional
quartersawing

ABOVE
Modern
quartersawing

Heart cut square
and discarded

LEFT
Plain or flat sawing

COMPRESSION WOOD *see* **REACTION WOOD**

CONVERSION The process of sawing trees or logs into smaller sections in readiness for use. There are several different ways in which a log can be cut. Some methods are very economical from the woodyard's point of view; others produce more wastage but yield more dimensionally stable timber and, in some species, a more attractive figure.

THROUGH-AND-THROUGH SAWING The log is sawn horizontally along its length, and this is repeated until all of the log has been cut. The boards have a wavy or natural edge running along their length. Another term for this is **slab-sawing**. Wastage is small, but the boards are liable to warp.

QUARTERSAWING Traditionally, boards were cut so as to radiate out from the heart of the tree, much as the spokes of a wheel radiate from the hub. Wood cut in this way is very stable, and in some cases – oak (*Quercus* spp.), for instance – the wood will yield an attractive ray figure. Because this method of conversion is expensive and wasteful, an alternative, more economical method is now used. It still produces the figuring mentioned above, but compromises the dimensional stability of the board a little.

PLAIN OR FLAT SAWING This is similar to through-and-through cutting, apart from the zone that includes the heart of the wood. The heart, because it is unstable, is cut out (**boxed**) and discarded, but the sections to either side of it are cut at a tangent to the grain (**riftsawn**).

23

CROTCH (FIGURE) The crotch is the area where a trunk or branch forks. The junction of the two stems creates a localized distortion of the grain which, when cut through along the grain, reveals a very distinctive figure pattern. The method of cutting has a major effect on the appearance of the figuring: if cut in the centre, it yields the normal crotch figure; if cut towards the edge, the figure shown will be what is called **swirl crotch**.

DETAIL A term used to describe the cutting of specific shapes such as beads, coves and V-cuts into the work. A wood is said to take 'fine detail' if small, delicate, refined, distinct shapes can be cut without **fracturing** or **tearout**.

DRY WEIGHT The dry weight of wood is typically measured at a moisture content of 12%; but take care when comparing figures from different sources, because different criteria may have been used.

DUTCH ELM DISEASE A fatal disease that affects many species of elm (*Ulmus* spp.) and is caused by the fungi *Ophiostoma ulmi* (syn. *Ceratocystis ulmi*) and the more virulent *O. novo-ulmi*, both spread by elm-bark beetles. The disease is so called because early research on it was carried out in the Netherlands; it is not named after the Dutch elm (*U. hollandica*).

END CHECKS or **ENDGRAIN CHECKS** Water travels more quickly along the grain than across it, so moisture is lost at a higher rate from the endgrain than from any other part of the wood. This area therefore shrinks at a faster rate than the rest, setting up uneven stresses that result in checks (cracks) developing radially in the endgrain.

END-REARING Storing boards vertically instead of horizontally. Certain woods, such as European sycamore (*Acer pseudoplatanus*), are liable to develop fungal staining if boards are laid flat for seasoning or storage. To avoid this, and to help retain the natural colour of

RIGHT
A crotch piece of yew (Taxus baccata) *seen from the outside*

RIGHT
Cutting through the centre of the crotch produces this classic crotch figure

BELOW
Close-up of detail cut into the wood

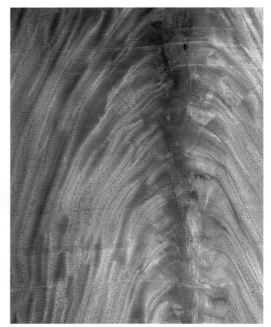

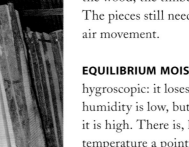

ABOVE
End-reared and stickered sycamore boards

the wood, the timber should be stored on end. The pieces still need to be **stickered** to allow air movement.

EQUILIBRIUM MOISTURE CONTENT Wood is hygroscopic: it loses moisture when relative humidity is low, but absorbs water when it is high. There is, however, at any given temperature a point at which no water is lost or taken back: this is the equilibrium moisture content.

EXTRACTIVES Substances such as metallic oxides and other chemical compounds deposited in the wood that give it its distinctive colour and resistance to decay.

FIDDLEBACK A type of figuring caused by wavy grain, in which the fibres of the wood continuously change direction in a regular manner. Fiddleback European sycamore (*Acer pseudoplatanus*) is traditionally used for the backs of violins, but the figuring can occur in other species as well.

FIGURE or **FIGURING** A term used to describe any decorative pattern on the surface of the wood created by colour variations, faults and defects, growth abnormalities and irregularities, and orientation of the grain. Figuring can be determined by the way the wood is cut, but also by pigment colouring and growth anomalies.

FLAME FIGURE Figuring that resembles a flame in appearance.

GENUS *see* **BOTANICAL NOMENCLATURE**

GIRDLING The practice of cutting away the bark around the circumference of a tree to cause the tree to die gradually and thereby reduce its moisture content prior to felling. Economic constraints mean that this technique is now rarely used.

GRAIN The arrangement of the fibres in the wood relative to the longitudinal axis of a tree or piece of wood. Many types of grain pattern are distinguished, such as fine, coarse, interlocked, wavy, etc. The word 'grain' tends to refer to the wood's regular pattern, whereas **figure** refers to interesting irregularities.

HARDWOOD Wood from a broad-leaved (dicotyledonous) tree. This is usually harder than softwood, but not always: balsa (*Ochroma pyramidale*) is a familiar example of a very soft hardwood. The species listed in this book are hardwoods except where otherwise stated.

ABOVE
Fiddleback figure in European sycamore (Acer pseudoplatanus)

HEART SHAKE A **shake** that starts at the pith of a log and radiates from there out towards the edge.

HEARTWOOD or **TRUE WOOD** The central part of the trunk, which provides support for the tree. It is the hardest, heaviest and most durable part of the timber, and usually the part of most commercial interest.

HEAT-CHECKING Minute splits, usually in the endgrain, caused by heat generated by friction when sanding. Excessive heat may be caused by the application of too much pressure or by using abrasives that are worn out and no longer sharp.

HONEYCOMBING or **HONEYCOMB CHECKS** A form of internal damage caused by case hardening that, as a result of stress, causes the tissues of the timber to break up and form internal checks. These are usually not visible from the outside.

INTERLOCKED GRAIN A configuration in which the fibres formed in successive stages of growth are laid down in different orientations. Certain combinations can produce a distinctive figure, such as **ribbon figure**.

IN THE ROUND A term used to describe a project that uses a whole section of the trunk, bough or limb of a tree, rather than a previously prepared blank.

LAMINATED WORK Gluing together layers of wood, or wood and other materials, of various thicknesses in order to create a distinctive pattern in the finished article.

LIMING Traditionally, a process in which the grain of an open-grained wood such as oak or ash (*Quercus, Fraxinus* spp.) was filled with a lime slurry that set in the wood's pores. Once dry, this was sanded back to reveal the natural colour of the wood on the surface, leaving the filled pores a distinctive, milky-white colour. Nowadays, tinted paste waxes of various colours, including white, green, black, terracotta and many more – also metallic pastes called gilt cream – are used to create a similar visual contrast, but the traditional term is still used.

MEDULLARY RAYS Sheets of tissue formed at right angles to the annual rings of the tree. In some species, such as oak (*Quercus* spp.), they are very distinctive; in others they are barely visible. How the wood is cut will have a big bearing on how these show on the cut timber. **Quartersawing** displays the medullary rays to great visual effect on oak and other timbers.

MOTTLE **Ripple figuring** that has been broken up by **interlocking grain**. It is, in effect, a broken-stripe figure with irregular interruptions caused by the wavy grain.

MOVEMENT A general term for the various ways in which wood shrinks and distorts as it seasons, due to moisture loss or the relief of inherent stresses within the wood.

NATURAL-EDGE WORK Any piece of work that retains part of the natural, unadulterated outer surface of the tree, often including the bark, to create visual contrast with the 'finished' surface.

RIGHT
Laminated peppermill
by Chris West

BELOW
Bowl in dyed ash
(**Fraxinus** *spp.*)
finished with gilt
cream by Mark Baker

BELOW
Natural-edged bowl
in European maple
(**Acer campestre**)
burr by Mark Baker

PENETRATIVE FINISH Any finish that penetrates the fibres of the wood and protects it – typically oils of various types, or some paste or liquid waxes. The finish may not set – some natural oils do not contain drying agents – but may still provide an effective barrier against moisture ingress, dirt and chemicals. Modern proprietary oil finishes combine natural oils with synthetic elements to increase the protection, and may incorporate dryers that will cause the penetrative finish to set and form a protective surface film in addition to the usual physical barrier. The degree of penetration depends on the density of the wood: with very dense woods such as lignum vitae (*Guaiacum officinale* or *G. sanctum*) they do not penetrate far at all, but still form an effective finish. Multiple coats are required to obtain a fine finish. Oils without dryers can be retouched whenever necessary; those with dryers must be sanded back before applying a fresh coat.

PERSONAL PROTECTIVE EQUIPMENT (PPE) Any items that are worn by individuals to minimize the risk of injury and exposure to potentially harmful substances. We turners need to protect our lungs from wood dust and chemicals, as well as protect our faces from chips, flying debris and, heaven forbid, work that comes loose from the lathe. PPE can sometimes be as simple as a pair of gloves worn to prevent splinters when handling large pieces of wood. When turning, we should wear, as a minimum, protection for the face, eyes and lungs; a powered respirator with full-face visor is the choice of most professionals.

PIERCED WORK Features voids cut into the wood to create a decorative effect. This is commonly done with a high-speed rotary carving unit in conjunction with special cutting bits and burrs of various sizes.

RIGHT
A striking example of pigmented striping in ebony (Diospyros *spp.*)

PIGMENT STAINING Not all **figuring** is caused by irregularities within the **grain**. Colours within wood, such as the stripes in ebony (*Diospyros* spp.), are caused by **extractives** within the **heartwood** that have coloured the wood.

PIPPY A term used to describe a burr pattern in which numerous small knots – 'eyes' or 'pips' – are present in a clustered or loosely spaced arrangement.

PLUCKOUT or **PULLOUT** The situation in which the tool pulls a clump of fibres away from the main body of the wood, resulting in a serious blemish that can run very deep. It often occurs when the wood has decayed a little and lost some of its strength, so the fibres are not so tightly bonded together.

BELOW
'Romeo' in turned, pierced and coloured European sycamore (Acer pseudoplatanus) *by Joey Richardson*

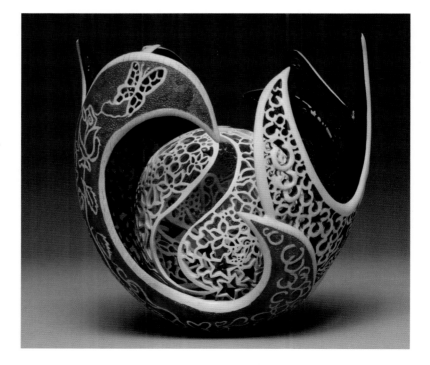

POSSIBLE HEALTH RISKS Many substances can cause allergic reactions in certain individuals, who may not be aware of the risk until they actually come into contact with the substance in question. Sometimes the effects are cumulative. Long-term exposure to dust can have serious effects on lung function, or result in conditions such as contact dermatitis; other reactions may be caused by chemical compounds in the wood. The possible risks mentioned in this book have been gathered from health and safety bodies around the world, and from anecdotal comments. Most published research has been done on readily available species, which is why anecdotal evidence has had to be included for many woods that are only available in small amounts and which have not been the subject of systematic study. *All* dust is potentially hazardous, so take sensible precautions to limit exposure to it, and take a shower afterwards to ensure that the dust is not in contact with your skin any longer than necessary. Be careful also of the finishes that you use: these can contain harmful chemicals.

POWER CARVING The process of using powered rotary or percussive tools to carve work.

POWER SANDING For this you need an arbor with a hook-and-loop face onto which is affixed abrasive, and a method of driving it, such as a drill. The revolving arbor is traversed across the surface of the work as it turns slowly on the lathe. Best results are achieved by having the arbor run in contrarotation to the work. Power sanding is devilishly quick, and a light touch is required so as not to create furrows in the wood.

QUARTERSAWING *see* **CONVERSION**

QUILTING *see* **BLISTER FIGURE**

ABOVE
Neil Scobie power carving a piece of work

BELOW
Power sanding a bowl

RADIAL CRACK This happens when the **tangential** shrinkage in a trunk, log or branch generates stresses that the wood cannot withstand, so that it splits along the grain. These cracks are usually very deep and can penetrate right to the heart of the tree. It is not uncommon to find more than one, starting from different positions.

RADIAL SURFACE A wood surface cut at right angles to the annual rings, as when a log is sawn through its centre. It seldom shows interesting grain patterning, except in woods that exhibit **ray fleck** or **ribbon figure**. Surfaces cut at an angle to the annual rings are described as **tangential**.

RAY FLECK Part of a **medullary ray** showing on a radial surface; this is usually regarded as a decorative feature, especially in oak (*Quercus* spp.).

REACTION WOOD An area of wood on a branch or a leaning trunk that shows distinctive characteristics because of the tensions and pressures due to gravity. It is denser but much more brittle than normal wood. In hardwoods it generally occurs on the upper side of the branch or trunk, and is called **tension wood**; on softwoods it forms on the underside and is known as **compression wood**.

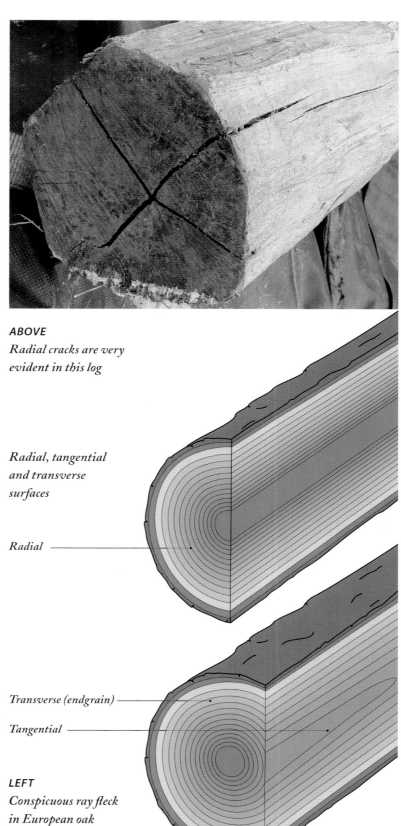

ABOVE
Radial cracks are very evident in this log

Radial, tangential and transverse surfaces

Radial

Transverse (endgrain)

Tangential

LEFT
Conspicuous ray fleck in European oak (Quercus petraea *or* Q. robur)

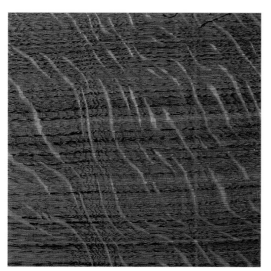

29

LEFT
Ribbon figure in African walnut (Lovoa trichilioides)

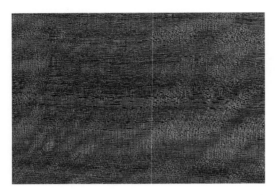

LEFT
Typical roe figure on radial surface of Queensland maple (Flindersia brayleyana)

LEFT
Routing on the lathe

BELOW
Using a scraper in the conventional trailing mode

RIBBON FIGURE A type of figuring produced as a result of **interlocking grain**. It only shows when the wood has been cut radially.

RING FAILURE or **RING SHAKE** A separation of the wood fibres, occurring parallel to and between the annual rings in the growing tree.

RIPPLE FIGURE An alternative name for **fiddleback** figure.

ROE or **ROEY FIGURE** Short, broken stripe or ribbon figure in certain **quartersawn** hardwoods, arising from **interlocked grain** interrupting a **ribbon figure**.

ROUTING The router is typically used to shape wood for joinery and cabinetry, but jigs are now available to hold a router in a horizontal position, which allows it to be used on the lathe bed in order to cut decorative effects while the work is stationary.

SAPWOOD The softer, less durable, less dense wood towards the outer surface of the trunk, confined in most species to a narrow band in relation to the **heartwood**. It is not always easily distinguished from the heartwood.

SCRAPERS Turning tools formed from a solid metal bar, either with a shaped end section, or with a fitment to which various-shaped cutting tips can be attached. Scrapers are used with a delicate touch to refine the surface of the wood once the primary shaping tool – typically a gouge – has done the main shaping. The profile of the end of the tool is chosen to suit the shape being worked on: a skewed or straight edge for external curves and a dome or French curve for internal curves. These are not **bevel-rubbing** tools: only the cutting edge is in contact with the work. They are typically presented to the work in a trailing manner; that is, the handle is held high and the tip is lower than the handle.

SEGMENTED Turning work constructed from a series of rings comprising glued-together sections of timber cut to highly accurate shapes and angles in order to create a specific visual effect. The piece may comprise different woods to create colour contrast, so that all the rings joined together create a geometric pattern or a picture. Some segmented items consist of tightly fitting pieces in a solid ring; others may feature gaps between the segments or blocks (known as open-segment work).

SENSITIZER Any substance which, after initial exposure, will cause an allergic reaction in the user when encountered again. In the case of some wood species, this reaction may take the form of dermatitis, other skin disorders, or respiratory and associated problems.

SHAKE A serious split in a piece of wood, which is not necessarily a result of the drying stresses.

SHEAR-SCRAPING A cutting technique in which a **scraper**, or the edge of a gouge, is presented at such an angle to the work as to cause shavings to peel off the cutting edge. There is no bevel rub during this cut. A good angle to begin with is 45°, with the tool trailed across the surface of the rotating work. The angle of approach can be varied: if you find that 45° is not right and you are tearing the wood, lessen or increase the angle until you achieve a fine peeling cut. The object is to clean up the surface and minimize the need for sanding with coarse grades.

SILVER GRAIN The figure created by lustrous **ray fleck** on **quartersawn** timber, especially oak (*Quercus* spp.).

SOFTWOOD Wood from a coniferous (gymnosperm) tree. It is generally softer than **hardwood**, but not always; yew (*Taxus* spp.) is a good example of a very hard softwood.

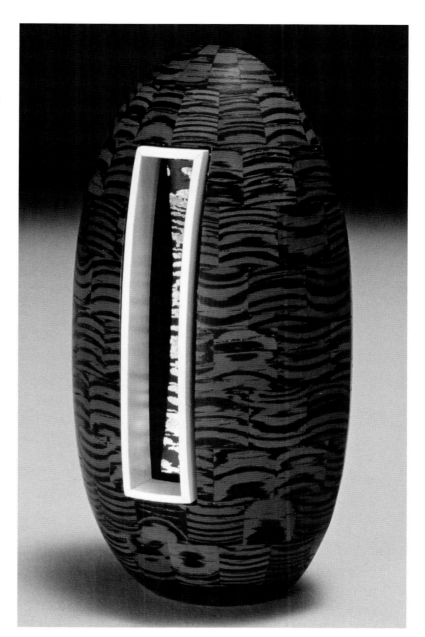

ABOVE
'The Gate' by Curt Theobald: segmented work in wengé (Millettia laurentii), *rock maple* (Acer saccharum) *and gold leaf*

RIGHT
Shear-scraping the outside of a bowl

SP., SPP. Abbreviations for species, singular and plural. '*Quercus* sp.' means 'an unspecified or unidentified species of the genus *Quercus*'; '*Quercus* spp.' means 'various species of the genus *Quercus*'.

SPALTED WOOD Wood that has been invaded by fungi, which produce various colour changes as they progress. When the colour changes occur without drastically reducing the inherent strength of the wood, the material is said to be spalted. This wood is, in effect, in the primary stages of rot. The same term is sometimes used for timber that is in a more advanced state of decay.

SPECIES *see* **BOTANICAL NOMENCLATURE**

SPECIFIC GRAVITY (SG) A measure of the density of a substance relative to that of water. Anything with a specific gravity of more than 1.0 is heavier than water, and sinks when placed in it; an example is satiné bloodwood (*Brosimum paraense*), which has a specific gravity of 1.15. Specific gravity may vary considerably, even within the same species, and the figures given in this book can only be regarded as averages.

STAINING AND DYEING The process of applying chemicals – natural or artificial – to wood in order to alter its appearance. It usually results in a different colour altogether.

ABOVE
Characteristic spalting pattern in European beech (Fagus sylvatica)*; vessel by Mark Baker*

RIGHT
Black bottle in dyed soft maple (Acer saccharinum) *by John Jordan*

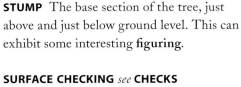

BELOW
Metal-patinated bowls in European sycamore (Acer pseudoplatanus) *by Mark Baker*

STUMP The base section of the tree, just above and just below ground level. This can exhibit some interesting **figuring**.

SURFACE CHECKING *see* **CHECKS**

SURFACE ENHANCEMENT Typically a catch-all phrase used to describe any alteration of the surface of the wood by any means after the wood has been shaped. This can include the application of a finish, but also carving, texturing, routing, colouring and so on.

SURFACE FINISH Any finish that does not deeply penetrate the wood, but forms a chemical or physical bond with the wood surface and provides a protective film or a base on which other finishes can be applied. Lacquers, shellac-based finishes (friction polish and French polish), varnishes of all types, hard block waxes and so on are some of the surface finishes available. Invariably they will require more than one coat to form an effective finish or base.

SYNONYM or **SYN**. Scientific names of plants are occasionally changed, as botanists revise their ideas of the relationships between individual species and genera. A synonym, in this sense of the word, is a botanical name that is no longer current in scientific use, but which may still be found in older textbooks or in less scholarly sources.

TANGENTIAL SURFACE *see* **RADIAL SURFACE**

TEAROUT A surface blemish caused when the fibres of the **grain** are broken or torn away from the surrounding fibres. It tends to occur when cutting against the grain, or where there are grain irregularities such as wavy or **interlocking grain**.

TENSION WOOD *see* **REACTION WOOD**

TEXTURED Used to describe a surface that is not smooth but has an indented, dimpled or wavy appearance created either by some form of carving or by specialist texturing tools utilizing spiked wheels, knurling tools, cogs, sprockets and suchlike (see also **chatterwork**).

ULTRAVIOLET (UV) INHIBITORS Additives included in certain finishes to block or retard ultraviolet light, which is the primary cause of colour degrade within wood. They act in the same way as sunblocks applied to the skin.

WANE or **WANEY EDGE** The natural edge of a plank or board, which may be irregular and have bark on it.

WET SANDING A sanding technique that employs a lubricant. I first saw it used by Ray Key, who applies paste wax to the finish-turned piece prior to sanding with fine abrasive. The dust and wax combine to form a slurry that gets pushed into the grain and acts as a grain filler. No further finishing is required, other than burnishing with a clean cloth. Oil or water can also be used as a lubricant; I mostly use oil. Simply turn the

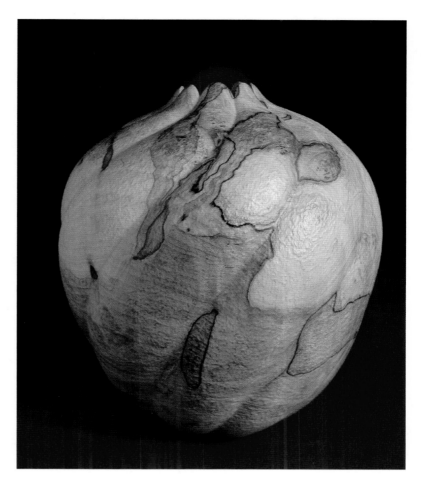

ABOVE
Red maple (Acer rubrum) *burr vessel with carved and textured surface by John Jordan*

work to the required profile and dry-sand any major blemishes away. Then apply a coat of oil or wax to the surface, and sand at a low speed. Work through the grades of abrasive and if you see dust forming, apply more lubricant. After sanding, use a clean cloth to apply a further coat of the oil or wax, then burnish to a smooth finish. One drawback is that this method can only be used when the wood colour is uniform: on a wood such as laburnum (*Laburnum anagyroides*), which has cream sapwood and dark heartwood, the sanding slurry will be dark and will contaminate the lighter sapwood.

WOOLLY GRAIN A fuzzy surface with frayed, rather than cleanly cut, fibres after cutting, resembling a mild form of **tearout**. Certain woods, such as the willows (*Salix* spp.), are very susceptible, especially when turned wet.

WOODS
IN DETAIL

There are so many timbers to choose from, it is difficult to list them all. So I consulted with turners around the world and created a list of some of the most commonly available timbers, which form a good foundation for people to use and work with.

European maple
Acer campestre

Other names
Field maple. Norway maple (*A. platanoides*) and Bosnian maple (*A. platanus*) are very similar and are also marketed as 'European maple'

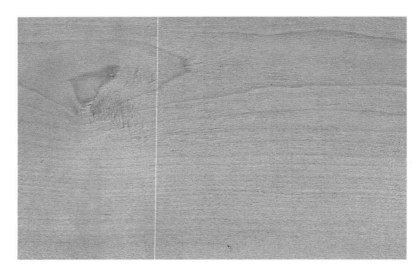

Try coating the endgrain sections of the rough-turned piece with PVA to slow down the drying process.

Seasoning
European maple exhibits little degrade or movement when air-dried slowly; however, rapid but careful kiln-drying is recommended for this timber (despite the slightly increased risk of movement) to preserve the creamy-white colour. Rough-turned pieces will not distort too much during the drying and stabilizing process, but this is dependent on the amount of figuring in the piece: the more figuring, the higher the potential for distortion. With crotch figuring, as with most highly figured areas of wood, there is a risk of splitting unless it is dried slowly.

Characteristics
Acers are wonderful woods to work with, and no turner should ignore them. A wide range of figured forms is available, and the uses to which the wood can be put are endless. The heartwood of field maple is creamy-white at first, but will mellow to a light tan colour with time. The sapwood is usually not distinguishable from the heartwood. The grain is normally straight but occasionally wavy or curly, with a fine, even texture. The grain pattern is delicate but clearly defined. Occasionally it will form ripple or curly figure; both of these are highly prized in the veneer trade, and heavily figured trees are usually snapped up very quickly, but turners may come across areas of figure in boards and precut blanks. This wood regularly produces burrs (burls) that more often than not comprise tightly packed clusters of small pippy knots.

Burr (burl) detail

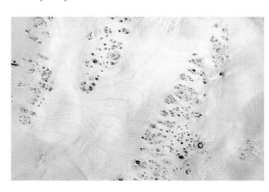

Grows
UK, mainland Europe, USA and parts of Asia
HEIGHT 60–65ft (18–20m)
TRUNK DIAMETER 1–2ft (0.3–0.6m)
SPECIFIC GRAVITY .69
TYPICAL DRY WEIGHT 43lb/ft³ (690kg/m³)

Field maple is typically only available in small to medium sizes, so it is generally more suitable for smaller projects such as bowls or hollow forms, rather than platters. It is often overlooked in favour of more flashy, brightly coloured woods. Being fine-grained, it is suitable for architectural, artistic, decorative and utilitarian work, including items that may come into contact with food. The burrs are wonderful for natural-edge work.

Working qualities

Acers are a large genus with over 100 species. Because there are so many, acers are available commercially in many countries, and form the backbone of many turners' wood requirements.

Field maple, along with rock maple (*A. saccharum* and *A. nigrum*) and soft maple (*A. rubrum* and *A. saccharinum*), is a beautiful wood to work with, wet or dry. This group of maples is a good one to develop your turning skills on. It is a fine-grained, medium-density wood that will hold quite fine detail. It has a slight blunting effect on cutting edges, but cuts well with both hand and machine tools. This wood will steam-bend, so can be used for making chair backs. It is an ideal timber for kitchen utensils.

It cuts cleanly with sharp tools when turning it wet or dry, but you may experience a little grain tearout when working highly figured areas and sometimes on endgrain areas, especially with scrapers. During turning it is easy to see from the finish off the tool whether the optimum cut is being achieved, and whether the tool is sharp. With care, it is possible to get a surface finish that requires very little sanding.

This is also an ideal timber for wet-turning – especially natural-edge work. Turn the piece to a thin, even wall thickness, apply your finish of choice, then let it dry. As it dries it will move and distort – more so if there is figure in it – to create a highly individual

Hint
Work with freshly honed or sharpened tools for the final cuts to create a surface that requires very little sanding

piece. Burrs, natural-edged or not, respond well to this technique. The burr, when dry, may take on a distinctive texture with a sort of 'hammered' quality to it.

If you want to pierce the timber with rotary carving tools, maple's ability to be turned thin makes it an ideal choice. This is also a great timber to use if you wish to carve, texture, rout or experiment with other surface enhancement effects, including dyes and stains. Another option is to use it in segmented or laminated work, as it glues well.

European maple takes surface and penetrative finishes well in most cases, but with dyes and stains, it can be 'hungry' for the finishes and occasionally blotchy if care is not taken. Once done properly it highlights figuring beautifully. The creamy-white colour of the freshly cut wood will be lost over time unless a finish with a light inhibitor is used. Oils and many surface finishes will have a slight darkening effect.

BELOW
Bowl in European maple burr finished with lemon oil by Mark Baker

Bigleaf maple
Acer macrophyllum

Other names
Maple, broadleaf maple, bugleaf maple, Californian maple, Oregon maple, Pacific coast maple, western maple, white maple

Characteristics
The wood is pale pinkish-brown to nearly white, normally with no clear distinction between heartwood and sapwood. It has a close, fine grain with uniform colour. Figuring variants are highly prized and the burrs, as with many timbers, are stunning.

Working qualities
This is one of those timbers that is a real treat to turn and excellent to explore. It can be worked readily in many ways, and has plenty of figured variants, the beauty of which never fails to amaze. Non-figured versions of this

POSSIBLE HEALTH RISKS
Allergic bronchial asthma, dermatitis and rhinitis

CONSERVATION STATUS
Not known to be at risk

Seasoning
The wood dries quite slowly with little degrade and exhibits medium movement when drying. Unless wet-turning a piece to a thin wall thickness – which this timber will accept readily – I usually rough-turn the pieces first and let them dry before reworking them using the normal allowance of 10–15% of the overall diameter for the wall thickness. I have yet to find any figured or plain timber that has required anything different, but, if in doubt, go to 15% for the figured pieces. You just have to let them dry longer before turning them.

Burr (burl) detail

Grows
USA and Canada, from California to British Columbia

HEIGHT 60ft (18m) plus

TRUNK DIAMETER 1–3ft (0.3–0.9m)

SPECIFIC GRAVITY .55

TYPICAL DRY WEIGHT 34lb/ft³ (545kg/m³)

timber turn easily, wet or dry. As with most timbers, it responds best to bevel-rubbing tools such as the gouge or the skew. If tools are sharp and presented correctly, you can get a great finish that requires minimal sanding afterwards if the wood is dry. If the wood is wet, you may experience a slight fluffiness on certain sections – endgrain or figured sections – that are cut, but you can minimize this by dropping the handle of the tool to create a more refined shearing cut.

Endgrain and figured sections may cause minor issues with grain pluckout if using scrapers or slightly dull-edged tools, but typically the wood turns beautifully and is able to hold reasonably fine detail. As with many timbers, avoid creating ultrasharp and fine edges. These will be prone to denting and potential chipping or fracturing.

This maple can be carved and textured relatively easily. Power carving with either rotary or percussive power tools is easier than hand carving, but of course generates a lot more dust and is noisier.

Hint

This, like many maples, is great for exploring natural edge work due to the bark being fine and stable enough to usually stay in place while working it

If you want to explore piecing work, maple is a good choice of wood. If you want to experiment with segmented or laminated work, this is a great timber to use and I have not experienced any problems when gluing it.

This is a timber that can be used architecturally, in furniture production and utilitarian and decorative turnings around the home. It sands well and takes most finishes well but, like its European cousin, can be a little finish-hungry, so a few extra coats might be required to get an even appearance, especially with dyes and other penetrative finishes. Above all, this a timber that lends itself to experimentation and, like all maples really, is one that I love to work with.

BELOW
Bowl by Mike Mahoney

Boxelder
Acer negundo

Other names
Ashleaf maple, Manitoba maple, maple, red river maple, cut-leaf maple

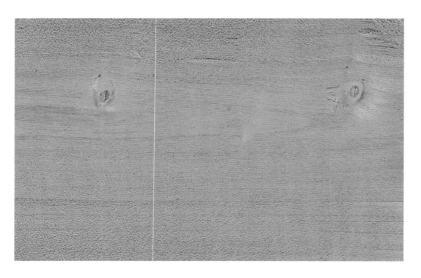

Seasoning

Boxelder dries with little degrade whether kiln- or air-dried, has a small to moderate amount of movement in drying and is stable in use when seasoned properly. As with most woods, when the work is required to maintain its shape after turning it is best to rough-turn the wood and then put it aside for some time to stabilize. It can, however, be wet-turned to completion to good effect and allowed to move so as to produce more 'organic' forms. The amount of movement is very variable – moderate with the plain timber but higher with the burr sections. If the wood is air-dried or stored for too long, blue staining may occur, and the results are often disappointing: muddy, greyish puddles or thin threads, rather than clearly defined bands or lines of colour.

Characteristics

Boxelder is a lightweight, porous but close-grained wood with a fine texture. It tends to have yellow-brown heartwood and green-tinged yellow sapwood. It does not have a clearly defined grain figure. It sometimes has wavy or curly figuring, which lifts its appearance no end. But boxelder is most highly prized when it has pink or deep red-purple streaks running through it. A fungal infection was, for a long time, cited as the possible cause of the colouring, but the current

Grows
Canada and USA
HEIGHT 60–65ft (18–20m)
TRUNK DIAMETER 1ft–3ft 6in (0.3–1.1m)
SPECIFIC GRAVITY .45
TYPICAL DRY WEIGHT 28lb/ft³ (450kg/m³)

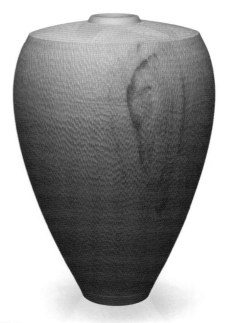

ABOVE
Vessel in bleached boxelder by John Jordan

thinking is that it is more likely produced as a function of the tree's natural defence mechanism when wounded.

Sadly, this colouring often fades when exposed to UV light and air – though I have a few examples where it has not. The application of finishes with UV inhibitors helps retard this process. When there is a lot of this colouring present, boxelder takes on a whole new persona, blossoming from a relatively bland timber into a glorious diva.

Working qualities

Boxelder's fine texture makes it ideal for both artistic and functional or utilitarian ware. It has a medium blunting effect on cutting edges and cuts reasonably well whether turned wet or dry. It can be wet-turned to a very thin wall thickness. On highly figured areas – especially when working with dry timber and more so if using scrapers – the grain may pluck out on endgrain areas, even if the tools are ultrasharp. It cuts best with bevel-rubbing tools such as gouges and skew chisels.

It has the capacity to hold reasonable detail – but not very fine detail – and it can be textured, carved, used for pyrography, pierced, stained, coloured, painted and bleached, so is ideal to experiment with. Some turners bleach the wood then apply lightfast dye over the coloured areas to replicate the natural look of the coloured staining in the wood. The dyed areas then contrast highly with the bleached timber. Boxelder also glues well, if you want to laminate work.

The wood is rather soft, and occasionally softer areas will be found within it, in which case aggressive sanding may create humps in the surface. A light, delicate touch when sanding is all that is needed.

RIGHT
'My Bowl is the Sky'
by Binh Pho

Being a porous wood, boxelder can be 'hungry' as far as finishes are concerned, requiring a few extra coats of surface or penetrative finish in order to build up a lustrous, silky surface. Dyes can be used to good effect to bring out the wavy or curly figuring.

Hint

If working with timber that is plucking out, prior to making the final cuts, apply two or three coats of thinned-down precatalysed lacquer or sanding sealer and allow to dry. This hardens the wood a little, which makes the final finishing cuts and sanding easier

BELOW
*Set of nesting bowls
in red boxelder by
Mike Mahoney*

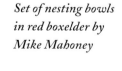

European sycamore

Acer pseudoplatanus

Other names
Sycamore plane, great maple, plane (in Scotland).
Not related to American sycamore (*Platanus occidentalis*), which is of the plane family

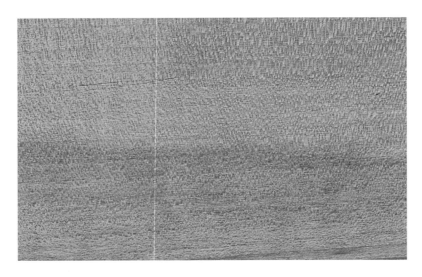

POSSIBLE HEALTH RISKS

Possible skin irritation, rhinitis, respiratory irritation

CONSERVATION STATUS

Not known to be at risk

Seasoning

The wood seasons well, whether kiln- or air-dried. Rapid kilning will help preserve the natural creamy colour.

When air-drying, the boards must be stood on end ('end-reared') to prevent staining. If the wood is laid horizontally and stickered, it will develop a silvery colour with green- or blue-tinged blotches; these are water and fungal stains, and can look quite attractive. This form is known as 'weathered sycamore'. A form known as harewood is

created artificially, using ferrous sulphate to colour solid wood and veneers; this gives a wonderful, translucent silver colour.

Rough-turning this timber will create very stable wood: there is a moderate amount of movement, and the usual guideline of leaving a wall thickness of 10% of the overall diameter should work fine.

Characteristics

A wonderful timber to work with, sycamore is creamy-white to yellowish-white in colour; the sapwood is not readily distinguishable from the heartwood. On exposure to light, the wood will darken to a tan or fawn colour. The grain is typically close and straight, but may have rippled, curly or lacy figuring and, very occasionally, burrs (burls). The characteristic ripple or 'fiddleback' figure is highly sought-after by violin makers and veneering companies; they snap up highly figured trees as soon as they become available, so you are more likely to encounter this type of figuring in small amounts – unless you know of a particularly helpful tree surgeon or timber

Figured sycamore

Grows
UK, mainland Europe, western Asia; now also planted in USA
HEIGHT 100ft (30m)
TRUNK DIAMETER 5ft (1.8m)
SPECIFIC GRAVITY .61
TYPICAL DRY WEIGHT 38lb/ft³ (610kg/m³)

supplier who will tell you when a suitable tree is coming down. Sycamore has a fine, even texture, is of medium density and will hold detail well.

Available in small and large sizes, this is an excellent wood for turning large platters and hollow forms, as well as smaller projects. It is a valuable wood for furniture turnery and baluster spindles, and is extensively used by cabinetmakers.

Working qualities

Sycamore is a wonderful timber to use in many different woodworking disciplines. I prefer it to European maple (*A. campestre*). To my mind, the non-figured timber is a bit of a shrinking violet: it does not shout 'Look at me!' but it is incredibly versatile to work with, can be used in many different situations and has an understated beauty that really shines when lovingly finished.

The wood cuts well wet or dry. Its ability to hold reasonably fine detail makes it useful for pieces that are to be carved, sculpted, textured or pierced in some way. I regularly carve, texture and, at times, rout it. It glues well if you want to create segmented work. In short, it is a very versatile timber to work with. Its close grain makes it ideal for use on items that will come into contact with food.

Hint

If you want to try piercing, carving or texturing, this is an ideal timber to use

RIGHT
Platter in figured sycamore by Mark Baker

BELOW LEFT
Natural-edged bowl by Bert Marsh

BELOW RIGHT
'Methusela', pierced and coloured sycamore by Joey Richardson

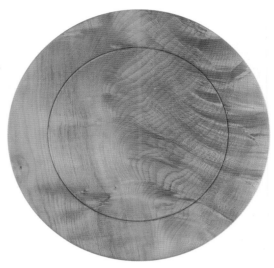

This is a great timber with which to experiment with wet-turning thin-walled items. Natural-edged vases, hollow forms and bowls are all worth trying. Since it is available in large sizes, there is plenty of scope to explore the full potential of this timber.

Any rippled or figured sections can be somewhat problematic due to the interlocking grain if the cuts are too heavy-handed or if tools are dull. As with most woods, gentle cuts with sharp tools will minimize grain tearout.

Sycamore accepts surface and penetrative finishes well, including dyes and stains.

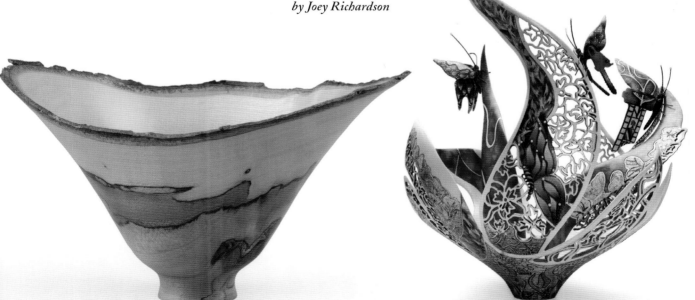

Soft maple
Acer rubrum and *A. saccharinum*

Other names
Red maple, Carolina red maple, Drummond red maple, scarlet maple, silver maple

POSSIBLE HEALTH RISKS
Dust may affect lung function

CONSERVATION STATUS
Not known to be at risk

Characteristics
This medium-density wood has light to dark reddish-brown heartwood, which may be faintly tinted with purple, grey or green. Usually straight and close-grained, soft maple can occasionally be wavy or curly. Quilting and burr forms are available from time to time. Very attractive pith flecks may be present. The sapwood varies from white to greyish-white. Heavily figured trees are bought for veneers. This wood is sometimes attacked by ambrosia beetles, and fungal spores colonize the tracks left by the beetle to form wonderful coloured patterns that make each piece unique. This is known as ambrosia maple.

Seasoning
This wood responds well to both air- and kiln-drying, with little degrade or movement – except for highly figured pieces, where movement is unpredictable. Occasionally there may be ring failure and honeycombing if the wood is wet. Blue staining may occur if there is not sufficient airflow during the drying process; this gives the wood a muddy appearance. The wood responds well to rough-turning followed by further seasoning, which is especially necessary with highly figured pieces.

Quilted figure

Grows
Canada and eastern USA
HEIGHT 60–100ft (18–30m)
TRUNK DIAMETER 2ft 6in (0.8m)
SPECIFIC GRAVITY *A. rubrum* .63, *A. saccharinum* .55
TYPICAL DRY WEIGHT *A. rubrum* 39lb/ft³ (630kg/m³), *A. saccharinum* 34lb/ft³ (550kg/m³)

Working qualities

This wood has many uses within the woodworking industry; because it works easily both wet and dry, it is valuable to turners for utility objects such as kitchenware, as well as artistic and decorative pieces, cabinetry and joinery work. Soft maple is also suitable for carving, texturing, piercing and other decorative effects.

Although not as durable and hardwearing as rock maple (*A. saccharum, A. nigrum*), the sheer variety of figure variants this timber is likely to form makes it a very interesting timber indeed.

Straight-grained soft maple cuts easily, finishes well and is capable of holding reasonably fine detail; but the quilted or curly-grained pieces, due to their erratic grain structure, can be a little difficult to work, so use delicate shearing cuts to help minimize potential grain tearout in the figured areas and on endgrain. The wood can be carved and routed and glued readily for laminated and segmented work.

Soft maples readily accept most surface and penetrative finishes – although they can, at times, be finish-hungry. All forms, except the ambrosia maple, respond well to wet or dry sanding. Because of the risk of colour contamination during wet sanding, ambrosia maple is best sanded dry.

RIGHT
Vessel in red ambrosia maple by John Jordan

Hint

Do not be tempted to skip grades of abrasive on this wood – or any other timbers, come to think of it. Little areas of imperfection have a nasty habit of showing up only after oiling or finishing, making it necessary to backtrack to the abrading stages again

RIGHT
Natural-topped hollow form in burr maple by John Hunnex

BELOW
Bowls in burl maple by Mike Mahoney

Rock maple
Acer saccharum and *A. nigrum*

Other names
Hard maple, sugar maple, white maple (*A. saccharum*); black maple, black sugar maple, hard rock maple (*A. nigrum*). Both species are sold as 'hard' or 'rock' maple

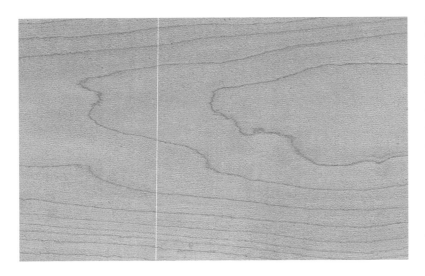

POSSIBLE HEALTH RISKS
Dust may affect lung function

CONSERVATION STATUS
Not known to be at risk

Seasoning
The wood dries slowly but is easy to season. It is classified as having a medium to high shrinkage rate and moderate tendency to warp. It responds very well to rough-turning before further seasoning, which is especially necessary with highly figured pieces; the rule of 1in (25mm) of wall thickness to every 12in (300mm) diameter, or 10% of the overall diameter, should be enough to cope with the likely degree of movement.

Characteristics
This beautiful timber is dense, close-grained and tough. The sapwood is white to cream in colour, with a red tinge. The heartwood is typically a uniform light tan to reddish-brown, with a nice pronounced grain pattern. It usually has a straight, tight, fine-textured grain that holds detail well without breakout. These maples produce the most highly figured variant forms, namely rippled or fiddleback, blister, leaf, burr (burl), bird's-eye and, occasionally, quilted. Bird's-eye maple comprises a creamy-white background covered with small, brown, eye-shaped dots. The burr forms can range from tight clusters of pippy dots through to swirling grain and striated patterns. The rock

Ripple figure

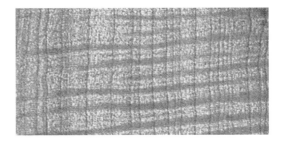

Bird's eye figure

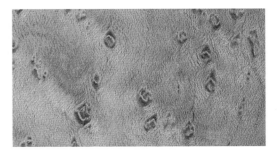

Grows
Canada and USA
HEIGHT *A. saccharum* 70–120ft (20–37m), *A. nigrum* 80ft (24m)
TRUNK DIAMETER 2–3ft (0.6–0.9m)
SPECIFIC GRAVITY .72
TYPICAL DRY WEIGHT 45lb/ft³ (720kg/m³)

maples, being considerably harder than the soft maples, are highly sought-after, and have myriad uses within the woodworking industry.

Working qualities

Rock maple is certainly one of the gems of the maple family. The variety of figured variants can keep many turners busy for a lifetime. This dense, tight-grained timber is a delight to work with. It cuts well when wet – to thin wall thicknesses – or dry. Even the highly figured forms respond well to a sharp tool and a light touch, yielding a finish that requires very little abrading. Its ability to hold detail and be turned to a thin wall thickness means that it can be used for complex turned work or it can be carved, textured, routed and pierced. This wood is hardwearing (it is used for flooring, squash courts and industrial rollers), so will stand up to arduous use in utilitarian articles such as chopping boards, pestles and mortars, or salad bowls, as well as being suitable for decorative or artistic work, cabinetry and joinery components.

ABOVE
Platter in rippled
maple by Mark Baker

BELOW
Bowls in rippled
maple by Mark Baker

The warm colour is enhanced further with a nice finish, oil being my favourite; but this depends very much on its intended use. It can accept penetrative and surface finishes well.

Rock maple is available in large sizes, and the varieties of dramatic figuring will constantly amaze. If you have not had the pleasure of trying this wood, please do – I know you will enjoy the experience.

Hint

A freshly honed or sharpened scraper, used gently, will produce nice delicate ribbons of shavings; this is a useful way to remove any minor ripples left after using a gouge, prior to sanding

Horse chestnut
Aesculus hippocastanum

Other names
European horse chestnut. Colloquially known in the UK as a 'conker tree', after the game called 'conkers' played with the fruit of the tree. Other *Aesculus* species are known as 'buckeye' in North America

POSSIBLE HEALTH RISKS

Not known, but take the usual precautions regarding dust

CONSERVATION STATUS

Categorized as 'near threatened' in Red List

Characteristics
The heartwood is normally creamy-white to yellow, with little or no demarcation between heart and sapwood. Winter-felled wood tends to be white, but that felled at other times can vary from yellow to light brown. It has a fine, close, uniform texture with a delicate grain pattern. Horse chestnut can becross-grained, spiral-grained or wavy-grained, and ripple or mottled figuring on longitudinal surfaces is not unusual. It is also prone to forming burrs.

Working qualities
Horse chestnut, and all variants, has a moderate dulling effect on cutting edges, and cuts well when freshly seasoned. Figured wood is a good candidate for wet-turning and I prefer turning the wet wood to the dry. This relatively light wood, despite having a fine grain structure, does not hold fine detail well; but it can be carved and routed to reasonable effect.

Seasoning
Horse chestnut dries quickly with little degrade, and can be air- or kiln-dried. It is, however, liable to distortion and end-splitting, and blue stain may occur if it is stored incorrectly. Rough-turning is definitely recommended, especially for burrs (burls). Weigh the rough-turned wood periodically: when it ceases to lose weight, it is ready to turn.

Buckeye figure

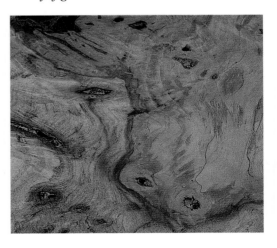

Grows
UK and mainland Europe; related species grown in the USA include **buckeye** (*A. glabra*, *A. flava* and other spp.)

HEIGHT 30–70ft (9–21m)

TRUNK DIAMETER 2–4ft (0.6–1.2m)

SPECIFIC GRAVITY .35–.51

TYPICAL DRY WEIGHT 25–31lb/ft³ (360–510kg/m³)

Hint

Try to get a fine finish straight from the gouge, followed by sanding to remove any minor imperfections. Scraping will likely cause grain tearout

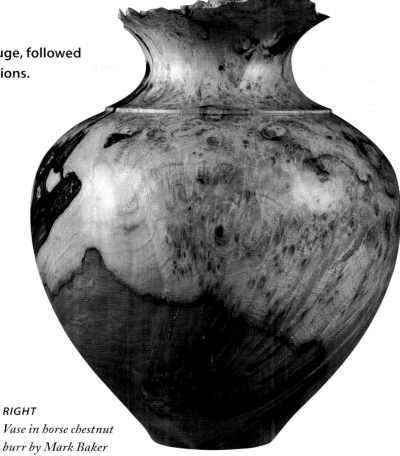

Though horse chestnut works wonderfully when wet, it can be a little problematic when seasoned, as it is prone to grain tearout when scrapers are used. Older pieces can be very dry, producing a lot of dust when turning, and very liable to grain pluckout. It is best to use bevel-rubbing tools and then go straight to abrasives to remove any minor blemishes.

If stored in damp conditions, the wood may be prone to fungal attack. A small amount of fungal staining may add interest, but if it goes too far and becomes rot it will seriously weaken this already soft wood, making it extremely tedious to work, with constant grain pullout.

RIGHT
Vase in horse chestnut burr by Mark Baker

BELOW
Bowl in buckeye burr by Ray Key

Being easy to work, horse chestnut has a variety of uses in the woodworking industry (cabinetmaking, interior construction and so on), but I think this bland-looking timber is best reserved for turning that is to be carved or sculpted, for which I find it very good. This does not apply to burred or figured pieces: these features really make the wood come alive. The burrs in particular are fantastic to work with.

Horse chestnut abrades well with the dry-sanding method. It finishes well (though it can be 'hungry' for finishes, bordering on greedy), and can be dyed to good effect. I find that a surface finish such as precatalysed lacquer is the most effective way to highlight the grain and figure.

She-oak

Allocasuarina fraseriana (syn. *Casuarina fraseriana*) and related species

Other names
Beefwood, Australian pine, horsetail tree, South-Sea ironwood, aru, ru, surra, agoho

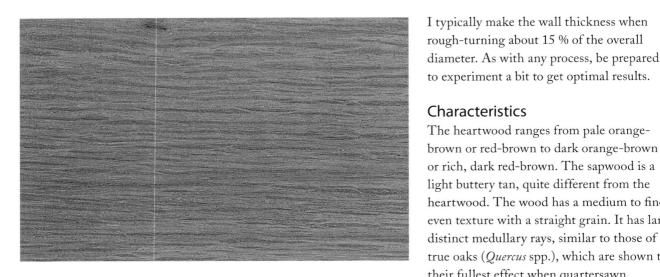

I typically make the wall thickness when rough-turning about 15 % of the overall diameter. As with any process, be prepared to experiment a bit to get optimal results.

Characteristics
The heartwood ranges from pale orange-brown or red-brown to dark orange-brown or rich, dark red-brown. The sapwood is a light buttery tan, quite different from the heartwood. The wood has a medium to fine, even texture with a straight grain. It has large, distinct medullary rays, similar to those of true oaks (*Quercus* spp.), which are shown to their fullest effect when quartersawn.

POSSIBLE HEALTH RISKS
Not known, but take the usual precautions regarding dust

CONSERVATION STATUS
Not known to be at risk

Seasoning
She-oak is difficult to dry; it is liable to warp and check, and shrinkage can be high. It is a lovely wood for wet-turning to completion: subsequent movement creates some fantastic twisted forms. It can also be rough-turned, allowing extra wall thickness to take account of the substantial shrinkage and distortion; coating the endgrain areas of the rough-turned piece with PVA helps slow down the drying and reduces the risk of splitting.

Lace figure

Grows
Australia, Africa, India, Indochina, Philippines, Polynesia
HEIGHT 120–150ft (37–45m)
TRUNK DIAMETER 2ft–2ft 6in (0.6–0.76m)
SPECIFIC GRAVITY .73
TYPICAL DRY WEIGHT 67lb/ft³ (1073kg/m³)

Working qualities

With its rich, beautiful colour, this timber is a true favourite of mine. She-oak turns well both wet and dry but, as with many timbers, you may encounter some pullout on endgrain areas, especially when scrapers are used – less so with bevel-rubbing tools such as gouges and skews. It is generally a very nice timber to work with. Since it can move a fair amount when drying, wet-turning this timber to thin wall thicknesses and then letting it dry will result in some nice distortion and wavy or twisted organic forms. The amount is variable, but this is well worth trying.

When cutting the timber it responds best to bevel-rubbing tools, but scrapers (except on very dry timber) produce a good-quality finish, too. She-oak can take reasonable detail such as fine 2mm beads, coves and V-cuts, and can be carved and routed, but I would advise against using details with ultrafine points or edges. Instead, leave micro-flats or very slightly radius the edges to minimize the risk of chipping, splintering or fracturing.

Hint

Try using oils to enhance the natural richness of colur and tonal qualities of the wood

This wood responds well to carving, routing and gluing up for laminating or segmented work, giving you more options to explore. I have not encountered any problems with sanding or applying surface finishes or oils and waxes of various kinds. I now mostly use oils and waxes on she-oak because I like the way that they enhance the tonal qualities and richness of the wood's colours. The wood sands easily and glues readily. It finishes well, accepting both penetrative and surface finishes without any problems.

My favourite finish on this timber is an oil finish, which is subsequently coated with a soft wax, then buffed – as on the finished pieces shown here.

BELOW
Lidded vessels by Mark Baker

Madrona
Arbutus menziesii

Other names
Strawberry tree, pacific madrone, coast madrone, arbutus, manzanita, madroño, jarrito

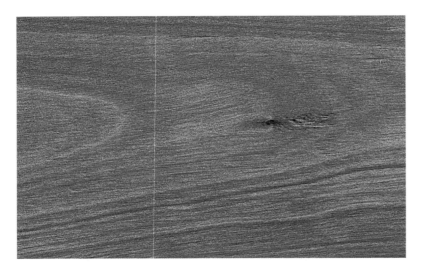

POSSIBLE HEALTH RISKS

Not known, but take the usual precautions regarding dust

CONSERVATION STATUS

Not known to be at risk

Characteristics

The light pink to pale red-brown heartwood can sometimes have red spots in it. The grain is fine, and may be either straight or irregular, with a smooth, uniform texture. Growth rings within the wood may form unusual, irregular patterns that can be particularly attractive.

The sapwood is whitish or sometimes cream, and may have a pink tinge. The burrs can be a riot of colour, ranging from creams through to vivid scarlet tints, with a variety of figuring, from swirling grain to knot clusters.

Not only the main trunk, but the branches and even the root system can be used, and the figuring and colour of root wood can be quite spectacular. These gnarled root forms are particularly prized by sculptors and turners.

Seasoning

This wood is difficult to dry. The very high moisture content of freshly cut wood can result in cell collapse, warping, excessive shrinking and checking as the wood dries. The shrinkage will be uneven, especially in burrs (burls). Rough-turning may work, but allow extra wall thickness and coat the piece with PVA to even out the drying. Even then, this method has a very high failure rate. As described later, this is a timber I find better turned when wet.

Burr (burl) detail

Grows
Canada and USA
HEIGHT 20–80ft (6–24m)
TRUNK DIAMETER 2–3ft (0.6–0.9m)
SPECIFIC GRAVITY .77
TYPICAL DRY WEIGHT 48lb/ft³ (770kg/m³)

Working qualities

This medium-density timber is a dream to work with when green. There will be long ribbons of shavings coming off the gouge, which is always a pleasant experience. Using scrapers on wet wood can be a little tricky, but light cuts with sharp tools will be OK. It can also be carved and routed well.

Madrona is also pleasant to work when freshly seasoned and dried, cutting cleanly with most tools but giving best results when bevel-rubbing tools are used. Old wood, however, may give rise to a great deal of dust. Areas of irregular grain require light cuts with a sharp tool to minimize grain pluckout.

I love turning this timber when it is wet to an even, very thin wall thickness – say $\frac{1}{8}$in (3mm) or less. The wood's tendency to shrink and warp will be utilized to maximum effect and, as it dries and twists, it can create some wonderfully warped organic forms. The amount of movement with this wood can be quite dramatic, even more so on figured wood.

When turning wet, I recommend a wet-sanding method using water as a lubricant and sanding it and keeping it wet through the sanding process. After sanding, let the wood dry, and then give it a final rub over using ultrafine abrasive to remove any 'woolly' areas prior to applying your finish of choice.

This timber can be carved and routed very easily and, when used on wet wood, everything moves and twists as it dries, the visual effect can be very interesting.

Seasoned wood sands well using either the wet or the dry sanding method. Madrona seems to accept all surface and penetrative finishes, including dyes, and can be polished to a high lustre if required. The burr forms are, to my way of thinking, shown off to full effect with a satin or gloss lacquer finish; oil finishes tend to dull the surface somewhat (unlike some other burrs, which are enhanced by oil), and a little of the natural vivacious sparkle is lost. Have a go and see what you think of it.

Hint

When turning wet wood, maintain an even wall thickness throughout, or you will very likely experience splitting due to differential drying and contraction rates

BELOW
Vase in madrona burr
by Mark Baker

Pink ivory
Berchemia zeyheri
(syn. Rhamnus zeyheri)

Other names
Red ivory wood, pau preto, umgoloti, mucarane, sungangona

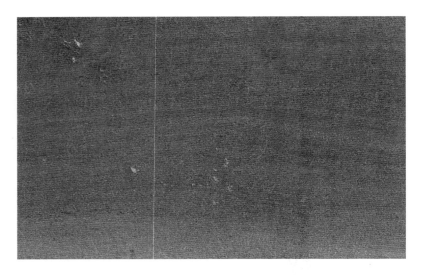

POSSIBLE HEALTH RISKS

Not known, but take the usual precautions regarding dust

CONSERVATION STATUS

Not known to be at risk

Seasoning

This wood is difficult to air-dry, and if you kiln-dry it you have to take care, or degrade can be severe. High differential shrinkage may cause major distortion, and the wood also shows large amounts of movement in use. It can be wet-turned to completion but, considering the type of projects usually undertaken with this wood, it is generally more appropriate to rough-turn it before further seasoning, allowing ¹⁄₄in (6mm) or more of extra wall thickness per 12in (300mm) diameter to account for the high distortion rate.

Characteristics

This beautiful wood is dense, hard and heavy. The heartwood is yellowish-brown to deep red in colour, while the sapwood is off-white to grey. It has straight to interlocked grain with a fine pore structure and a fairly fine and even texture. It has a pinkish striped figure that is created by alternating bands of dark and light wood in the growth rings.

Since it is only available in small sizes, either as precut blanks or as logs, typical uses would include small boxes or hollow forms. When heartwood and sapwood are used in combination, the colour contrast can be very effective. The wood can hold very fine detail. It has a medium to severe blunting effect on cutting edges, and bandsaw blades do not last long when dimensioning this wood.

Sadly, the wood loses a lot of the richness of its pink-red colour over time and mellows to a soft brown with a pink tinge. The use of finishes with UV inhibitors retards this process but does not stop the colour degrade fully.

Oiled finish

Grows
Mozambique; also southern and southeastern Africa
HEIGHT 20–40ft (6–12m)
TRUNK DIAMETER 7–12in (0.2–0.3m)
SPECIFIC GRAVITY .90
TYPICAL DRY WEIGHT 56lb/ft³ (900kg/m³)

Working qualities

This is a great wood to work with. It cuts well with gouges and scrapers, which produce fine shavings and leave a very fine finish straight off the tool. Skew chisels can be a problem if interlocking grain is present, but light cuts will usually solve this. If the wood is old it can be dusty to work, but it is not usually so. Sharp tools are vital, and they will need frequent sharpening while working this wood.

It is dense enough to be used for thread-chasing by hand, but if interlocking grain is present there is a risk of the threads fracturing or chipping out.

Pink ivory is a nice wood to carve (power tools are easier than hand-carving) or rout. Careful sanding is required to avoid heat-checking. The grain on wet-turned wood may fluff up a little, so, after sanding, allow the piece to dry and then sand again by hand prior to applying the finish of your choice. Surface finishes or oils or waxes can be used, and the wood can be taken to a very high polish.

ABOVE
Box in pink ivory and ebony (diospyros *spp.*) *by Ray Key*

BELOW
Bowl by Bert Marsh

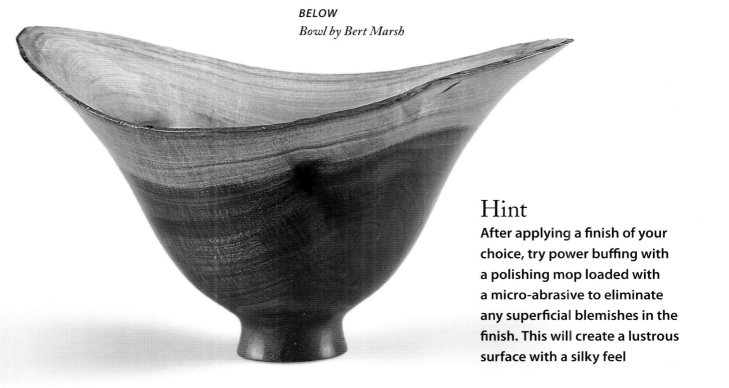

Hint

After applying a finish of your choice, try power buffing with a polishing mop loaded with a micro-abrasive to eliminate any superficial blemishes in the finish. This will create a lustrous surface with a silky feel

Silver birch

Betula pendula (syn. *B. verrucosa*),
B. pubescens, B. alba

Other names
**European birch; downy or hairy birch
(*B. pubescens* and *B. alba*); also English, Finnish,
Swedish birch, and, additionally, according to
figure: flame, ice, curly, masur birch**

Characteristics
The heartwood and sapwood alike can range
from creamy-white to pale brown. The wood
is usually straight- and fine-grained with
even texture, and has a lustrous appearance
and a delicate grain pattern. Irregularities
in the grain can cause both flame and curly
figuring. Birch is also prone to spalting, which
can create dramatic colouring and patterning
effects in the wood.

This underrated timber has a wonderful
silky lustre that turners can exploit to the full.
It will mellow to a light tan after a while, but
will retain its natural lustre.

Masur birch is the term used to describe a
distinctive flecked, flame-like figuring in the
wood. This was once ascribed to beetle attack
but it is now known to be a hereditary genetic
variant of birch, termed *B. pendula* var. *carelica*.

POSSIBLE HEALTH RISKS

Dermatitis and
respiratory health
problems

CONSERVATION STATUS

Categorized as 'least
concern' in Red List

Seasoning
The wood must be dried rapidly to avoid
fungal attacks. It is also slightly prone to
warping. Rough-turning followed by further
seasoning is a must for larger work, so as to
avoid undue movement.

Ripple figure

Grows
Europe, including UK and Scandinavia; grows further north
than any other broadleaved tree
HEIGHT 60–70ft (18–21m)
TRUNK DIAMETER 2–3ft (0.6–0.9m)
SPECIFIC GRAVITY .66
TYPICAL DRY WEIGHT 41lb/ft³ (660kg/m³)

Working qualities

This is a hard, tough wood of medium density that cuts well in most instances, provided care is taken with figured pieces. It doesn't always produce nice ribbon-like shavings, but not all woods do. It is available in reasonably large sizes, so a range of projects can be undertaken, my favourites being platters and hollow forms using figured wood. Plain close-grained timber is suitable for kitchenware. Birch cuts well with bevel-rubbing tools most of the time, though occasionally it can be a bit woolly – especially when turned wet – and tearout may occur in the vicinity of crossed or interlocking grain or knots. Shear-scraping can sometimes improve a gouge-cut surface; conventional scraping, even with a delicate touch, may cause the grain to pluck out.

If birch is felled and left for a while, it may spalt. However, spalted birch can degrade quickly, so a balance must be struck between having enough spalting to make it interesting and becoming too rotten to work with. Spalted wood also creates a problem with sanding: you may well have to reinforce areas with sanding sealer or superglue (cyanoacrylate) to harden them before turning or sanding.

The timber can be carved, routed and glued up for laminated and segmented work, making it a versatile timber worth exploring.

Sanding and finishing plain or masur-figured timber is no problem. If you are working with spalted timber, you might end up with the spalting contaminating the clean timber and making it look dirty. I find soaking the wood in a thinned-down shellac or lacquer mix to penetrate and seal the fibres, letting it dry and then sanding it, minimizes this risk.

Birch readily accepts all finishes and glues well, but can be a little 'hungry', requiring several coats to avoid a blotchy look. Dyeing is effective, especially on figured pieces, to accentuate the figure. Oil is particularly good at enhancing the already warm lustre of the wood.

RIGHT
Box in spalted birch
by Mark Baker

BELOW
Tall hollow vessel
in masur birch
with black accent
by Ray Key

Hint

When working with spalted wood that is on the soft side, saturate the wood with a 40–50% thinned solution of sanding sealer. Allow it to dry fully, and then turn to a fine finish. The sealer will harden the fibres of the wood enough to allow you to turn it without too much pluckout

Boxwood
Buxus sempervirens

Other names
Box; often identified also by country of origin, e.g. Iranian box

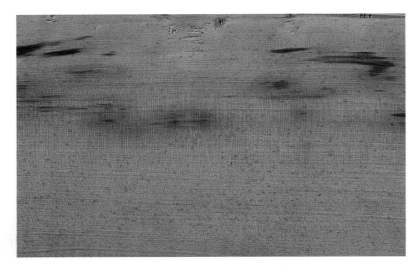

Characteristics
Varying in colour from butter to lemon yellow, boxwood is dense, hard and heavy. It has a beautiful, fine, uniform texture, and the heart and sapwood are not clearly differentiated. Tight, pippy knots and fungal staining are fairly common. It is usually straight-grained but can occasionally be irregular. Only available in small pieces, boxwood is commonly used for boxes, small hollow forms and bowls. Its ability to hold very fine detail without breaking out means that it is also prized for small carved work, and it is one of the timbers ideally suited to exploring the creation of hand-chased screw threads.

Working qualities
This is a fantastic timber to work with, and one of the nicest you are likely to encounter. It's just a shame that it's not available in larger sizes.

POSSIBLE HEALTH RISKS

Dermatitis; dust is an irritant to eyes, nose and throat

CONSERVATION STATUS

Not known to be at risk

Seasoning
Owing to its small diameter, box is mainly dried in the round. End-coating with PVA is essential to minimize splitting but, in truth, even with very slow air-drying under cover, it is very common to experience splitting along the length of the piece, rendering the wood unusable except for small items. It may be necessary to rough-turn the wood to stabilize it prior to finish-turning, especially when making boxes with close-fitting lids. For other types of project you might consider using partially seasoned timber, bearing in mind that it will move a little.

Grows
UK, mainland Europe, Turkey, western Asia
HEIGHT 20–30ft (6–9m)
TRUNK DIAMETER up to 8in (0.2m), but usually less than 6in (0.15m)
SPECIFIC GRAVITY .91
TYPICAL DRY WEIGHT 57lb/ft³ (910kg/m³)

BELOW
Natural-edged bowl in boxwood burr by Ray Key

Hint

When chasing threads, a little paste wax will act as a lubricant, making cutting easier still

What boxwood lacks in size it more than makes up for in its beauty to turn, its ability to hold very fine detail and the ease with which it can be turned.

It cuts well with all tools: even with a conventional scraper, long ribbon shavings can be produced, leaving a surface that may not require anything but a small amount of sanding using fine grades. If creating fine detail you do not want to use coarse grades anyway or all your hard work creating that detail will be wasted and the detail blurred or worn away.

For thread-chasing, use clean, stain-free wood. Fungal infection or spalting can make the wood a little softer than normal and cause the chased threads to break out.

Its ability to hold fine detail make this timber a superb candidate for carving and routing and the endgrain will also hold a chatter pattern well.

Being only available in relatively small sizes, it is excellent as a timber to be used in conjunction with another to create visual contrast. African blackwood *(Dalbergia melanoxylon)* and boxwood, for example, contrast brilliantly with each other. This is a wood that can be wet-turned to good effect; an even, thin wall thickness is necessary to reduce the risk of splitting.

Box responds well to sanding; wet-sanding will reduce the frictional heat and the risk of heat-checking. When the wood is dry, it accepts all finishes but, being dense, nothing penetrates too far into the wood. Lacquers, oils and waxes all work well.

BELOW
Box in spalted figure
by Mark Baker

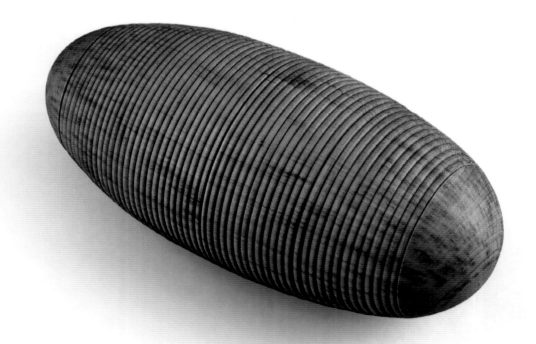

Sweet chestnut
Castanea sativa

Other names
European chestnut, Spanish chestnut

Characteristics
A delightful wood, the heartwood of which is is light brown to yellow-brown; it is not dissimilar to oak in appearance, but with finer or less prominent rays on quartersawn surfaces. The sapwood of this timber is very thin and pale, and distinct from the heartwood.

The grain is usually straight but it is not unusual to see spiral grain in older trees. (Spiral growth is often visible on the outside of the trunk also.) The colouring is distinctive and very beautiful; it sometimes has darker brown streaks running through it. The texture is coarse, and shakes can frequently be found in older trees. Although chestnut rarely forms burrs, figuring is not uncommon, and adds a further dimension to this wonderful timber.

Available in large sizes, sweet chestnut is suitable for many projects. It is often used in the cabinetmaking trade as a substitute for oak. Other common uses include artistic and ornamental turning, domestic ware and furniture parts.

POSSIBLE HEALTH RISKS
Dermatitis, possibly caused by bark lichens

CONSERVATION STATUS
Not known to be at risk

Seasoning
This wood is difficult to dry. It is best dried slowly, and is liable to degrade, suffering from cell collapse and honeycombing. The movement in service is small. Where accuracy is required, rough-turning is a must, to stabilize the wood prior to finish-turning. Alternatively, wet-turn it to completion and then allow the piece to move.

Grows
Europe, chiefly southwest and Mediterranean areas
HEIGHT 100–115ft (30–50m)
TRUNK DIAMETER 5ft (1.5m)
SPECIFIC GRAVITY .54
TYPICAL DRY WEIGHT 34lb/ft³ (540kg/m³)

Figured sample

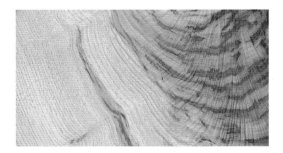

Working qualities

Though chestnut resembles oak, it is easier to work. It is a medium-density wood. Wet or dry, it cuts cleanly with freshly sharpened tools, though scrapers are likely to pluck out endgrain areas. Having said that, this timber is very forgiving to turn.

The wood has a sweet smell when freshly cut. Because of the tannin in it, it may stain hands and steel blue. If left in contact with steel too long it can corrode it, causing surface pitting, so clean the lathe and tools well after using this timber.

Chestnut can be carved and routed with ease but avoid ultrafine sharp edges. It is relatively soft and can be dented easily. It does not present any problems when gluing so is good for laminated and segmented work.

It sands well with either wet or dry sanding methods, and accepts finishes well with penetrative or surface finishes.

If you require an absolutely smooth surface finish you will need to fill the grain. Either apply many coats of a surface lacquer, cutting back between coats to fill the open grain (this is my preferred option), or treat with a grain filler before applying the finish of your choice.

Due to the tannin content this is a timber that responds very well to fuming, so you can create a deeper, richer colour.

This is another underrated wood that I recommend you try.

Hint
You can deepen the colour of sweet chestnut by fuming it with ammonia

ABOVE AND BELOW
Platter by Mark Baker,
finished with oil

61

Ziracote
Cordia dodecandra

Other names
Ziricote, zircote, sericote, siricote, canalete, peterebi, laurel

POSSIBLE HEALTH RISKS

Not known, but take the usual precautions regarding dust

CONSERVATION STATUS

Not known to be at risk

Seasoning

The wood is slow-drying and fairly difficult to season. It is prone to surface checking and may develop end splits. Rough-turning and then setting it aside to season further is recommended. Coating the whole piece or just the endgrain in PVA will even out the drying process and reduce the likelihood of checking or splitting. It is a timber that can be turned from start to finish when wet or partially seasoned. In my experience it does not move massively, so very warped forms are unlikely.

However, if you want to turn nicely fitted lids on boxes you will have trouble unless you rough-turn it and set it aside to dry first before finish-turning.

Characteristics

The brownish-yellow sapwood is clearly distinguished from the heartwood. The latter is a reddish-brown colour with irregular, wavy, dark streaks. Dark markings on the wood often run at an angle to the main axis of the tree, making a pattern that is unique and highly decorative. The erratic nature of these markings means that you are never quite sure what the piece will be like until you start to cut it; the result can be a real treat. It usually has straight or interlocked grain, a fine to medium texture and an average lustre. Ziracote is a medium-density timber that holds fine detail well. Not often found in large sizes, this wood is mainly used for artistic and decorative turning.

BELOW
Box by Bert Marsh

Grows

Belize, Guatemala, Mexico
HEIGHT 60–90ft (20–28m)
TRUNK DIAMETER 2ft 6in (0.75m) max.
SPECIFIC GRAVITY .65–.85
TYPICAL DRY WEIGHT 41–53lb/ft³ (650–850kg/m³)

Working qualities

Ziracote cuts well with gouges and scrapers when wet or dry, but you will need to sharpen the tools regularly. It will, more often than not, produce chips and dust rather than ribbon shavings when turning dry timber; this is a result of the interlocking grain, and does not indicate that the grain is pulling out. Ziracote blunts bandsaw blades quickly. Chatterwork is possible on the endgrain, but the wood is not quite hard enough to hold a fine hand-chased thread, although I have had some success with 10 tpi (threads per inch) or coarser. It can be carved by hand reasonably well, but even though it is dustier, power carving and routing are easier. Ziracote is suitable for wet-turning to completion, and produces little dust, but you might get slightly fewer chips and maybe a few short shavings when turning it wet.

Dry rather than wet sanding is recommended to avoid colour contamination if the sapwood is present. But be careful: seasoned wood produces a lot of acrid, choking dust when turned or sanded, and it is prone to heat-checking. Use fresh abrasive

Hint

Chatterwork on endgrain is difficult to clean up once created. Use sharp tools to start with, to make sure that you get a clean cut that will only require polishing

when sanding, and work through the grades; the natural oils in the wood may clog the abrasives. The wood can be brought to a very fine finish before any finishes are applied.

Surface finishes such as lacquers and shellac, as well as oils and waxes, do not appear to present any problems on this timber. If you are making segmented or laminated work, this timber usually presents few problems regarding gluing or bonding it to other timbers.

This is a beautiful wood. Its colour pigmentation never fails to delight. Some woods come alive in large-scale work, but I think ziracote is a real gem when used to create well-crafted, delicate, small pieces.

BELOW
Bowl by Bert Marsh

Brazilian tulipwood

Dalbergia decipularis, D. frutescens
and related species

Other names

Pau rosa, bois de rose, pinkwood, pau de fuso, jacarandá rosa. Not to be confused with American tulipwood (*Liriodendron tulipifera*), which is not related

Characteristics

A wood that shouts it presence far and wide, Brazilian tulipwood is dense, hard and heavy, with an oily feel to it. The very distinctive creamy-yellow sapwood contrasts well with the heartwood, which has a variegated striped figure in various shades of soft pink, rose, violet or maroon on a cream or straw-coloured background. This really is one of the peacocks of the wood world. After exposure to light, the fantastic colouring will mellow down a little, the rich markings remaining distinct but losing a little of their fresh-cut vibrancy. The grain can vary from straight to roey and can be erratic, irregular and interlocking. The wood is fine in texture and has a natural high lustre. It is a timber capable of holding fine detail and can be hand-thread chased down to about 16tpi if careful. I have seen finer threads on this wood, but have experienced problems creating finer than 16tpi myself.

The small sizes available may be thought to restrict its possible uses, but if this vibrant wood were available in sufficient size for a platter, imagine how gaudy it would be! Smaller is definitely better, to maximize the visual impact of this stunning wood.

POSSIBLE HEALTH RISKS

Not known, but take the usual precautions regarding dust

CONSERVATION STATUS

Not listed by CITES or Red List, but special licence may be required from country of origin

Seasoning

This wood usually dries without any problems, with a low risk of twisting and checking.

To avoid movement, rough-turning and setting it aside to season further is recommended. Alternatively, the wood can be turned to completion wet or partially seasoned, but will distort a bit.

RIGHT
Box by Mark Baker

Grows

Mainly northeast Brazil, Colombia, Guyana and Venezuela

HEIGHT AND DIAMETER As the tree is small and the trunk irregular in shape, it is generally sold in small billets

SPECIFIC GRAVITY .96

TYPICAL DRY WEIGHT 60lb/ft³ (960kg/m³)

Working qualities

Popular uses for this wood include small boxes, bowls, vases and other decorative items. Tulipwood can be a little tricky to work: although close-grained and dense, it is liable to splinter or fracture a little if you attempt to form sharp, fine edges. This problem is most common when using it for furniture-making, but it can occasionally happen when turning. Having said that, for the most part this is a well-behaved wood and a pleasure to work.

Brazilian tulipwood often yields a fine finish straight from the tool, which may require only minimal sanding to remove minor blemishes. It generally produces a nice cut from scrapers, too.

It is often used in segmented and laminated work, but due to its slightly oily nature, it might be prudent to dewax it before bonding it to other timbers. This is a timber that can be carved and routed well; these might be elements you want to explore and integrate into your work.

ABOVE
Box by Bert Marsh

BELOW
Bowl by Bert Marsh

Dry sanding will produce a lot of very fine dust that has a peppery smell and, because the wood is slightly oily or resinous, it will readily clog abrasives. It can heat-check on endgrain if you sand so heavily that excess heat is generated, so care is needed when sanding.

The wood can be finished to a high polish with both penetrative and surface finishes, and surfaces can be further enhanced and brought to a fine lustre by buffing. The colours may fade over time, but using finishes with UV inhibitors will help retard this process.

Hint
Use a fine-bristled bronze brush to clean clogged abrasives. This will extend their useful life

Sonokeling rosewood
Dalbergia latifolia

Other names
Indian rosewood, East Indian rosewood, Bombay blackwood, Indian palisander, Java palisander, malabar, shisham, biti, eravidi, kalaruk

POSSIBLE HEALTH RISKS

Dermatitis, asthma and respiratory problems

CONSERVATION STATUS

Categorized as 'vulnerable' in Red List; export from India is prohibited unless plantation-grown

Seasoning
The wood dries quite quickly with very little degrade. However, let it dry too quickly and end-splitting and surface checking may occur. It responds well to rough-turning and setting it aside to stabilize and dry further. Turners often use this timber in small sizes for making boxes with close-fitting lids, in which case it is essential to stabilize it by rough-turning so as to maintain the fit. It is suitable for wet-turning, if you can get large enough pieces.

Characteristics
This beautiful wood is hard, dense and heavy. The heartwood varies from rich rose to a deep brown with dark purple-black lines streaking through it, resulting in a very attractive pattern. It has a narrow, interlocking, cross grain with a moderately coarse and uniform texture. When quartersawn, it can display a wonderful ribbon figure. The sapwood, which is distinct from the heartwood, has a yellowish-white tinge, sometimes with a hint of purple colouring. Fresh-cut wood has a pleasant smell, but this wears off as it dries. The name 'sonokeling' is used for wood that is plantation-grown. When finished well this is a beautiful-looking wood. Sonokeling rosewood is used extensively in the furniture trade, for high-class joinery and for artistic and decorative turnings.

BELOW
Vessel by John Jordan, detail of carving

Grows
India and southeast Asia

HEIGHT 100ft (30m)

TRUNK DIAMETER 2ft 6in (0.75m), sometimes broader

SPECIFIC GRAVITY .85

TYPICAL DRY WEIGHT 53lb/ft³ (850kg/m³)

Working qualities

This hard, dense wood frequently contains mineral deposits that will blunt bandsaw blades and other cutting edges quickly, sometimes severely. That said, it turns satisfactorily with most tools. The best cuts are achieved with bevel-rubbing tools, but frequent sharpening may be necessary to maintain an effective edge.

Having a moderately coarse texture, it does not, in my experience, hold very fine detail without breaking out on points or fine, sharp edges. However, it can be carved and routed to good effect; use power carving to make life easier for yourself.

The wood will darken with age, mellowing to a rich, deep brown that will continue to show the dark streaks running through it. Finishes with UV inhibitors will help retard the darkening process. If you are fortunate to get a section of log or a natural-edge bowl blank that includes contrasting sap and heartwood sections, you can make a piece that creates even more of a spectacle – not that this timber isn't stunning enough in the first place.

This rosewood usually sands reasonably well, but heat-checking may occur if excessive heat is generated. The grain may need filling if a super-smooth surface is required.

RIGHT
Box by Chris Stott

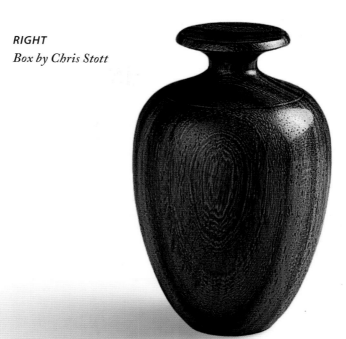

Hint

When cutting detail, leave a micro-flat on the edge or crown to minimize the risk of breakout or fracturing

BELOW
Vessel by John Jordan

Wet sanding causes the grain to fill with the sanding slurry, and this should be sufficient, though this method does have a slight darkening effect on the timber. It is receptive to both surface and penetrative finishes.

African blackwood
Dalbergia melanoxylon

Other names
Mozambique ebony, mpingo, African grenadillo, pau preto

Characteristics

This very dense, dark, oily wood is sometimes referred to as an ebony, but in fact it is related to the rosewoods. (The real ebonies are *Diospyros* spp.) The sapwood is narrow and a soft yellow-cream in colour, providing a stark contrast to the heartwood, which is a dark, rich purple-brown with black streaks. The grain is often straight, but can vary. It is one of the blackest, darkest, densest timbers a turner is likely to encounter. Most people assume it is solid black, but if you look closely you will see that there is a delicate but distinct grain pattern. The wood can be slightly oily to the touch, and is very fine and even-textured, heavy and hard.

It is only available in small sizes, which limits the turning possibilities, but its looks are stunning, especially when heartwood and sapwood are contrasted. It is used for woodwind instruments, decorative or artistic turning and cabinetmaking.

POSSIBLE HEALTH RISKS

Sneezing, conjunctivitis, acute dermatitis

CONSERVATION STATUS

Categorized as 'lower risk/near threatened' in Red List. Special licence required from country of origin

Seasoning

This is a very slow-drying wood and it can take 2–3 years to be fully seasoned. It is part-seasoned in log or billet form, then converted, end-coated and stacked under cover. Problems with heart shakes and end splitting mean that only small sections are commonly available. Rough-turning and setting the pieces aside for further drying is recommended.

Unfinished surface

Grows

Eastern Africa

HEIGHT 15–20ft (4.5–6m)

TRUNK DIAMETER Rarely more than 1ft (0.3m)

SPECIFIC GRAVITY 1.2

TYPICAL DRY WEIGHT 75lb/ft³ (1200kg/m³)

Working qualities

African blackwood is a wonderful wood to work with. Being dense and very fine-grained, it will hold very fine detail and is ideal to use for thread-chasing by hand. These qualities also enable it to be carved and routed well. The wood cuts well but blunts tools quickly, and has a severe blunting effect on bandsaw blades. Long ribbon shavings are rare; instead, you are likely to get small curls, sometimes chips, and quite a lot of dust. The dust is a real pain, but the results are worthwhile. Try turning a natural-edge piece, incorporating some sapwood: the vivid contrast with the heartwood gives a stunning effect.

It is often used with other woods, to provide a contrasting accent. White or cream woods such as holly (*Ilex* spp.) or boxwood (*Buxus sempervirens*), and red or orange woods such as padauk (*Pterocarpus* spp.), work particularly well. It might need degreasing before gluing it to another piece of wood.

It is an excellent wood to carve and rout, although power caving is considerably easier than hand carving. Blackwood is prone to heat-checking, so care is needed when sanding. If no sapwood is present it can be sanded wet or dry, although dry sanding will produce a lot of noxious dust. If sapwood is present you have to be careful not to let the dark heartwood dust contaminate the cream sapwood. Finishing is easy and the wood can be taken to a high lustre using penetrative or surface finishes. Although penetrative finishes do not penetrate that far, they still work well on this wood.

Hint

Minute splits and checks can be filled with superglue (cyanoacrylate) and sanded while the adhesive is still wet; the mixture of dust and adhesive will set and fill the crack

ABOVE
Ogee bowl by Bert Marsh, showing both heartwood and sapwood

BELOW
Natural-edged bowl by Bert Marsh

Cocobolo
Dalbergia retusa

Other names
Granadillo, Nicaraguan rosewood, pau preto, caviuna, nambar, cocobolo prieto, palo negro, palo sandro

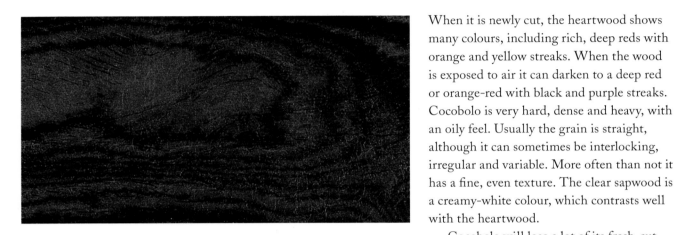

When it is newly cut, the heartwood shows many colours, including rich, deep reds with orange and yellow streaks. When the wood is exposed to air it can darken to a deep red or orange-red with black and purple streaks. Cocobolo is very hard, dense and heavy, with an oily feel. Usually the grain is straight, although it can sometimes be interlocking, irregular and variable. More often than not it has a fine, even texture. The clear sapwood is a creamy-white colour, which contrasts well with the heartwood.

Cocobolo will lose a lot of its fresh-cut vibrancy on exposure to light. The wood will darken considerably over time, taking on a much richer brown colouring; the streaks remain visible. It is available in reasonably large sizes, but more often than not it is used to make highly decorative small pieces, where the beauty of the grain is shown to its fullest.

POSSIBLE HEALTH RISKS

Skin irritation from dust; conjunctivitis, nausea, asthma and irritation to the nose and throat

Seasoning
Cocobolo dries very slowly, with a tendency to split and check, and should be air-dried rather than kilned. The wood is stable in use, as the natural oil content acts as a barrier to water absorption. However, rough-turning and setting it aside to season further is essential to prevent undue movement if you are making fine or delicate items such as boxes.

CONSERVATION STATUS

Vulnerable. Special licence may be required from country of origin

Characteristics
This rosewood species is another one that draws attention to itself: both visually and physically, it is a beautiful wood. Cocobolo is a close-grained wood that will hold fine detail and can be carved and routed to good effect.

BELOW
Box by Bert Marsh

Grows
Pacific areas of Central America
HEIGHT 45–60ft (13–18m)
TRUNK DIAMETER 1ft 6in–2ft (0.5–0.6m)
SPECIFIC GRAVITY 1.10
TYPICAL DRY WEIGHT 68lb/ft³ (1100kg/m³)

Working qualities

This is a wood that cuts well on the lathe, producing small curled shavings rather than long ribbons from the gouge. It can create quite a bit of fine dust, which is oily, clings to surfaces, and will also stain clothing. The finish from the cut can be exceptionally good. It cuts well with scrapers, but best with gouges and skews. If the oily dust sticks to the bevel of the tool, it needs to be cleared from time to time to ensure a controlled cut. The wood takes very fine detail and can be carved and routed. It can also be used for chasing threads by hand, although it is not as good as boxwood (*Buxus sempervirens*) or African blackwood (*Dalbergia melanoxylon*). It is suitable for carving and routing. Power carving is better than hand carving on this timber but carving this timber can yield stunning results.

Cocobolo is prone to heat-checking if one is not careful with sanding, so take care and work through the grades with fresh, sharp abrasive and a light touch. As long as sapwood is not present, it can be wet-sanded; this will avoid the fine, choking dust that is produced by dry sanding. Because of its oily nature, some surface finishes (lacquer, for example) may occasionally fail to adhere firmly; it can also gum up bandsaw blades a little.

RIGHT
Beaded vase
by Mark Baker

Hint

If applying a surface finish such as lacquer, wipe the work over first with a cellulose thinner to clean the surface and remove any oiliness

BELOW
Bowl by Ray Key

Adhesion can also be a problem when trying to glue cocobolo if one hasn't dewaxed the surface of the wood first. There is no difficulty in using oil and waxes as a finish.

Tasmanian oak

Eucalyptus delegatensis, E. obliqua and *E. regnans*

Other names
Alpine ash, white-top or gum-top stringybark, woollybutt (*E. delegatensis*); messmate stringybark, brown-top stringybark (*E. obliqua*); stringy gum, swamp gum, Victorian ash (*E. regnans*). All three species are sold as 'Tasmanian oak'

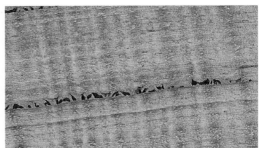

Ripple figure

POSSIBLE HEALTH RISKS

Dermatitis, asthma, sneezing, irritant to eyes, nose and throat

CONSERVATION STATUS

Not known to be at risk

Seasoning

This wood dries quite rapidly, but if care is not taken there is a high risk of distortion, surface checking, internal checking and cell collapse. As the wood moves quite a lot it is an ideal candidate for wet-turning. If stable timber is needed, rough-turn your piece, leaving a wall thickness equal to 15% of the overall diameter to allow for the increased level of warping and distortion that is likely with this wood. Seal the endgrain areas with PVA to cause the wood to dry more slowly, then set it aside to dry further before turning to completion.

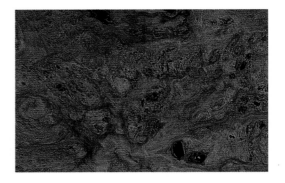

Burr (burl) detail

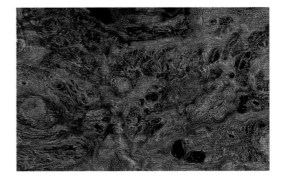

Burr with oiled finish

Grows
Southeast Australia and Tasmania
HEIGHT 200–300ft (60–90m)
TRUNK DIAMETER 3–7ft (1–2.3m)
SPECIFIC GRAVITY .62–.78
TYPICAL DRY WEIGHT 39–49lb/ft³ (620–780kg/m³)

Characteristics

This medium-dense wood has a slight blunting effect on tools. The heartwood is usually a pale creamy-tan to pale brown colour with a pinkish tinge. The sapwood is paler and not distinct from the heartwood. The grain is usually straight but can be wavy or interlocked.

It has a coarse, open, even texture and the growth rings are often clearly visible. The wood is neither a true ash nor a true oak; it resembles plainsawn European oak (*Quercus robur* or *Q. petraea*), but without the silver grain. It produces delightful burrs (burls) and, as with many woods, there is a lot of colour variation from piece to piece – especially in the burrs, which can range from a rich orange-tan to a soft brown. Sometimes gum veins are present. It mellows quickly on exposure to light, and loses its fresh-cut look. Available in quite large sizes, it can be used for a variety of projects.

Working qualities

This is a nice wood to work with. It does tend to blunt tool edges a little, especially bandsaw blades, but does not present the turner with any major problems. As with any wood, sharp tools are required to achieve a clean cut. If you use scrapers you are likely to pull or fluff up the grain a bit. A delicate cut with a gouge, followed by a freshly sharpened gouge used with the handle held lower than normal so you get more of a shearing cut, should be all that is necessary to remove wood and refine the surface prior to sanding. The wood can be wet-turned to create thin walls and then allowed to move as it will. Tasmanian oak also carves well with hand tools, but better still with power tools.

Sanding and finishing are not a problem. Sanding is easy and it readily takes dyes and other penetrative and surface finishes to achieve the required look and feel.

BELOW
Bowl by Bert Marsh

Hint

Tasmanian oak stains well, and staining can be used to enhance the grain when figuring is present

Jarrah
Eucalyptus marginata

Other names
(Formerly) Swan River mahogany

Characteristics

Jarrah is a medium-dense, hard, heavy wood, the heartwood of which varies from pink through rich orange-red to brownish-red colours. It is sometimes marked by short, dark flecks on the endgrain, with crescent-shaped flecks on the flatsawn surface. It often has dark brown or black streaks, and sometimes has bark inclusions (pockets of ingrown bark).

The colour of the wood is variable, and can change to a rich mahogany-red on exposure to light. Over time, the wood darkens considerably with exposure. The grain is usually straight but can be interlocked or wavy, and it has a moderately coarse, even texture. Veins and gum pockets are commonly found. The sapwood is a creamy-yellow colour and is distinct from the heartwood, but darkens with age. It often forms burrs (burls), and both burrs and trunk wood are available in nice large dimensions, enabling a wide range of projects to be undertaken. The burr form is stunning.

POSSIBLE HEALTH RISKS

Irritation to eyes, nose and throat

CONSERVATION STATUS

Not known to be at risk

Seasoning

Jarrah needs careful drying, and it is best to air-dry before kiln-drying. Wide stock may check or warp while drying, and cell collapse can often occur. To minimize movement, rough-turning to allow the wood to stabilize and dry is recommended. This is also a great wood to use if you want to turn your work wet and then let it move as it wants. Wet-turned burrs will dry to create a nice 'hammered' effect across the surface, which is very pleasing to look at and to touch.

Burr with oiled finish

Grows

Southwest Australia

HEIGHT 100–150ft (30–45m)

TRUNK DIAMETER 3–6ft (0.9–1.8m)

SPECIFIC GRAVITY .80

TYPICAL DRY WEIGHT 50lb/ft³ (800kg/m³)

Working qualities

This is a gorgeous wood to work with, especially the burrs or figured timber. It can be a little tricky to turn, however. Seasoned timber does not produce long ribbon shavings; instead it usually makes short, curly shavings or chippings, all of which are accompanied by a dirty dust, especially on seasoned and very old timber. This applies to both the figured and the standard forms of the wood. If you turn it wet, it is much more likely to give you better shavings, but again, it produces chippings rather than nice ribbons. The interlocking grain and the figured areas with irregular grain are prone to plucking out, and the edges of the work may be brittle and inclined to splinter. Scraping tools used in the conventional mode will often pluck the grain – but even gouges will do that. Occasionally a delicate scrape will give a better result than a good gouge cut. With light cuts this will not cause much tearout, and what there is can be dealt with by sanding afterwards.

It can be power-carved and routed, but be wary of creating very sharp edges and peaks as these might fracture or chip.

Hint

Fissures, cracks, resin pockets and suchlike can fill up with sanding dust and finishes. Clean the dust out prior to applying a finish, and wipe off the gathered finish before it gels

RIGHT
Bowl in jarrah burr by Bert Marsh

BELOW
Platter by Mark Baker

Jarrah can be sanded wet or dry. With burr wood, wet sanding may result in the open structure filling with sanding slurry, which can be unsightly and may need to be cleaned out before applying the finish. Because the wood may have gum pockets, especially in burrs, oil is my favoured form of finish for this timber. Good results can be achieved with either surface or penetrative finishes.

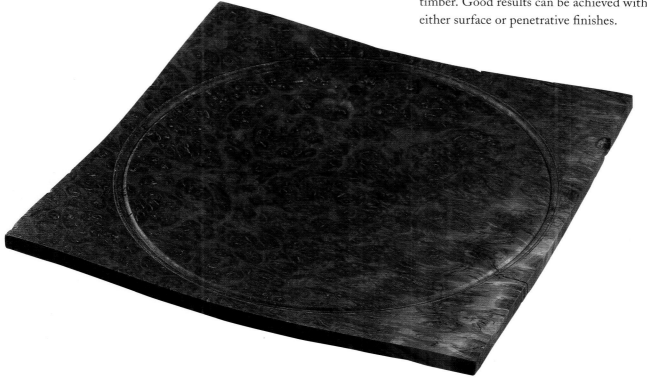

European beech
Fagus sylvatica

Other names
English, Danish, French, Romanian beech, depending on country of origin

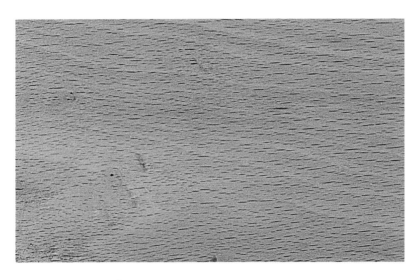

POSSIBLE HEALTH RISKS

Dermatitis, eye irritation, decrease in lung function, rare incidence of nasal cancer

CONSERVATION STATUS

Not known to be at risk

Seasoning

The wood dries fairly rapidly but may warp, check and shrink, so care is needed whether air- or kiln-drying. Spindle work for furniture and joinery can be made from well-seasoned air-dried beech that has been stored in a heated workshop, or from kiln-dried stock of about 10–12% moisture content; but for items such as hollow forms, boxes or bowls, rough-turning followed by further seasoning is advisable.

Characteristics

Beech is a moderately dense wood, the heartwood of which is very similar in colour to the sapwood. The colour of both can vary from a creamy white to a very pale tan; it may even darken to a pale pink or a pale brown. Steaming may produce a pinkish red. Sometimes the wood has a dark red heart, or darker veining. It has a straight grain with a fine, even texture, and a characteristic fleck. When quartersawn, it may exhibit an attractive broad ray figure on radial surfaces. It can hold quite fine detail.

Beech will regularly spalt, given the right conditions. The amount of spalting varies considerably from piece to piece, and can result in an exquisite marble-like appearance.

Beech also occasionally forms burrs (burls), which can vary in colour from the parent wood; I have had some beech burr that is pink. This is a good timber for wet-turning. It is commonly used in the woodworking and furniture industries to create anything from chairs to architectural features.

Beech burr (burl) detail

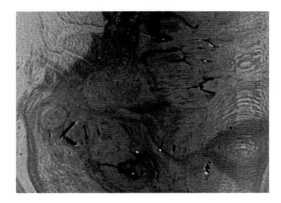

Grows
Throughout central Europe and Britain; also western Asia
HEIGHT 100ft (30m)
TRUNK DIAMETER 4ft (1.2m)
SPECIFIC GRAVITY .72
TYPICAL DRY WEIGHT 45lb/ft³ (720kg/m³)

Turners use beech a great deal, but the spalted wood is most in demand for use in artistic or decorative items.

Working qualities

Non-spalted beech is ideal for kitchenware and utilitarian work in general, and for turning furniture parts. It is easy to turn when using wet or dry wood and cuts well with all tools, though bevel-rubbing tools give the best results. Beech can be carved or routed easily and it takes reasonably fine detail. This is a timber often used in laminated and segmented work, and gluing rarely presents any problems.

Spalted beech can exhibit softer areas, so care is needed when cutting and sanding; soft patches may need 'hardening' to enable proper finishing cuts to be made. Try coating the whole piece with shellac, cellulose-based sanding sealer or cyanoacrylate (depending on what the finished item is to be used for), and then letting it dry prior to finish-turning. This method should harden the surface sufficiently to allow a reasonable cut without excessive grain tearout. Try not to use scrapers on the spalted timber; if you do, tearout is highly likely.

Non-spalted timber sands easily. Spalted wood should be sanded dry to reduce the risk of colour contamination in the lighter wood from the darker spalted areas. To minimize this risk, seal the wood first with thinned-down sanding sealer and let it dry before sanding. Spalted timber might have softer areas, so sand carefully to avoid abrading the softer wood more than the solid sections.

Hint
Don't use cyanoacrylate (superglue) to 'spot'-seal soft wood. The resulting spot coating will remain conspicuous. Instead, treat a zone within the marked spalt lines so you will not see where the cyanoacrylate was placed

BELOW
Hollow form in spalted beech with black accent by Ray Key

Beech can be dyed to good effect and penetrative and surface finishes are easily applied. The spalted form might be a little 'hungry' for finishes in the softer areas, so be prepared to use a few coats to get the result you want.

American ash

Fraxinus americana, F. pennsylvanica and F. nigra

Other names
White ash, northern ash, southern ash (*F. americana*); **green ash, red ash**

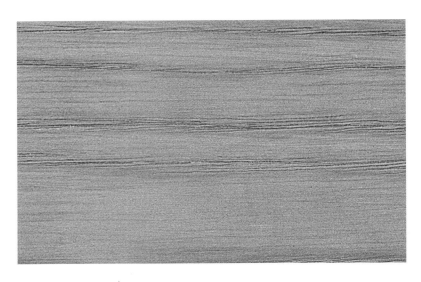

Characteristics

American white ash, in particular, is a wonderful wood to work with. It does not shout its presence, but is very attractive. This wood looks similar to European ash (*F. excelsior*), but is a little less dense. The sapwood is off-white, and the heartwood can vary from pale cream or tan to dark brown in colour with a pinkish tinge. The other two species vary in colour from a light greyish-tan to grey-brown. Occasionally, olive green to brown colouring is seen and this is referred to as 'olive' figuring.

The grain is generally straight, with a coarse but uniform texture. American ash is usually available as through-cut boards and predimensioned blanks, and can be found in reasonably large sizes. It is suitable for joinery and cabinetmaking components, artistic and functional ware.

Seasoning

American ash dries fairly easily with minimal degrade, and there is little movement in use. Grey-brown stains and surface checks can occur. Wet-turning to completion, working from partially seasoned stock, or rough-turning and setting it aside to season are all feasible routes to explore.

Olive figuring

Grows
Canada and eastern USA

HEIGHT 80–120ft (25–36m)

TRUNK DIAMETER 2–5ft (0.6–1.5m)

SPECIFIC GRAVITY .66 (*F. nigra* .56)

TYPICAL DRY WEIGHT 41lb/ft³ (660kg/m³) (*F. nigra* 35lb/ft³ (560kg/m³))

Working qualities

All three species have similar working qualities. They turn well wet or dry and produce a clean finish off the tool, even with scrapers – though expect occasional pulling of the endgrain when using scrapers.

The timber carves and routs satisfactorily, but due to the open grain structure you should avoid creating sharp peaks or edges – they are prone to chipping or fracturing and may end up looking like a serrated knife. Radius or create a micro-flat on any such edges. Otherwise, it really is a very versatile and much-underrated timber. It sands well and will readily accept dyes and both penetrative and surface finishes. It also bleaches well.

You can really play with the beautiful coarse grain structure and clearly defined growth rings by wire-brushing it, then colouring it and finally applying gilt cream or liming paste to accentuate the grain. Black and white is a particularly effective colour scheme for this timber.

RIGHT
Black and white
vessels by John Jordan

Hint

A bronze brush is better than a steel wire brush to open up the grain: it just removes the softer areas of the grain and does not mark the harder growth

BELOW
Nest of bowls
by Mike Mahoney

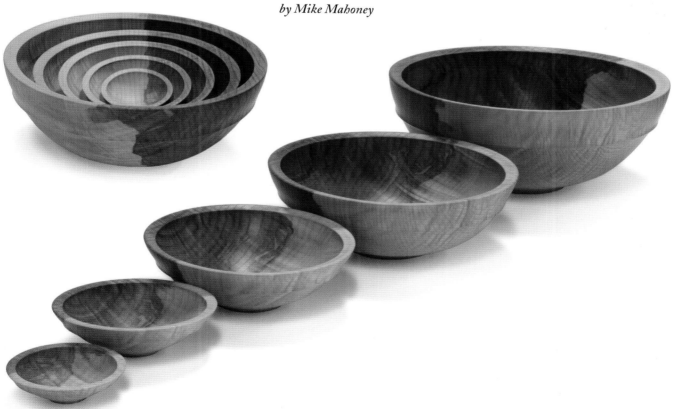

European ash
Fraxinus excelsior

Other names
Usually distinguished by country of origin

Characteristics
Ash is a fantastic wood to work with. It is tough, heavy, straight-grained, open and reasonably coarse but even in texture. The grain pattern is very distinctive. Available in large sizes, it is a great wood for utilitarian items such as platters and bowls, as well as more 'artistic' turning. It is often used for handles and for architectural work such as balusters and spindles, but this belies the full quality, beauty and versatility of this wood. This is a nice wood for wet-turning, where the piece is brought to a thin, even wall thickness and then allowed to distort as it dries.

POSSIBLE HEALTH RISKS
Decrease in lung function, rhinitis, asthma

CONSERVATION STATUS
Not known to be at risk

Seasoning
This wood dries fairly quickly but care is needed to avoid splitting and checking. The figured parts, especially the crotch area, are particularly prone to splitting, and this can be problematic if the wood is left in thick sections to dry. Rough-turning, using a wall thickness allowance of 10% of the overall diameter, has always worked for me with this timber.

Ripple figure

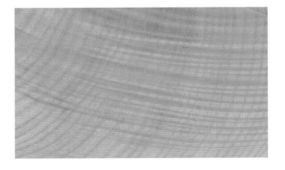

Finish with oil and wax

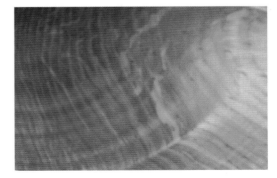

Grows
Europe, North Africa, western Asia
HEIGHT 80–120ft (25–35m)
TRUNK DIAMETER 2–5ft (0.6–1.5m)
SPECIFIC GRAVITY .71
TYPICAL DRY WEIGHT 44lb/ft³ (710kg/m³)

The sapwood is not easily differentiated from the heartwood; both are usually a creamy to light tan colour. Sometimes it has a mid to dark brown or black-streaked heartwood, which resembles olivewood (*Olea europaea*) and is therefore referred to as olive ash; this is **not** caused by rot, and can be denser than the standard form. Rippling can also occur quite frequently, but burrs (burls) are not so common. Ash is available in large sizes, which gives the turner a lot of scope to experiment and play. The wood mellows quickly from its fresh-cut whitish-cream to a tan colour.

Working qualities

The coarse, open-grained texture is not something that turners need to worry about – it cuts nicely with all tools, as long as they are sharp and you don't force them through the cut. Ash is a great wood to work with, wet or dry. As with many wet woods, using scrapers may produce a woolly surface, particularly on endgrain areas.

Despite its fairly coarse texture, ash is often used to produce utilitarian pieces for domestic use. Its high resistance to shock makes it ideal for making handles for such things as turning tools and mallets.

It power carves and routs easily, too. It sands easily, using either a dry or a wet sanding method, and can be finished to a high polish with both penetrative finishes – including dyes and bleaches – and surface

ABOVE
Bowl in rippled ash
by Ray Key

treatments. Like other ashes – and, indeed, oaks (*Quercus* spp.), which have a similar coarse grain structure and distinct growth rings – it lends itself to the technique of staining the wood, then filling the open grain with a contrasting 'liming' or coloured paste wax.

BELOW
Bowl in stained ash
with gilt cream
by Mark Baker

Hint

Small areas of figuring on hollow forms can be highlighted to wonderful effect using dyes, which will be absorbed unevenly by the figured wood

Bubinga
Guibourtia demeusei

Other names
African rosewood, akume, essingang, buvenga, ovang, waka, okweni; rotary-cut veneers are known as kevasingo

POSSIBLE HEALTH RISKS

Dermatitis and skin lesions

CONSERVATION STATUS

Not known to be at risk

Seasoning

This wood seasons reasonably well, with little degrade, but contains a gum that sometimes causes problems. It is advisable to season it slowly to prevent distortion and checking. Rough-turning, followed by further seasoning, works well to minimize distortion and gives more predictable results than air-drying the wood in board form. On highly figured pieces it may be prudent to coat the endgrain or the whole piece with PVA to even out the drying process. Kiln-drying works well when flat boards are required, such as for platters or for cabinetry.

Characteristics

Bubinga is a dense, hard and wonderfully decorative wood. The sapwood is normally greyish-white, ivory or streaked ivory-white, or sometimes brownish-white. The heartwood is altogether different, featuring light to medium reds, orange-browns and mid-toned browns, often with lighter veining in red or purple. The grain is normally straight or interlocked, and the annual rings are conspicuous. Fine pores, which can contain a reddish gum, may be found throughout. The texture is variable: it may be coarse but is usually fine to medium, and the surface can be highly lustrous. The wood will darken a lot over time, losing the orange-red vibrancy and mellowing down to a mid-brown tone. The grain pattern, which varies greatly from piece to piece, will remain distinct.

Because it contains silica, this wood has a medium to severe blunting effect on cutting edges. Bubinga is available in large sizes, giving turners a lot of scope to experiment with different types of projects.

Oiled finish

Grows
Central and west central tropical Africa
HEIGHT 70ft (21m)
TRUNK DIAMETER 4ft (1.2m)
SPECIFIC GRAVITY .88
TYPICAL DRY WEIGHT 55lb/ft³ (880kg/m³)

Working qualities

Bubinga cuts well when wet or dry with all tools but better with gouge and skews; occasionally the interlocking grain will pluck out, but sharp tools and a delicate cut will usually solve this. There is a risk of splintering at the edges of work; a gentle cut will minimize but not wholly solve this potential problem. Using a freshly sharpened or honed scraper after using gouges will help remove fine ripples and undulations relatively easily. But a shearing cut is a better option, and will usually remove any minor grain blemishes or tearout as well. The wood can produce long shavings, but is more likely to give short, curly shavings with some very fine, irritant dust.

It can hold reasonable detail so a $^1/_8$in (3mm) bead or slightly smaller is possible without any issues, and it can be power-carved or routed nicely. Try not to create sharp peaks, or edges due to the risk of fracture. Bubinga sands well, but it will clog up abrasives if sanded dry. It also wet-sands well,

Hint

If making square-edged bowls from this wood – or any brittle wood which is prone to splintering at the edges – glue some wastewood strips to the square edges and let them set. Turn the bowl, sand and finish to completion, then plane or sand off the remaining wastewood strips. The edges will just need minor sanding to remove any sharpness; then apply your finish of choice

BELOW LEFT
Box in figured bubinga by Chris Stott

BELOW RIGHT
Box by Mark Baker

as long as no sapwood is present to cause colour contamination. If sapwood is present, dry sand only and, prior to doing so, seal the wood with thinned-down sanding sealer and allow to dry before sanding. This timber can be taken to a nice lustre with both surface and penetrative finishes.

American black walnut
Juglans nigra

Other names
American walnut, eastern black walnut, gunwood, Virginia walnut

Characteristics
The heartwood colour can range from a light grey-brown to a dark chocolate or purplish-black. The sapwood is naturally whitish-yellow or brown, but can be stained or steamed to match the heartwood, or left to provide a nice visual contrast to it instead. The grain is usually straight and slightly open, but curls or waves may occur. The texture of the wood is generally coarse; the dull lustre develops to a more glossy patina in time. Spectacular figuring is common, including pippy knots, knot clusters, mottled, curly, rippled and wavy figures. Burrs (burls), stumpwood and crotches are areas in which figure is likely to occur, but veneer companies will buy up highly figured trees before other woodworkers get a look-in.

American black walnut is used in joinery and cabinetmaking, and for artistic and utilitarian turning.

POSSIBLE HEALTH RISKS
Irritation to eyes and skin

CONSERVATION STATUS
Not known to be at risk

Seasoning
This wood dries slowly, and care has to be taken to avoid degrade. Faults that may occur include checking, iron staining, ring failure, honeycombing and cell collapse. Kiln-dried and air-dried wood in a variety of sizes are readily available for the construction, architectural and cabinetmaking industries.

Rough-turning is recommended if you wish to maintain the shape of the work with minimum movement.

Ripple figure

Grows
Canada and USA
HEIGHT 70–90ft (21–27m)
TRUNK DIAMETER 2–4ft (0.6–1.2m)
SPECIFIC GRAVITY .64
TYPICAL DRY WEIGHT 40lb/ft³ (640kg/m³)

Working qualities

This wood cuts beautifully whether wet or seasoned; a very fine finish can be achieved off the tool, although it does have a distinct blunting effect on cutting edges. The slightly open grain does not present a problem, but grain filling may be necessary, especially in cabinet work, to produce an ultrafine finish. It cuts well with all tools, but very gentle cuts are necessary with a scraper to prevent tearout. Old wood tends to be very dusty, but freshly seasoned timber produces nice curly shavings with very little dust.

This is an excellent candidate for wet-turning, where the wood is turned to a thin wall thickness and then allowed to move freely. Its ability to be wet-turned to a thin wall thickness and hold detail makes it a nice timber for pierced work, too.

Burrs and rippled wood can tear out a little more than the plain wood, but gentle cuts with very sharp tools soon make light work of any potential problems. American walnut is capable of holding quite fine detail; it carves and textures beautifully with either hand or power tools and it can also be routed.

ABOVE
Vessel in rippled walnut by John Jordan

BELOW AND RIGHT
Carved vessel by John Jordan

Hint

Sharpen tools regularly to achieve the best finish possible straight from the cutting edge

The wood sands well with both wet and dry sanding methods, although wet sanding should be avoided when sapwood is present, because of the risk of colour contamination. It readily accepts both surface and penetrative finishes, and a very high gloss can be achieved if desired.

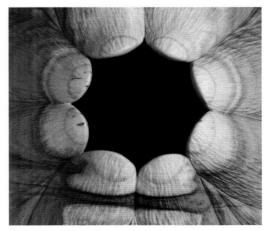

European walnut
Juglans regia

Other names
**Usually differentiated according to origin:
Persian, French, Black Sea walnut, etc.**

Characteristics
European walnut is a stunning wood to look at. The heartwood is normally greyish-brown in colour with some irregular dark streaking. The sapwood is paler, and clearly different from the heartwood. The colour mellows quite a bit with time, but the grain pattern remains distinct. This is a medium-dense wood that usually has straight grain but which can also be wavy. It has a coarse texture. Walnut crotch, burr (burl) and stumpwood can produce attractive figuring, but highly figured trees are likely to be snapped up by veneer manufacturers.

POSSIBLE HEALTH RISKS

Dermatitis, nasal irritation and nasal cancer

CONSERVATION STATUS

Categorized as 'near threatened' in Red List; population decreasing

Seasoning
European walnut dries well but can take a long time. Air-dried wood is most commonly available, but kiln-dried stock can be found. Honeycombing can occur in larger stock if it is dried too quickly. Allow extra wall thickness when rough-turning, to take movement into account. Spindles, balusters and other such work can be made from kiln- or air-dried timber of about 10–12% moisture content.

Burr (burl)

Ripple figure

Grows
Europe, Turkey, southwest Asia
HEIGHT 100ft (30m)
TRUNK DIAMETER 2–3ft (0.6–0.9m)
SPECIFIC GRAVITY .64
TYPICAL DRY WEIGHT 40lb/ft³ (640kg/m³)

Working qualities

This wood works very similarly to American black walnut (*J. nigra*) and is capable of holding reasonably fine detail, so carving, texturing, routing and piercing are all viable options for this timber.

It has a moderate blunting effect on cutting tools and is an ideal candidate for wet-turning (though the finish off the tool can be a bit woolly). Seasoned wood cuts well with gouges and skews, permitting a nice finish off the tool. It scrapes reasonably well, but you may experience grain tearout or fluffing up of the endgrain with all but the most delicate of shear cuts. Take extra care with figured timber.

This is a timber that takes carved and routed detail well and can be pierced easily if the wall thickness is very thin.

Wet and dry sanding both produce excellent results, the former giving a slightly finer finish and less dust. Both penetrative and surface finishes work well on walnut, although it may be necessary to fill the grain, or to cut back between multiple coats of surface finish, in order to achieve a flat, smooth surface.

As with its American cousin, this is an excellent timber to work with and well worth looking out for.

ABOVE
Fountain pen in walnut burr by Walter Hall

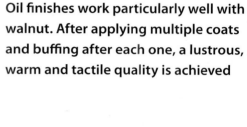

Hint
Oil finishes work particularly well with walnut. After applying multiple coats and buffing after each one, a lustrous, warm and tactile quality is achieved

RIGHT
'Pink Pony' teapot in sycamore and walnut by Joey Richardson

Wengé
Millettia laurentii

Other names
Awoung, bokonge, dikela, mibotu, nson-so, palissandre du Congo

POSSIBLE HEALTH RISKS

Dermatitis, dizziness, drowsiness, visual problems, stomach cramps; irritation of the eyes, skin and respiratory system; splinters go septic

CONSERVATION STATUS

Categorized in Red List as 'endangered'

Grows
Congo, Cameroon, Gabon, Tanzania, Mozambique
HEIGHT 50–60ft (15–18m)
TRUNK DIAMETER 2ft 6in–3ft (0.75–1m)
SPECIFIC GRAVITY .88
TYPICAL DRY WEIGHT 55lb/ft³ (880kg/m³)

Characteristics

This is a dense, heavy wood of striking appearance, with a clear differentiation between the white to pale yellow sapwood and the dark brown heartwood with fine, close, near-black veins and white or cream lines. The grain is fairly straight, and it has a medium to coarse texture with a low lustre. The wood darkens to a much deeper brown on exposure, but the veins remain distinct.

The wood has a small to moderate blunting effect on cutting edges. It is available in reasonable sizes, mostly as dimensioned boards or precut bowl blanks; it is rarely found as blanks or sections suitable for large hollow forms, or as trunks, which can be cut to suit one's own requirements. Because it is so dark, large pieces can look very imposing and sombre. You will often find wengé used as an accent, to set off another, lighter wood; it is also used for turned components in joinery and cabinetmaking. It is capable of holding quite fine detail.

Working qualities

Wengé is not the easiest wood to work, but is worth persevering with because few other woods offer such a fine display of contrasting markings combined with the deep brown colour. It cuts reasonably well with all tools – bevel-rubbing tools giving a slightly better finish – but long shavings are rare. It is more common to achieve small chips and quite an amount of dust unless the wood has a high moisture content, in which case there may be slightly larger, curly shavings and less dust. The wood tends to splinter at the edges of the work; a light, slow cut will solve this problem.

Seasoning

This wood seasons quite slowly and is fairly difficult to dry. It is highly prone to surface checking and has a slight tendency to distort. It shows a small amount of movement in use. The technique of rough-turning followed by further seasoning works well, but is only necessary for artistic work; kiln-dried wood is fine for furniture and joinery items.

The dust is unpleasant and very fine, so extract it properly, as close to the source as possible, to prevent inhalation or ingestion.

This is not a wood that I would recommend for wet-turning and allowing it to move. That is not to say that it will not work (and you may want to set a trend!), but it is more common to season and stabilize it fully before finish-turning. It can be carved (preferably with power tools) and routed, and is a timber highly prized by segmented turners to create high visual contrast.

Wengé is prone to heat-checking when sanding. Dry sanding gives off lots of dust, while wet sanding produces a slurry that fills the pores and diminishes the fine, light markings that are such a distinctive feature of the grain. On balance, I would recommend dry sanding, using fresh abrasives and a light touch so as not to generate too much heat.

I commented to Curt Theobald when discussing this timber that I thought that the wood was a foul concoction of nasty fibres and didn't like the process of cutting it, but the end results were well worth it. I will leave you to make up your own mind about this one. I still think the end results are beautiful.

The wood can be finished with both penetrative and surface finishes, but the open, coarse grain may need filling for an ultra-smooth feel. I find the open texture pleasant and like the tactile quality of it, so I do not fill the grain; instead I often seal the wood with thinned-down sanding sealer, then use oil and buff with a power buff. Using oil on its own darkens it too much in my mind. Curt has used bleach on the piece shown, to brilliant effect. Give it a try and see what you think.

ABOVE
Bowl by Bert Marsh

BELOW
'The Promise': vessels in bleached wengé with gold leaf by Curt Theobald

Hint
Wengé is a great wood to combine with maple (*Acer* spp.) or ash (*Fraxinus* spp.) in segmented turning

European olive
Olea europaea

Other names
**None. Related to East African olive
(*O. hochstetteri*), which is a much larger tree**

POSSIBLE HEALTH RISKS

The dust can be an irritant to the eyes, skin and respiratory system

CONSERVATION STATUS

Not known to be at risk

Seasoning

The wood dries very slowly and has a tendency to warp, check, split and honeycomb if you try to rush it, especially when dried in the round or in large pieces. Large sections will need part-turning followed by further seasoning. I have only ever encountered air-dried wood, which varies greatly in moisture content. The logs and branches are variable in quality and need checking over very carefully; they are rarely free from minor splits or checks. Predimensioned timber, though more expensive, does give you a clearer idea of what you are purchasing.

I use olive mainly for wet-turning: it responds well to being turned thin and then allowed to distort freely, with or without bark. It can be rough-turned, coated with PVA and set aside to season – but expect some failures.

Characteristics

This is a truly stunning timber: strong, hard, heavy and oily, with a clear differentiation between sapwood and heartwood. The sapwood is gold or creamy-yellow, and often striped. The heartwood is usually tan, pale brown or yellow-brown, and it can be streaked with black, grey or brown. The grain is close and shallowly interlocked, with a fine, even texture that is capable of holding fine detail. Figuring may appear on tangential surfaces. The annual rings are clearly seen.

Olive is not usually available in large sizes, as the tree is invariably stumpy and gnarled. The wood is essentially a by-product of the olive-oil industry. Boughs and trunks become available from time to time, but it is more commonly sold as predimensioned blanks and small branch sections.

Oiled finish

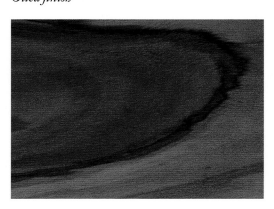

Grows

Mediterranean region, Middle East and North Africa
HEIGHT 25ft (8m) max.
TRUNK DIAMETER Typically 1ft (0.3m) but can reach 3ft (0.9m)
SPECIFIC GRAVITY .80
TYPICAL DRY WEIGHT 50lb/ft³ (800kg/m³)

The shavings will stain your hands and any steel that they come into contact with blackish blue, so make sure that you clean up thoroughly after using it. The wood has an oily feel that takes a long while to disappear, and a strong smell. Olive can be used by turners for utilitarian and decorative work.

Working qualities

Wet olivewood is particularly easy and pleasant to work: long ribbon-like shavings positively fly off the tool. Scrapers can be used to good effect, too. The irregular grain does not usually present any problem when working the wood wet. Old or well-seasoned wood is a different matter: the interlocking, irregular grain often plucks out, the edges of the work are liable to splinter and it is often very dusty to turn. Sharp tools and a slow, deliberate steady cut (in a shear-cutting mode if necessary) will help overcome some of the problems encountered when turning dry wood.

Boxes with finials should always be made from straight-grained wood; any cross or interlocking grain in the finial will cause problems and may result in breakage.

The wood responds well to carving, although powered rotary or percussive carving suits it best. If you want to carve it, try to use the straighter-grained sections for best results. It can also be routed easily, too.

The wood is prone to heat-checking if you are heavy-handed with sanding, so take care. It is liable to clog the abrasive if you sand it dry, but responds well to wet sanding and can be brought to a fine finish with abrasives. The oils in the wood tend to make it resistant to some surface finishes, but it finishes well with oils and waxes.

Hint
Small areas of figuring on hollow forms can be highlighted to wonderful effect using dyes, which will be absorbed unevenly by the figured wood

RIGHT
Finial box
by Mark Baker

Purpleheart
Peltogyne porphyrocardia
and related species

Other names
Amaranth, amarante, guarabu, morado, nazareno, pau roxo, saka, tananeo, violetwood

Characteristics
This is a wood that you certainly cannot overlook when you see it. Newly cut heartwood is a dull, soft brown colour, but on exposure to light it changes to a bright purple. Sadly, this is a wood that loses its vibrancy of colour, mellowing down to a purplish mid-brown tone. There can also be some difference in colour between one board and another within each species, and minerals in the wood may cause uneven colour. The grain is typically straight but can be roey, wavy, interlocked or irregular. It has a medium to fine, even texture and a high lustre, and is capable of holding quite fine detail. The heartwood is clearly distinct from the sapwood, being an off-white colour. It is available in large sizes, either as predimensioned blanks or as boards of varying thickness, so a wide variety of work can be created from it. However, large turnings in purpleheart can be quite imposing and 'in your face', so choose your projects wisely.

POSSIBLE HEALTH RISKS

Dust can cause irritation and nausea

CONSERVATION STATUS

Not known to be at risk

Seasoning
This wood usually dries fairly quickly with little degrade, but it can warp or split. The moisture content in the centre of thicker stock can be a problem, so if you are making bowls, boxes, hollow forms and platters you will get better results by rough-turning it and then setting it aside to season further before final turning. Coating the endgrain with PVA will even out the drying and minimize the risk of splitting or surface checking.

Oiled finish

Grows
Central America and northern South America
HEIGHT 100–150ft (30–45m)
TRUNK DIAMETER 2–4ft (0.6–1.2m)
SPECIFIC GRAVITY .86
TYPICAL DRY WEIGHT 54lb/ft³ (860kg/m³)

Try smaller bowls, hollow forms or boxes, then work your way up to larger pieces and see what you think. Purpleheart is also a good choice as an accent or contrasting colour against a lighter or darker wood and, since it glues up nicely, can be excellent for laminated and segmented work.

Working qualities

This is not as easy to turn as some of the other woods featured in this book. It is somewhat brittle, so is liable to splinter, especially near the edges of the work, and any irregular or interlocking grain is likely to tear out.

Sharp gouges, used on seasoned wood with a slow, delicate cut, will normally produce chips with a small amount of dust but not too much tearout. Scraping will likely pluck fibres on endgrain surfaces, but not too much in other areas. If a scraper doesn't work, make the best finishing cut you can with the gouge and then go straight to abrasives. But do not be tempted to skip grades; the scratches will show up when finished.

Wet-turning works better than dry-turning, but we usually get part-seasoned or kiln-dried material so rarely have the chance to do this.

Hint

For an ornamental piece that is not to be used with food, consider applying an oil or surface finish to the wood, then give it a spray of silicone-free cockpit spray (used to clean dashboards and other plastic fitments on cars). These products have very strong UV inhibitors, and a fresh coat every other month or so, sprayed on and wiped over with a soft cloth, can have a big impact on helping to maintain the wood's vibrant colour

The wood can be carved and routed, but needs to be done carefully. Working it with power tools is better than using hand tools.

Purpleheart is prone to heat-checking when dry sanding, and abrasives clog up quickly when the wood is sanded dry, so clean them regularly and use minimal pressure to prevent heat build-up. If you want any chance of keeping the purple colour for any length of time, use a finish that incorporates a UV inhibitor. However, the wood does finish well with either penetrative or surface finishes.

BELOW
Bowl by Mark Baker

Snakewood
Piratinera guianensis,
syn. *Brosimum guianense*

Other names
Letterwood, letterhout, amourette, gateado, palo de oro, burokoro, cacique carey, leopardwood, speckled wood

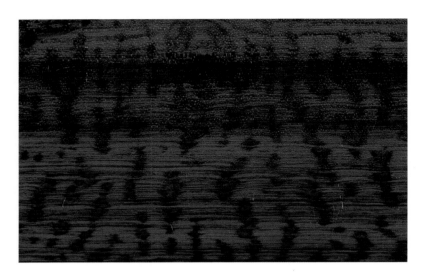

POSSIBLE HEALTH RISKS
Thirst, salivation, respiratory tract irritation and nausea

CONSERVATION STATUS
Not known to be at risk

Seasoning
Drying can be difficult, and there may be warping and degrade. Snakewood shows medium movement in use. I strongly recommend rough-turning the blank and coating it with PVA to even out the moisture loss and minimize checking and warping, then setting it aside to season further before finish-turning. The wood can be turned wet or partially seasoned for items such as bowls, but lidded boxes will need to be rough-turned to ensure stability.

Snakewood is not available in very large sizes. It can be bought as logs or as a whole tree trunk, but frequently exhibits splits. It is more commonly sold as predimensioned blanks. However you purchase it, store it in an area with a uniform moisture content and temperature, to minimize checking.

Characteristics
This wood is naturally high in resin and has markings resembling snakeskin or a spotty leopard – hence its alternative names. The heartwood is dark red to red-brown, with irregular black spots or stripes, which can appear on their own or with interspersed speckles. It will darken with time, but the black markings will always remain distinct. The border between heartwood and sapwood is irregular. The sapwood is thick, creamy or yellow-white, and is rarely used because it often contains splits. When a piece is found without splits, it can be used to provide an effective contrast with the darker heartwood. The grain is moderately fine, uniform and straight, with a medium to high lustre.

Grows
Central America and tropical South America
HEIGHT 80ft (25m)
TRUNK DIAMETER 1–3ft (0.3–0.9m)
SPECIFIC GRAVITY 1.30
TYPICAL DRY WEIGHT 81lb/ft³ (1300kg/m³)

Working qualities

This is a wonderful wood to turn. A fine finish can be achieved with all sharp tools. Because it is naturally resinous, a high shine is produced with bevel-rubbing tools such as gouges and skews. Cutting with these tools produces small chips instead of shavings, with a little dust. This is one of those few timbers on which a scraper, used in either the conventional or the shear-scraping mode, is likely to produce a shaving better than that from a gouge; but such a cut will be accompanied by a little dust. If interlocking grain is present I prefer the scraper to minimize tearout.

This dense, hard and heavy wood – one of the heaviest that a turner is likely to encounter – is capable of holding quite fine detail, but can be brittle. It can be power carved and routed. Rotary carving tools yield better results than percussive or hand carving tools.

Snakewood is prone to heat-checking on the endgrain, so be careful when sanding; wet sanding will help minimize this, as long as no sapwood is present to pose a risk of colour contamination. Dry sanding will result in the production of a lot of nasty dust, as well as regular clogging of the abrasive with the wood's natural resin.

The high resin content can resist surface finishes, but wiping over with a solvent first should sort the problem out. Alternatively, use oil or wax as a finish and power-buff it to a fine lustre.

Hint

If tiny splits are present, thin cyanoacrylate (superglue), run into the split and then sanded while wet, will fill and colour it to blend it in with the solid sections

ABOVE
Box by Ray Key

RIGHT
Box by Chris Stott

European plane
Platanus hybrida, syn. *P. x acerifolia*, *P. x hispanica*

Other names
London plane, English plane, French plane.
Related species include *P. orientalis* in southeast
Europe, Iran and Turkey; *P. occidentalis*
(American plane), known as buttonwood or
(confusingly) American sycamore

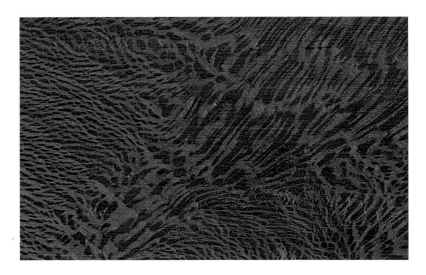

POSSIBLE HEALTH RISKS

Not known, but take
the usual precautions
regarding dust

CONSERVATION STATUS

Not known to be
at risk

Seasoning
Plane dries quickly, but care is needed
to prevent splitting and distortion. Once
seasoned, it is stable in use. It can, depending
on the intended end use, be turned wet and
thin walled to completion and will move a
considerable amount at times, especially on
figured wood, but movement is not consistent
and the result are variable. Alternatively,
rough-turn and set it aside to season before
finish-turning; my usual rule of thumb,
allowing a wall thickness of 10-15% of the
overall diameter when rough-turning, has not
let me down yet with this wood. But nothing

is a given as far as timber is concerned.
David Bates, the owner of Stiles and Bates,
a woodturning supply company, once said to
me: 'Whenever I give an opinion on timber,
there is always a tree that says I am lying.' That
statement has proved very true over the years.

Characteristics
The heartwood ranges from cream to pinkish-
tan or coppery-brown. On quartersawn stock
the numerous, very conspicuous rays give a
distinctive and very attractive fleck figuring,
known as lacewood. Plane has straight grain
and a fine to medium texture and is capable
of holding reasonably fine detail.

BELOW
*Burr London plane hollow
form by Mark Baker*

Grows
Europe
HEIGHT 100ft (30m)
TRUNK DIAMETER 3–4ft (0.9–1.2m)
SPECIFIC GRAVITY .62
TYPICAL DRY WEIGHT 39lb/ft³ (620kg/m³)

Hint

Experiment with various finishes to see what suits the intended use best and also to see what best shows up the wood to its maximum potential

Working qualities

Plane can be used for decorative or utilitarian turning and for furniture parts. I think it is a much-underrated timber.

In truth, there isn't much not to like about this timber. The lacewood is lovely to look at, and the wood cuts well with sharp tools, whether wet or dry. That said, it does cut better with bevel-rubbing tools rather than scrapers. Scrapers tend to fluff up the grain a little, usually on endgrain or wet timber. Unless the wood is very old or dry only a little tearout (usually endgrain) seems to occur.

Be aware that small pieces around the fleck figuring may flake off. The best way to avoid this is to use sharp, bevel-rubbing tools presented in a shear-cutting mode and using a delicate cut.

Plane carves and routs well and can be glued readily, so segmented and laminated work are options for you to consider.

This wood sands easily with both dry or wet sanding methods. It can be finished with surface or penetrative finishes, but my preference is to use an oil finish to accentuate the grain and colour.

BELOW
Bowl in European
plane burr
by Bert Marsh

Poplar
Populus

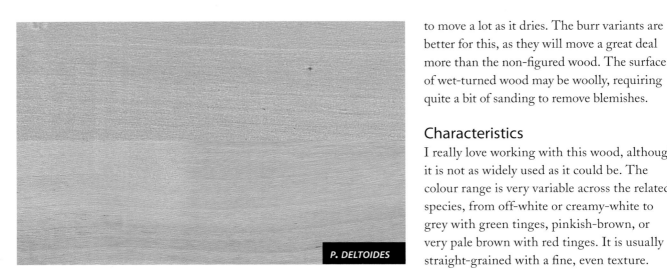

P. DELTOIDES

to move a lot as it dries. The burr variants are better for this, as they will move a great deal more than the non-figured wood. The surface of wet-turned wood may be woolly, requiring quite a bit of sanding to remove blemishes.

Characteristics

I really love working with this wood, although it is not as widely used as it could be. The colour range is very variable across the related species, from off-white or creamy-white to grey with green tinges, pinkish-brown, or very pale brown with red tinges. It is usually straight-grained with a fine, even texture.

Burr (burl) detail

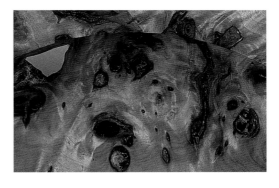

Ripple figure

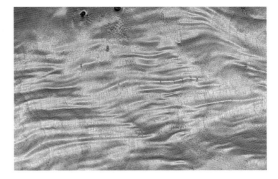

POSSIBLE HEALTH RISKS

Asthma, dermatitis, bronchitis, sneezing, eye irritation

CONSERVATION STATUS

P. nigra categorized as 'least concern' in Red List

Seasoning

Poplar dries reasonably quickly with little degrade, but may retain pockets of moisture. The knots are prone to split, but otherwise it will respond to kiln- or air-drying, or to the rough-turning method. If you are undertaking architectural work (balusters, stair spindles and so on) kiln-dried wood will be fine; but for items such as bowls, boxes or vases it is advisable to rough-turn and set aside for further seasoning. Poplar can be turned wet to a thin, even wall thickness to good effect, but is not one of the best choices if you want the work

Grows

UK and mainland Europe, North America

HEIGHT 100–115ft (30–35m)

TRUNK DIAMETER 3–4ft (0.9–1.2m), but varies according to species

SPECIFIC GRAVITY .45

TYPICAL DRY WEIGHT 28lb/ft³ (450kg/m³), varying according to species

It is a soft to medium-density wood that can be a bit fibrous and woolly. Being soft it can mark quite easily if mishandled. It is used for turned components in the construction and joinery industries, but more commonly for decorative or utilitarian ware.

Turners can make use of the wide variety of available sizes, some of which are large. Poplar produces lovely burrs, which vary in figure from 'pippy', with a mass of knots, to swirling grain. Rippling can also occur.

Working qualities

When working with seasoned or dry wood, try to get as good a finish as you can using a sharp gouge; if it is not sharp, the finish off the tool is likely to be fluffy. Reasonably long shavings will be produced if the cut is made correctly, and if the wood is freshly seasoned there will be little dust; old stock will produce dust. It is quite a lightweight wood and can be soft and easily marked at times, even with a fingernail.

Poplar's woolly nature can cause a problem if any but the most careful of cuts are used. Shear-cutting minimizes, but will not wholly eliminate, grain tearout or woolliness.

Hint

If using water-based stains or dyes on this wood, wet the surface before applying the colour. This will even out the absorption rate of the dye or stain, and should result in a more even coverage and colour

Try moving straight on to the abrasive after the gouge or skew chisel rather than using a scraper. Poplar does not splinter in cutting or in use, which makes it a good choice for items used in contact with food. This timber can be carved and routed, too, but don't create very fine edges; radius them or create a narrow flat to minimize breaking or crushing.

Poplar sands satisfactorily with both wet and dry techniques, but be mindful if power-sanding to move the arbor across the work with a very fluid motion. This is always important with power sanding, but poplar is particularly soft and you can quickly create sanding hollows that will mar the surface. Poplar accepts both penetrative and surface finishes fairly well but can be a bit 'hungry'. But, if using stain to accentuate the figuring, the resulting look may be a little blotchy if care is not taken.

BELOW
Nest of bowls in figured poplar by Mike Mahoney

European cherry
Prunus avium

Other names
Gean, wild cherry, mazzard, fruit cherry

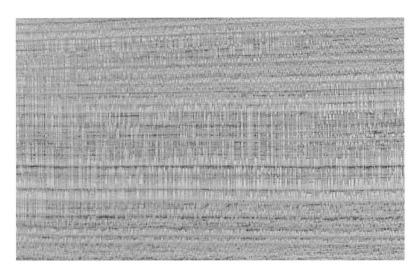

POSSIBLE HEALTH RISKS

Not known, but take the usual precautions regarding dust

CONSERVATION STATUS

Not known to be at risk

Seasoning

Cherry dries quickly but is prone to warping, and may develop end splits if not seasoned carefully. The knots are particularly prone to splitting, but otherwise it will respond to kiln- or air-drying or to the rough-turning technique, provided care is taken not to dry it too fast.

Cherry can also be wet-turned to good effect. The bark is fine enough to remain in place if you want to incorporate it into the design for natural-edge work.

Characteristics

The heartwood is an orange-red or brown colour and is clearly distinct from the pale cream to buff-white sapwood. When exposed to light, it will lose some of its fresh-cut red hue. Usually straight-grained with a fine and even texture, cherry is a medium-density wood, which occasionally exhibits dark streaks running through it. Burrs are not uncommon, and ripple or roey figuring can occur. The root structure, if large enough, is also worth considering for turning, though its very high moisture content makes it prone to splitting. Also, make sure you clean it thoroughly: pressure wash it to remove debris or you could end up in serious trouble if something comes loose when turning.

Cherry is available in reasonably large sizes in predimensioned blanks. The wood is suitable both for decorative or artistic work and for utilitarian wares.

Working qualities

All the fruitwoods I have tried are a pleasure to work with. They may vary considerably in colour and density, and some have a slightly coarser texture, but all, without exception, are worth trying.

European cherry cuts well when seasoned, but the grain fibres may fluff up a little when wet-turning or drying it, so make sure the tools being used are sharp. Scrapers may also cause the grain fibres to tear out, especially when wet; but figured areas around knots and so on may be a problem even when dry. It is capable of holding reasonably fine detail, so small beads, V-cuts and coves can be easily created on dry timber – not so easily on wet timber.

Grows

UK and mainland Europe, western Asia and North Africa

HEIGHT 60–80ft (18–24m)

TRUNK DIAMETER 2ft (0.6m)

SPECIFIC GRAVITY .61

TYPICAL DRY WEIGHT 38lb/ft³ (610kg/m³)

Most fruitwoods are well worth exploring as far as natural edge work is concerned. Branches, trunks, roots and burr sections can yield beautiful results.

Like most fruitwoods, cherry's ability to hold reasonably fine detail means that it carves and routs well and I thoroughly recommend exploring those options, but don't think this has to be extensive and intricate: small coves, V-cuts and suchlike can have a great impact. But make sure you keep everything uniform, using an indexing plate to mark things accurately and work to the marks, otherwise any errors will immediately show

Hint
If you have to use cyanoacrylate (superglue) to reattach a bit of bark that has come off natural-edge work, apply some thinned-down sanding sealer to seal the wood first

ABOVE
Bowl by Mark Baker

up. Alternatively, don't follow a grid or aim for uniformity; make things look more 'hand done' and rustic instead.

Cherry sands quite well; make sure the first grit grade used removes all damage before moving on to finer abrasives. Both surface and penetrative finishes work well.

LEFT
Hollow vessel with micro V-groove decoration by Mark Baker

American cherry
Prunus serotina

Other names
Black cherry, cabinet cherry, choke cherry, Edwards Plateau cherry, wild cherry, rum cherry, whisky cherry, New England mahogany

Characteristics
The heartwood is pale creamy-pink to light or mid coppery-brown, darkening on exposure to a rich, deep red-brown. It sometimes has attractive darker flecks and streaks running through it. The much paler, quite thin sapwood is typically a creamy colour but may be pinkish to reddish brown. The grain is usually straight, the texture fine and even. It occasionally forms burrs (burls), which are highly sought-after.

Working qualities
American cherry, like its European cousin, is a treat to work with. It looks attractive and works well; I recommend trying it for both decorative and utilitarian work. It is available in quite large sizes, which gives wide scope for experimenting.

It is an easy wood to work with, both wet and dry. As far as technique is concerned, when turning wet wood, bevel-rubbing tools produce a very fine finish off the tool; scrapers less so, with a risk of tearing out the endgrain or creating fluffy grain – especially in the endgrain areas if the tools are anything but sharp. Dry timber cuts cleanly with occasional pull on the endgrain. You will sometimes encounter interlocking grain on the plain timber, as well as on pieces with ripple or roe figuring. This can be a little tricky, but delicate, fine cuts will help you get a smooth finish; use scrapers sparingly on this type of timber.

POSSIBLE HEALTH RISKS
Wheezing and dizziness

CONSERVATION STATUS
Not known to be at risk

Seasoning
American cherry dries rapidly, but overfast drying can cause severe distortion. Shrinkage is common and ring shakes can occur. It can be air-dried or kiln-dried, but the rate of drying must be carefully controlled. If turning for joinery or cabinetmaking applications, working straight from kiln-dried stock is fine. For turners, it can be turned wet or partially seasoned, or rough-turned and set aside to dry further before turning.

Grows
Eastern and midwestern USA, southern Canada
HEIGHT 80–100ft (24–30m)
TRUNK DIAMETER 2–5ft (0.6–1.5m)
SPECIFIC GRAVITY .58
TYPICAL DRY WEIGHT 36lb/ft³ (580kg/m³)

Hint

Small areas of figuring on hollow forms can be highlighted to wonderful effect using dyes, which will be absorbed unevenly by the figured wood

LEFT
*Vessel in figured cherry
by John Jordan*

BELOW
*Jar with fossil
walrus ivory inlay
by John Jordan*

American cherry is capable of taking reasonably fine detail and that makes it suitable for carved and routed effects, too. The two examples shown show how things can be carved and textured to create effect. Also, in the case of the piece above by John Jordan, note the pleasing contrast between the darker heartwood and sapwood areas.

Cherry sands well and takes both penetrative and surface finishes readily, but take care with dyes and stains to minimize a blotchy look.

African padauk
Pterocarpus soyauxii

Other names
Barwood, bosulu, camwood, corail, mbe, mututi, ngula

POSSIBLE HEALTH RISKS

Sawdust can cause skin and respiratory problems, swelling of the eyelids, itching and vomiting

CONSERVATION STATUS

Not known to be at risk

Seasoning

This wood dries with hardly any degrade and shows little movement in use. It can be wet-turned and finished straight away, but because it is usually supplied as through-cut boards rather than logs it is more common to convert it into blanks first, then rough-turn it and set it aside to stabilize before finish-turning. Kiln-dried wood is fine for architectural or furniture turnings.

Characteristics

This dense wood is one of the most strikingly coloured ones that turners are likely to encounter. It is capable of holding quite fine detail without breaking out. When the wood is freshly cut the heartwood is a bold red-orange, but it will change over a period of time to a strong red or pink-red with dark streaks. It can darken even further to a red-purple, or even black. The colour will later fade with age, losing the bright red and mellowing to a mid reddish-brown tone. The grain ranges from straight to interlocked, with a fine to medium texture and a natural surface lustre. The sapwood is easily differentiated from the heartwood: when freshly cut it is white, but it will turn grey-brown or yellow after a time on exposure to light.

Working qualities

At some stage or other you are likely to have the opportunity to turn this lovely wood. African padauk is a nice wood to work, and cuts cleanly if the tools are sharp and used sensitively. You may well be able to get a fine finish, straight off the tool, that requires very little sanding. That is more likely when using bevel-rubbing tools, but scrapers that are sharp and used well, in most instances, give a reasonably fine result, too. The wood has a slight blunting effect on cutting edges. The worst aspect of this wood is the peppery dust it produces. There is a lot of it, and it is sticky – the wood is slightly oily in nature, clinging to almost everything it touches, and it can stain clothes and hands.

Grows

Tropical west and central Africa

HEIGHT 100–130ft (30–40m)

TRUNK DIAMETER 2–4ft (0.6–1.2m) or wider

SPECIFIC GRAVITY .72

TYPICAL DRY WEIGHT 45lb/ft³ (720kg/m³)

The wood can hold reasonably fine detail; it carves well with both hand and power carving tools and works well if routed. Good results are achieved with either the dry or the wet sanding method – but avoid wet sanding if sapwood is present, or you will cause colour contamination. You might, depending on the finish used, experience colour leaching in the finish. Penetrative finishes such as oil have a marked darkening effect on this wood. If you wish to retain the vibrant red colour, consider using a surface finish with a UV inhibitor in it; this will not prevent colour loss completely, but will slow it down.

Hint

I am known to have a penchant for using oils and waxes, but actually I think this timber is shown off better by using a hard-curing surface finish and then buffed, with the possible addition of wax or an oil on top

RIGHT
Bird-box ornament by Chris Stott in maple (Acer sp.) *and padauk*

BELOW
Hollow form by John Hunnex

American white oak

Quercus alba, Q. prinus, Q. lobata, Q. michauxii, Q. lyrata

Other names
Chestnut oak, swamp chestnut oak (*Q. michauxii*); overcup oak (*Q. lyrata*)

POSSIBLE HEALTH RISKS

Asthma, sneezing, nose and eye irritation, nasal cancer

CONSERVATION STATUS

Q. alba, Q. lyrata, Q. michauxii categorized as 'least concern' in Red List

Characteristics
The heartwood is creamy brown to mid-tan or pale brown, sometimes tinged with light red. The sapwood is cream to greyish off-white. The grain is straight and open with a medium-coarse texture, with large rays that give it a silver-grained appearance; the quartersawn surface shows numerous rays and is very attractive. Various types of figuring can occur, including swirls, crotch figure and burrs (burls). It can be used for many applications, including furniture and joinery components, utilitarian and artistic turned items.

Working qualities
This is a gem of a wood that I find easier to work than European oak (*Q. robur* or *Q. petraea*). Using either wet or dry timber,

Figured oak

Seasoning
These species can be kiln- or air-dried but have a tendency to split, check and honeycomb. The wood can be turned to completion from wet or from a partially seasoned state, but it does warp, so expect some interesting shapes once dry. Rough-turning it works beautifully if you want stable timber. Kiln-dried wood is fine for joinery or furniture components.

Grows
Central North America and Canada
HEIGHT Up to 100ft (30m)
TRUNK DIAMETER 0.9–1.2m (3–4ft)
SPECIFIC GRAVITY .76
TYPICAL DRY WEIGHT 47lb/ft³ (760kg/m³)

it seems to cut cleanly in most circumstances with sharp gouges or skews and reasonably well with scrapers. Endgrain tearout is possible when quartersawn or figured stock is used, especially when using scrapers on very dry wood. Other than that, it works well, leaving a relatively clean finish off the tool.

This is a wood that can be readily carved or routed to good effect, and surprisingly, given its moderately open grain structure, can hold reasonably fine detail. Avoid very sharp edges; this minimizes breakage and fracturing risks and also creates a serrated edge.

I must admit that I love wet-turning this wood to a thin wall thickness and letting it move – the more figuring the timber has, the more movement there is likely to be.

Surface and penetrative finishes do not appear to present any problems in use. If you require a very fine, smooth surface, grain filling may be required.

As with all oaks, the shavings can stain iron, so make sure you clean the lathe and tools after turning.

LEFT
Figured vessel by
John Jordan

Hint

White oak can be fumed with ammonia to deepen the colour. Like its European cousin, this oak can also be limed; use a bronze brush to open up the grain a bit prior to applying the liming wax

BELOW
Bowl in Q. lobata *by*
Mike Mahoney

European oak
Quercus robur and *Q. petraea*

Other names
Pedunculate oak (*Q. robur*); sessile oak, durmast oak (*Q. petraea*).
Syn. for *Q. robur*: *Q. pedunculata*;
for *Q. petraea*: *Q. sessiliflora*

For architectural work, kiln-dried stock is fine. European oak is a great wood for wet-turning to completion – especially the burr forms, which may move a lot as they dry, creating fantastic undulating forms.

Characteristics

A true king among woods, European oak has a heartwood varying in colour from light tan or biscuit to deep chocolate brown. The wood mellows a lot with time and can darken to a deep brown, or take on a reddish or orange-brown tone. It has obvious alternating bands of earlywood and latewood.

POSSIBLE HEALTH RISKS

Sneezing, dermatitis, nasal cancer

CONSERVATION STATUS

Not known to be at risk

Seasoning

This wood is slow to dry, and likely to check, split, warp and honeycomb, especially when air-dried from the natural state. The likelihood of shrinkage is also high. Movement in service is medium. When rough-turning, allow an extra ¼in (6mm) in addition to the standard 1in (25mm) of wall thickness per 12in (300mm) diameter to take into account the likelihood of warping, and coat it with PVA before seasoning.

Brown oak

Burr (burl) detail

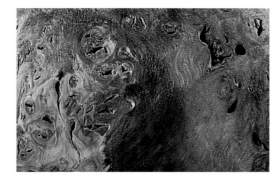

Grows

UK and mainland Europe, Turkey, North Africa; also southeastern Canada and northeastern USA

HEIGHT 60–100ft (18–30m)

TRUNK DIAMETER 4–6ft (1.2–1.8m)

SPECIFIC GRAVITY .72

TYPICAL DRY WEIGHT 45lb/ft³ (720kg/m³)

The sapwood is somewhat lighter, and about 1in (25mm) wide. This is a tough, reasonably heavy, dense wood, the grain of which is typically straight, but irregularities and cross grain can occur. Though the texture is coarse, it is still capable of holding reasonably fine detail. When the wood is quartersawn the rays and growth rings show a lovely figure with a metallic sheen, known as 'silver grain'.

Brown oak results from fungal attack in the growing tree. This wood is a deep purplish-brown, and is slightly less strong than ordinary oak. Fungal activity stops when the wood is seasoned.

Oak often forms burrs (burls), which are highly prized by turners and cabinetmakers. The figure in these ranges from small, tight clusters of pippy knots, to whole tightly packed sections of mid-sized knot formations and whorls of swirling grain. The list of uses for this wood is immense, but suffice to say that its availability in large sizes means that turners can use this timber in a variety of ways: architectural items such as columns, spindles and balusters; turnery for cabinetmaking; utilitarian and artistic forms.

Hint

Oak contains tannins, so wet shavings from all the oaks (as well as ash (*Fraxinus* spp.), false acacia (*Robinia pseudoacacia*), sweet chestnut (*Castanea sativa*) and a few others) will turn steel black and also stain your fingers to some extent – so clean up and oil your lathe's bed bars and toolrest once turning is finished

Working qualities

Oak cuts well in most situations, but has a moderate to severe blunting effect on cutting edges. Frequent sharpening will be necessary. Occasionally it may splinter off at the edges of the work, or suffer from grain tearout when there is cross, irregular grain or knots; gentle cuts with very sharp tools are necessary to minimize the risk of this. However, most of the time it will cut very well with gouges, leaving a fine finish straight off the tool. Scrapers, too, if freshly honed, can produce a good finish, but not so good as gouges or, for that matter, the skew chisel.

If the wood is freshly seasoned, it produces little dust when turned. Old wood, however, can generate lots of dust, which is quite choking and has a musty smell. Oak's ability to produce a clean finish straight from the tool is particularly prized by carvers – it can also be routed to good effect. Many ancient buildings, and furniture both old and new, have turned items or carvings made from oak.

Oak sands well with power or by hand, and both surface and penetrative finishes can be used with ease. This timber also responds to fuming with ammonia to darken the colour. The open-grained texture makes oak a great candidate for liming; this is usually reserved for furniture and joinery work, but can be used to good effect on turned pieces.

BELOW
Bowl in oak burr by Mark Baker

False acacia
Robinia pseudoacacia

Other names
Acacia, locust, black locust, white locust, yellow locust, robinia

Characteristics

The sapwood is thin and yellow, and the heartwood ranges from greenish-yellow to dark or golden-brown. On exposure to light it darkens to golden-brown or russet. The wood has a straight grain with a coarse texture, and shows a marked contrast between the dense latewood and large-pored earlywood. It is a tough wood of medium density, and has a moderate blunting effect on tools.

This wood frequently produces burrs (burls), ranging from tight pippy figuring to violently swirling grain. These burrs are quite stunning and are a great favourite of mine. Sadly, it is not available in very big sizes, but it can be bought in branch or trunk sections, precut blanks or through-cut boards, which gives the turner a lot of scope to experiment.

POSSIBLE HEALTH RISKS

The dust can be an irritant to the eyes and skin, and cause nausea and malaise

CONSERVATION STATUS

Categorized as 'least concern' in Red List

Seasoning

This is a slow-drying wood and dries with little degrade. Movement is minimal if the timber is straight-grained. There can be end and surface checking, and it shows small to medium movement in use. Minute splits are frequently found in logs. Rough-turning works well when stability is required.

Burr (burl), finished with oil

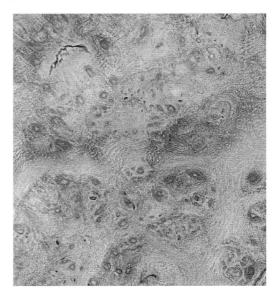

Grows

Mainly Canada and USA; also Asia, Europe, New Zealand and North Africa

HEIGHT 40–80ft (12–24m)

TRUNK DIAMETER 1–2ft (0.3–0.6m)

SPECIFIC GRAVITY .72

TYPICAL DRY WEIGHT 45lb/ft³ (720kg/m³)

Working qualities

Both plain and burr forms of this wood are pleasant to work when wet or partially seasoned. It cuts well, producing long ribbon shavings, and leaves quite an attractive finish off the tool, which may require only a light sanding to remove minor blemishes. Dry wood, I find, is prone to producing short shavings, small chips and a bit of dust. Interlocking grain is likely to pull or tear out. There can be a bit of splintering towards the outer edges of the work, so proceed carefully with light cuts and sharp tools.

It is a wood that can be wet-turned to completion and cut to create very thin wall thicknesses and left to move. I prefer turning wet figured pieces such as burrs, which move more erratically and take on a 'hammered' effect due to uneven drying of the knots and figured areas, compared to the plainer surrounding parts.

Because the sap and heartwood are different colours, natural-edge work allows you to exploit a wonderful visual contrast,

Hint

If working with burrs that have voids in them, always clean them as best you can before turning and check them over to see if the wood is stable enough to withstand turning. Small cracks and checks can easily go unnoticed and cause potential problems

which is accentuated further on natural-edged burr pieces due to the very irregular bark edge. This is a wood that responds well to carving and routing techniques. If carving it, I prefer to use power rather than hand carving tools.

Sanding can be carried out using either wet or dry methods, and the wood accepts surface or penetrative finishes well. It also can be glued easily so this wood can be used on laminated and segmented work.

LEFT
Hollow form in
false acacia burr
by Mark Baker

111

Redwood
Sequoia sempervirens

Other names
Californian redwood, coast redwood, sequoia.
Burrs are sometimes sold as **vavona burr (burl)**

Characteristics
This is a true giant among softwoods –
though it must not be confused with the
giant redwood (*Sequoiadendron giganteum*).
Massive sections of timber are available,
allowing the turner a lot of scope to tackle
almost any project imaginable: architectural,
cabinetmaking, artistic or utilitarian. The
sapwood is a near-white or pale whitish-yellow
colour, and the heartwood ranges from a light
red to a deep red-brown. This is not a very
heavy or dense wood. It is straight-grained
and has a texture ranging from fine to coarse,
but is not capable of holding fine detail. The
complementary earlywood and latewood form
a clear growth-ring figure.

Burrs up to 6ft (1.8m) in diameter are
fairly common, and are fantastically beautiful.
They vary enormously in figuring, and will
not disappoint anyone who wants to try them
out. Be prepared to pay a big premium for
them: they are highly sought-after by the
cabinetmaking industry for veneers.

POSSIBLE HEALTH RISKS
Dermatitis, asthma,
nasal cancer and
hypersensitivity
pneumonia; the
dust is a respiratory
irritant

Seasoning
Although the timber holds a lot of water when
felled, redwood dries quickly and easily with
hardly any degrade. It also shows minimal
movement in use. Redwood can be wet-
turned to completion and allowed to distort,
or rough-turned and set aside to season fully
before final turning.

CONSERVATION STATUS
Categorized by Red
List as 'endangered'

*Burr, finished with
acrylic lacquer*

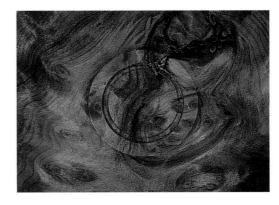

Grows
California and Oregon, USA
HEIGHT 200–325ft (60–100m)
TRUNK DIAMETER 10–15ft (3–4.6m), achieved during a lifespan of
800 years or more
SPECIFIC GRAVITY .42
TYPICAL DRY WEIGHT 26lb/ft³ (420kg/m³)

Working qualities

This is a lovely wood to work with. Wet timber cuts beautifully. Seasoned timber cuts well with sharp gouges and skew chisels, but shear-scraping is preferable to conventional scraping, to lessen the likelihood of grain tearout or of leaving a woolly surface.

A certain amount of dust is produced when turning seasoned wood, so be careful to extract it properly. Burrs and figured wood can be a bit tricky, grain tearout being the major problem; to minimize this, use sharp tools with a delicate, deliberate cut, avoid scraping and use abrasives to remove minor blemishes. This wood responds well to carving with both hand and power tools.

Abrasives can clog quickly when dry-sanding, especially if knots are present; knots may be quite resinous.

Hint

Small areas of figuring on hollow forms can be highlighted to wonderful effect using dyes, which will be absorbed unevenly by the figured wood

BELOW
Hollow form in redwood burr by Mark Baker

Since the wood is very soft, take care not to sand too heavily in any one spot, but keep the abrasive moving all the time; failure to do this will result in hollows and surface depressions. Surface and penetrative finishes can be used to good effect to enhance the lovely grain pattern of this wood. However, the wood is quite 'hungry', so you may need quite a few coats to achieve a fine, even finish, especially on burrs.

Yew
Taxus baccata

Other names
European yew, yewtree

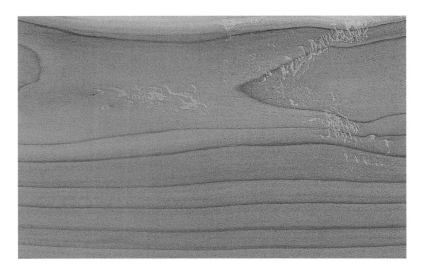

POSSIBLE HEALTH RISKS

Headaches, nausea, fainting, intestinal irritation, visual disturbances, lung congestion

CONSERVATION STATUS

Categorized as 'least concern' in Red List

Seasoning

This wood dries quickly and well, and there should be little degrade. Slight distortion may occur, and new shakes may form or existing ones widen. The wood shows hardly any movement in use. It is a lovely wood to turn wet to completion. The bark is thin, and can be retained in the finished work: heart, sap and bark make a truly stunning combination. The movement in wet-turned pieces varies considerably. It can also be rough-turned and set aside to season fully before finish-turning.

Grows

UK and mainland Europe, Turkey, northern Iran, North Africa, the Caucasus, the Himalayas and Myanmar (Burma)

HEIGHT 50ft (15m)

TRUNK DIAMETER Typically 1–3ft (0.3–0.9m); old trees can be very wide but tend to become hollow

SPECIFIC GRAVITY .67

TYPICAL DRY WEIGHT 42lb/ft³ (670kg/m³)

WARNING

Many parts of the tree are considered to be highly toxic, so take great care when handling wet and dry timber, and also make sure you take precautions to avoid ingestion of dust

Characteristics

The sapwood is a soft creamy-white and contrasts strongly with the darker heartwood, which ranges in colour from a golden orange-brown to a darker reddish-brown, and is commonly streaked with violet, red and purple. The wood will lose some of its fresh-cut vibrancy, mellowing to a darker orange-brown, but the darker streaking will always be present and distinct from the main body colour. There are frequently clusters of small knots and bark inclusions (pockets of ingrown bark). Although this medium-textured softwood is usually straight-grained, it can also be wavy, curly and irregular. Burrs are not uncommon, and can range from masses of tightly packed knots through to multicoloured, swirling grain. In short, you can never be truly sure what you will end up with until you start cutting. All of these features make it a truly exceptional wood, which is much sought-after for architectural, cabinetmaking and artistic turned work.

Since the living tree and wood are regarded as toxic, there is much debate as to whether the dry wood is safe to use for items that will come into contact with food. I would recommend using it for artistic work only.

Yew trees can live for over a thousand years. The wood is available in large sizes, affording considerable scope to the turner, but expect to find minute cracks or bark inclusions in larger pieces.

Working qualities

I love working with this wood: it has to be one of my all-time favourites. It cuts well most of the time, though irregular, sometimes interlocking grain can cause problems for skews and scrapers, resulting in grain tearout. Be aware of this and choose your projects wisely, matching the wood to the project rather than trying to force it to do something that it is not suited for. If you experience tearout with the skew chisel, change to a gouge and make very fine shearing cuts.

Hint

If irregular or interlocking grain is present, don't attempt any projects that involve very fine detail or delicate finials. The grain is liable to tear out, and finials are likely to snap because of short grain

I find that most turners are more confident with a gouge than a skew, so use the tools you feel happy with. Long ribbon shavings are produced when the wood is wet; seasoned wood is more likely to produce small shavings with dust. The dust is very fine, with a peppery smell, so make sure that you can extract it as close to source as possible and, as with all turning, wear appropriate PPE. The wood can be carved with both power and hand tools, but the former are recommended if irregular or interlocking grain is present. Yew is prone to heat-checking, so be careful when sanding to use fresh, sharp abrasive. It sands well with both dry and wet methods. Use water or oil as a sanding lubricant (water for wet-turning), but be careful to avoid colour contamination if there is sapwood present. Both penetrative and surface finishes can be used; my preference is for oil, which I power-buff to a fine, silky lustre.

LEFT
Vase by Ray Key

BELOW
Natural-edged bowl in yew burr by Ray Key

Thuya
Tetraclinis articulata

Other names
Thuya burr, thuyawood, thyine wood, citron burl, sandarac tree

Characteristics
This softwood is spectacular to look at. The part of the tree that is used by woodturners is a root burr (burl) created by the repeated removal of the coppice growth, which stimulates increased growth underground. The burrs are a rich golden orange-brown or red-brown in colour, very knotty and contorted, with a fine, interlocked grain. The colour will darken over time to a mid-brown tone, losing its orange-red tint. The figuring is usually bird's-eye or mottled, and can be very attractive. This wood has a distinctive resinous or oily smell, which you will either love or hate. I do not like it, and unfortunately for me it is long-lasting.

Thuya burr is not available in very large sizes, and the rootstock is a highly irregular shape. It is expensive and mostly used for decorative veneers, carving, or other artistic work such as turning.

Burr (burl)

POSSIBLE HEALTH RISKS
Not known, but take usual precautions regarding dust

CONSERVATION STATUS
Categorized as 'least concern' in Red List

Seasoning
The natural oil in the wood retards moisture loss, which makes seasoning easier. Kilning the wood slowly is strongly recommended. Thuya can either be wet-turned to completion, or rough-turned, coated with PVA and set aside to season further before finish-turning.

Grows
North Africa and southern Spain; also east Africa, Cyprus and Malta

HEIGHT 50ft (15m)

TRUNK DIAMETER 1.3ft (0.4m)

SPECIFIC GRAVITY .67

TYPICAL DRY WEIGHT 42lb/ft³ (670kg/m³)

Hint

Because the wood is naturally resinous and oily, sand the work to completion and then power-buff using a polishing mop loaded with very fine abrasive held in a wax compound. This will produce a very fine lustre and, depending on the end use, may be the only finish that is needed

Working qualities

This resinous wood exudes an all-pervading smell when cut; I find this very 'heady' after a while, and it lingers for days. The contorted grain with lots of small knots means that grain tearout is very likely. Skews are difficult to use on this wood, and gouges produce by far the best finish, but the resin is liable to build up on the bevel, which must be cleaned and sharpened frequently. Light, shallow cuts will minimize grain tearout, but will not prevent it. A very light cut in conventional scraping mode can sometimes give a better finish than a gouge; shear-scraping works also. This is a wood that can be carved with both hand and power tools.

Abrasives clog readily with the resinous dust, but both dry and wet sanding methods produce a very fine finish, though checking can occur if too much heat is generated. Because of its oily nature, the wood can be resistant to surface finishes, so wipe it over with a solvent first to clear away the resin. It finishes well with oils and waxes, and can take a very high polish.

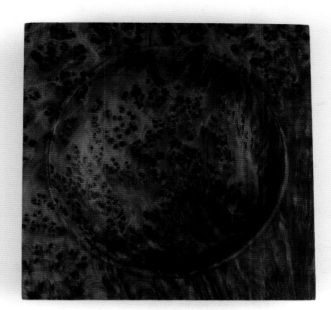

ABOVE AND BELOW
Square-edged, round-bottomed bowl by Mark Baker

117

Myrtle
Umbellularia californica

Other names
Acacia, baytree, bay laurel, California laurel, mountain laurel, Oregon myrtle, pacific myrtle, Californian olive, pepperwood, spice tree

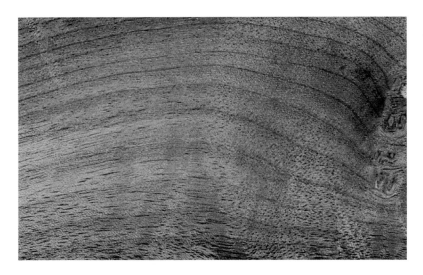

Characteristics
This wonderful wood can be quite stunning when it has figuring in it. Even without figure, the wood itself is pleasant, with a subtle colour and grain pattern. The heartwood is a creamy, golden toffee-brown, often with a greenish tinge. The sapwood is a very similar colour and not easily distinguishable from the heartwood. The wood will darken considerably over time to a mid-brown tone. This is a dense, heavy wood. Its grain – which is compact, smooth and close – is usually straight, but can be wavy or irregular. Myrtle frequently has ripple, feather, mottle or roe figuring.

It is a wood that can be used for utilitarian ware, artistic pieces and architectural work such as balusters and chair legs. It is frequently used in cabinetmaking. It is available in quite large sizes, giving turners ample opportunity to explore this wood with many different types of project.

POSSIBLE HEALTH RISKS
Not known, but take usual precautions regarding dust

CONSERVATION STATUS
Not known to be at risk

Seasoning
Care must be taken when drying this wood to avoid checking and warping. It can be wet-turned to completion, or rough-turned and set aside to dry further. Rough-turning and setting it aside to season before finishing works well. To minimize the risk of checking, coat the endgrain or the whole of the rough-turned piece with PVA adhesive to even out the drying process.

The wood is sometimes submerged in water to bring about colour changes.

Figured sample

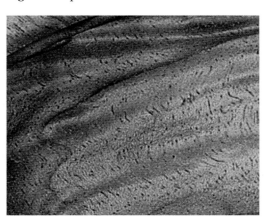

Grows
Oregon and California, USA

HEIGHT 40–80ft (12–24m)

TRUNK DIAMETER 1ft 6in–2ft 6in (0.5–0.8m)

SPECIFIC GRAVITY .85

TYPICAL DRY WEIGHT 53lb/ft³ (850kg/m³)

Hint

Try wet-turning figured forms of this timber and letting it move. The amount of movement is variable and I love the organic forms produced

Working qualities

This is a lovely wood to turn. Myrtle is capable of holding quite fine detail, and is well worth considering if you want to make finial-topped boxes or other work that requires fine embellishment.

It can, however, be a little tricky when the grain is irregular, especially when using a skew chisel on spindle work. Freshly sharpened gouges used with a light touch will minimize any tearout. Shear-scraping is a better option than conventional scraping; both will fluff up the grain a little, but if light cuts are made the damage should be slight.

If the grain is straight, long ribbon shavings can be obtained from seasoned and wet wood alike. Very little dust is produced when cutting freshly seasoned wood, but old wood is a different matter. The dust is somewhat dirty and has an acrid, peppery smell to it. Myrtle can be carved with either hand or power tools.

It will sand well with either wet or dry sanding methods, but dry sanding will produce a lot of dust. Myrtle can be finished with both surface and penetrative finishes.

BELOW
Bowl by Bert Marsh

WOODS

IN BRIEF

Even if you work with wood a lot, nature will always
come up with amazing surprises, and that is ever more
evident in the variety of timbers we have to work with.
In this section of the book I have included timbers that
you may well encounter. The main working qualities and
characteristics are listed, but I have not gone into
so much detail as in the previous section.

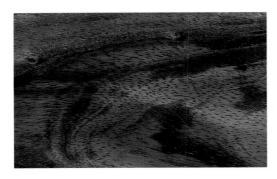

Koa

Acacia koa

OTHER NAMES Black koa, curly koa, koaia, koa-ka, Hawaiian mahogany

GROWS Hawaiian Islands

HEIGHT 80–100ft (24–30m)

TRUNK DIAMETER 3–4ft (0.9–1.2m)

SPECIFIC GRAVITY .57

TYPICAL DRY WEIGHT 41lb/ft³ (670kg/m³)

POSSIBLE HEALTH RISKS Not known

Seasoning Koa dries easily but there can be checking on thicker sections. It can be wet-turned to completion, or rough-turned and set aside to season if you need to ensure minimal movement.

Characteristics The light brown sapwood is distinct from the heartwood, which is mostly red-brown but can vary from pale cream through golden-brown to a deep reddish-chocolate colour. Koa yellows quickly in sunlight. The curly and wavy grain is interlocked, which can produce beautiful fiddleback and roe figure. The growth rings show as black lines on longitudinal surfaces. Koa has a moderately coarse texture.

Koa is a delightful wood to work with and highly prized. It cuts well with sharp gouges, skew chisels and scrapers, giving a surface that will require only a little abrading to remove blemishes. If there is interlocking grain present you may encounter tearout. Gentle, delicate cuts will minimize this. It can take quite fine detail and can be hand and power carved easily. Routing it presents no problems. As with many woods, very dry wood may produce a fair amount of dust. It seems to respond to gluing up reasonably well for laminating or segmenting work. It sands well, though with a risk of heat-checking, and finishes well. It takes surface and penetrative finishes well.

Australian blackwood

Acacia melanoxylon

OTHER NAMES Black wattle

GROWS Eastern Australia, including Tasmania

HEIGHT Generally 33–80ft (10–24m) but can reach up to 115ft (35m)

TRUNK DIAMETER Generally 1ft 8in (0.5m) but can be up to 5ft (1.5m)

SPECIFIC GRAVITY .66

TYPICAL DRY WEIGHT 41lb/ft³ (665kg/m³)

POSSIBLE HEALTH RISKS Dermatitis, sensitizer asthma, nose and throat irritation

Seasoning Blackwood has relatively low shrinkage and remains moderately stable in service. It can be wet-turned to completion, or rough-turned and set aside to season before finish-tuning. When tunring it wet, I have found that, like oak, it turns my hands and the lathe bed black due to the tannin content.

Characteristics The heartwood is generally golden-brown to darker brown, sometimes with a reddish tint and with dark brown, brown-black or reddish streaks. The sapwood is pale and up to 4in (100mm) wide. The grain is usually straight, with a medium, even texture, but sometimes interlocked, producing a fiddleback figure when quartersawn. It exhibits high natural lustre. Weight and hardness vary, the heavier timber generally coming from Tasmania.

This beautiful wood is a joy to turn, and will not present any problems to anyone who has mastered the basics other than it blunts tool edges quite quickly so keep the tools sharp. On figured work, light shearing cuts will minimize any tearout. It takes fine detail and can be carved with hand or power tools. It readily takes glues if you want to do laminated and segmented work.

It sands well, but be careful of endgrain heat-checking. It takes surface or penetrative finishes well. As with many acacias and timbers with a decent tannin content, fuming is an option if you want to explore different tonal qualities of the colour of the wood.

Seasoning Afzelia can be kiln-dried slowly from green, with a risk of slight distortion, the extension of existing shakes and some fine checking. This is a wood best rough-turned and then set aside so that it can season fully.

Characteristics The orange or red-brown heartwood, which matures to a deep red-brown on exposure to air, is distinct from the pale straw-coloured sapwood. The grain of this dense, heavy wood is irregular and interlocked, giving a coarse yet even texture. Yellow or white deposits may cause staining. Afzelia is generally used for decorative turnery and burr and figured forms are highly prized.

It is resistant to cutting with hand tools but turns reasonably well with gouges and skews but expect some grain tearout if anything but sharp tools and a well-presented cutting edge are used. If using scrapers, there is a risk of fluffing up the endgrain (that is, creating a woolly surface). It can be power carved and routed, and if you venture into segmented or laminated work, be aware that there are occassional issues with bonding pieces together. It can be power carved and routed and sands relatively easily but is prone to heat-checking if excessive heat is generated. Surface finishes and oils and waxes seem to work well.

WAX FINISH

Afzelia
Afzelia spp.

OTHER NAMES Doussié, apa, aligna, lingué, chamfuta, mkora, bolengo, m'banga, papao
GROWS Tropical West Africa and East Africa
HEIGHT 80–100ft (25–30m)
TRUNK DIAMETER 4ft (1.2m)
SPECIFIC GRAVITY .82
TYPICAL DRY WEIGHT 51lb/ft³ (820kg/m³)
POSSIBLE HEALTH RISKS Dermatitis and sneezing

Seasoning Dries reasonably well but can warp; stable once seasoned. Can be turned wet or partially seasoned to completion, but the finish off the tool may be woolly and require quite a lot of sanding; expect some movement. Kiln-dried wood can be turned for furniture or joinery parts. When there is a need for precision, it responds well to rough-turning and setting aside to season.

Characteristics First impressions are that it is quite bland, a closer look reveals subtle colour patterns that are very pretty. This lightweight softwood is useful for decorative and utilitarian turning. The heartwood varies from a creamy toffee colour, through darker pinkish-red hues to dark brown. It mellows quickly to a more uniform reddish-brown. Normally straight-grained with a fine, uniform texture, it can exhibit a streaked or mottled figure.

It cuts cleanly and easily with sharp bevel-rubbing tools and a slow traverse rate. It carves easily. Scrapers are likely to tear the grain, so, after gouges or skews, move straight to abrasives to remove blemishes. It sands well, as long as you do not skip grades. Oil darkens the wood a lot, and imparts an orange tinge; lacquer finishes with UV inhibitors darken less.

CONSERVATION STATUS (see icons, right) **1** *A. dammara* vulnerable; **2** *A. microstachya* near threatened; **3** *A. robusta* slight concern

Kauri pine
Agathis spp.

OTHER NAMES New Zealand kauri (*A. australis*), Queensland kauri (*A. robusta*, *A. palmerstonii*, *A. microstachya*), East Indian kauri (*A. dammara*), Fijian kauri (*A. vitiensis*)
GROWS Australia, New Zealand, Papua New Guinea, Philippines, Fiji, Indochina, Indonesia
HEIGHT 150ft (45m)
TRUNK DIAMETER 5–6ft (1.5–2m)
SPECIFIC GRAVITY .48–.58
TYPICAL DRY WEIGHT 30–36lb/ft³ (480–560kg/m³)
POSSIBLE HEALTH RISKS Not known

Pau marfim

Agonandra brasiliensis (formerly also *Balfourodendron riedelianum,* which is now endangered)

OTHER NAMES Marfim, gutambu, pau liso, moroti, kyrandy, ivorywood

GROWS Brazil, Panama

HEIGHT 25–50ft (8–15m)

TRUNK DIAMETER 1–4ft (0.3–1.2m)

SPECIFIC GRAVITY .86

TYPICAL DRY WEIGHT 50lb/ft³ (800kg/m³)

POSSIBLE HEALTH RISKS Dermatitis, rhinitis and asthma

Seasoning This wood dries easily with little degrade. There is only small movement in service. Rough-turning is recommended before turning it to completion.

Characteristics Both heartwood and sapwood look much the same, the colour ranging from almost white to pale yellow-brown or off-white to creamy-yellow. Sometimes there is a hint of grey, and darker streaks. The grain may be straight or irregular, and can be interlocked. The texture is fine and the wood has a medium lustre. This is a very hard, dense wood, and has a moderate to severe blunting effect on tool edges. It can be carved, and is available in reasonably large sizes, but the cost can be high, so it is more frequently used for smaller decorative items.

This wood is a delight to work with, as long as it is straight-grained: it cuts well with all tools, but frequent sharpening will be necessary. When the grain is irregular, tearout is likely – especially when using scrapers – so light, delicate cuts are required. It can be hand or power carved and also routs well. It sands satisfactorily, but is prone to heat-check on the endgrain. Gluing seems to present no issues and I have not encountered any problems using surface or penetrative finishes.

CONSERVATION STATUS (see icons, left) **1** *Balfourodendron* endangered; **2** *A. brasiliensis* not at risk

---

Common alder

Alnus glutinosa

OTHER NAMES Black alder, grey alder, Japanese alder

GROWS From North Africa to northern Russia, most of Europe and UK, and Japan

HEIGHT 50–90ft (15–27m)

TRUNK DIAMETER 1–4ft (0.3–1.2m)

SPECIFIC GRAVITY .53

TYPICAL DRY WEIGHT 33lb/ft³ (530kg/m³)

POSSIBLE HEALTH RISKS Dermatitis, rhinitis and bronchial problems

Seasoning Dries quite rapidly, well and with little degrade as long as log are quickly converted after cutting down. It can readily be turned wet and thin walled and left to move – although it doesn't move much – or rough-turned and set aside to dry before finish-turning. You can apply end seal to the endgrain areas on rough-turned work to retard drying, but I haven't found it necessary with this wood.

Characteristics There is little difference between the sapwood and the heartwood. The wood is generally a flat-looking light cream or pinkish-orange, but sometimes a light burnt orange or red-brown. On exposure to light and air, it changes to a duller, more muted light-mid orange or reddish brown. It has straight grain and a fine, close texture, though it can be a little fibrous or woolly. It is quite a soft wood and its surface can be marked with a fingernail quite easily.

It is a relatively easy timber to work with, wet or dry, but if using anything but sharp gouges or skews you might encounter fluffing up of fibres or pulling on the endgrain – especially when using scrapers. It can hold reasonable detail without problem, but don't go too fine or create too sharp an edge. It is nice for hand or power carving and routing it is easy. Sanding does not present any issues and it readily accepts dyes and stains and other penetrative finishes as well as surface finishes.

Seasoning Red alder dries fairly rapidly and easily with almost no degrade. It moves very little once seasoned. It can be wet-turned to completion or rough-turned and set aside to dry prior to finish-turning following the normal guidelines for these methods.

Characteristics Red alder is a lightweight wood, fairly straight-grained, of uniform texture. The heartwood is pale yellow to reddish-brown, and the sapwood is not clearly differentiated. It has a pleasant but not outstanding visual appeal. This wood is suitable for utilitarian or artistic work.

This wood turns well, with few problems when using sharp tools presented properly to the wood other than a slight risk of endgrain tearout, especially when using a scraper in conventional scraping mode. Because it is soft, it is easily marked, and failure to keep the abrasive moving when sanding will cause hollows. Red alder will accept both surface and penetrative finishes. Alder glues well so laminated and segmented work are worth exploring.

Having said all that, unless one encounters figuring, both this timber and its relative common alder *(Alnus glutinosa)* are quite bland in appearance, so it might be worth exploring carving or routing them. You won't have any issues if you want to carve and sculpt it by hand or power tools, and such details may well lift this from being a nice timber to something special.

American or red alder
Alnus rubra

OTHER NAMES Western alder, Oregon alder, Pacific coast alder
GROWS Pacific coast of USA and Canada
HEIGHT 70–120ft (21–36m)
TRUNK DIAMETER 1–4ft (0.3–1.2m)
SPECIFIC GRAVITY .53
TYPICAL DRY WEIGHT 33lb/ft³ (530kg/m³)
POSSIBLE HEALTH RISKS Dermatitis, rhinitis and bronchial problems

Seasoning This dries slowly and is likely to split if dried in large sections. It can be turned to completion from wet or partially seasoned timber with some movement occurring – this is variable but usually not much. Rough-turning it and setting it aside to season before finish-turning is the method I have had most success with.

Characteristics The heartwood often features pale to mid-brown, and, very commonly, brown-black streaks. On exposure the wood turns a darker, deeper colour. The sapwood colour ranges from yellow to pale reddish-brown. The grain is irregular and often interlocked, and the wood has a fine, even texture. Because it is prone to splitting, through-cut boards are not commonly available. You can buy flooring boards; more often than not, for turners this wood is sold as air-dried, predimensioned blanks.

It turns and carves well, and holds fine detail. A 12tpi (teeth per inch) hand-cut thread is possible – but do not leave any sharp points on the cut teeth or edges of work because they may break off. A very high finish can be obtained directly from bevel-rubbing tools (gouges or skew chisels). It can be sanded satisfactorily, but don't generate too much heat or you might end up with endgrain heat checks. It can be taken to a fine finish with either penetrative or surface finishes and can be glued readily.

Curupay
Anadenanthera colubrina
var. *cebil,* syn. *A. macrocarpa*

OTHER NAMES Not known
GROWS Brazil
HEIGHT 80ft (24m)
TRUNK DIAMETER 2–3ft (0.6–0.9m)
SPECIFIC GRAVITY 1.02
TYPICAL DRY WEIGHT 66lb/ft³ (1050kg/m³)
POSSIBLE HEALTH RISKS Not known

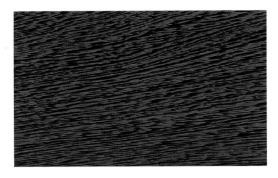

Red kabbas

Andira inermis

OTHER NAMES Red cabbage bark, partridgewood, pheasantwood, angelin, angelim, andira, macaya, maquilla
GROWS West Indies, Mexico, Central America, northern South America, Peru, Bolivia, Benin
HEIGHT 90–120ft (27–37m)
TRUNK DIAMETER 1ft 8in–2ft 4in (0.5–0.7m)
SPECIFIC GRAVITY .64
TYPICAL DRY WEIGHT 40lb/ft³ (640kg/m³)
POSSIBLE HEALTH RISKS Not known

Seasoning Red kabbas dries slowly, with a slight risk of checking and distortion. You are most likely to encounter partially seasoned wood in predimensioned blanks, but occasionally boards may be available. If you turn it when partially seasoned it will distort, which can be interesting. Rough-turning works well also.

Characteristics This is a strong, tough, hardwearing wood that is very interesting to look at. The pale sapwood is clearly demarcated from the pale yellow, mid-brown to deep red-brown heartwood. The heartwood also features lighter striping that, combined with the darker areas, resembles the pattern found on a partridge feather. Red kabbas has a coarse texture and the grain is straight, but usually irregularly interlocked.

The wood cuts well, but when very dry it is somewhat dusty. It carves well, too, with power tools and routers. But keep all cutters and tools sharp. Scrapers work reasonably well despite its coarse texture. But when turning the wood, despite its ability to hold reasonably fine detail, it can be a bit brittle and is liable to fracture at the edges and where sharp detail is used. It can readily be glued, so works well for laminated and segmented work, and is a timber that can be sanded without problems other than avoiding heat build-up. Surface finishes, oils and waxes work well to bring out the best in this wood.

Paraná pine

Araucaria angustifolia

OTHER NAMES Brazilian pine, pinheiro do Brasil
GROWS Brazil, Argentina, Paraguay
HEIGHT 80–100ft (24–33m)
TRUNK DIAMETER 5ft (1.5m)
SPECIFIC GRAVITY .54
TYPICAL DRY WEIGHT Varies widely, but approx. 33lb/ft³ (540kg/m³)
POSSIBLE HEALTH RISKS Not known

Seasoning This softwood, which is not a true pine, is difficult to season. The darker wood may distort, split and take a long time to dry. It shows moderate movement in service, but is prone to distortion if moisture conditions change. Kiln-dried stock can be turned for most projects, but when more stability is needed, rough-turn to even out the drying process then finish-turn it once seasoned.

Characteristics The cream to soft brown heartwood has a darker inner core and may be streaked attractively with dark pink, red or red-brown. The grain is usually straight, and the wood has a close, uniform texture. Small, tight knots may be present. It can be used for architectural work, balusters, spindles and so on; for utilitarian items such as pepper mills; and for artistic work.

Due to its status, this timber is now becoming much scarcer and is typically encountered in smaller sections than before, often old stock and from salvaged timber used previously in construction.

This underrated wood behaves more like a hardwood than a softwood. It works well with sharp bevel-rubbing tools, but will suffer from grain tearout using scrapers. It can be carved and routed easily. Sanding will not present a problem as long as you keep your abrasives moving. The timber readily accepts surface and penetrative finishes.

Seasoning Norfolk Island pine dries quickly and well, without degrade. Take care to avoid blue stain, unless you like the effect; rapid but controlled drying will usually prevent it. The wood can be wet-turned to completion or rough-turned and set aside to dry.

Characteristics The heartwood can vary from white through to pale yellow-brown. The creamy-white sapwood, which is not clearly differentiated, is up to 6in (150mm) thick. The grain is straight, with a fine, uniform texture. This soft, light softwood is not a true pine.

It cuts well when wet, but if using seasoned timber you will need ultrasharp tools; otherwise a woolly or torn surface is likely. Bevel-rubbing tools will give a better cut than scrapers, which can pluck out fibres or create fluffy grain. The wood sands easily, but care needs to be taken so as not to form hollows and grooves. It can be finished with surface or penetrative finishes.

Norfolk Island pine
Araucaria cunninghamii

OTHER NAMES Hoop pine, Australian araucaria, arakaria, Dorrigo pine, colonial pine
GROWS Australia and Papua New Guinea
HEIGHT 100–150ft (30–45m) and above
TRUNK DIAMETER 2–4ft (0.6–1.2m) or more
SPECIFIC GRAVITY .56
TYPICAL DRY WEIGHT 35lb/ft³ (560kg/m³)
POSSIBLE HEALTH RISKS Not known

Seasoning Severe splitting and checking are common during drying. Rough-turning before drying will not guarantee a split-free piece of wood. Wet-turning to completion, with a thin, uniform wall thickness, is a better option, but the inevitable distortion means that boxes with tight-fitting lids, for example, are inadvisable. If you must, try rough-turning, then coating the whole piece in PVA before setting it aside to dry, but expect a high failure rate.

Characteristics The heartwood is red-brown to red, and the narrow sapwood is light brown. There is often attractive figure and grain. This is a hard, strong wood with a fine texture. It is easy to turn when wet, slightly harder and dustier when dry. It takes quite fine detail; bevel-rubbing tools, as well as scrapers, can produce a fine finish. It can be carved and routed easily, and I have not encountered any issues with sanding or applying any finishes.

Root sections, available in many shapes and sizes, are usually a deep red-brown or maroon, sometimes with a dramatic swirling figure. These contorted, twisted forms are highly prized by carvers. Turners, however, need to find larger sections that they can dimension as necessary. I find it best to wet-turn the root sections to a thin wall thickness to completion. Finishes of all types can be readily used.

Manzanita
Arctostaphylos spp.

OTHER NAMES Not known
GROWS Mexico; USA (Oregon, Sierra Nevada and California)
HEIGHT 12ft (4m)
TRUNK DIAMETER 4–10in (100–160mm)
SPECIFIC GRAVITY .70
TYPICAL DRY WEIGHT 55lb/ft³ (881kg/m³)
POSSIBLE HEALTH RISKS Not known

Peroba rosa

Aspidosperma polyneuron, syn. *A. peroba*

OTHER NAMES Rosa peroba, red peroba, palo rosa, amarello, amargosa, ibri romi

GROWS Argentina and Brazil

HEIGHT 90ft (27m)

TRUNK DIAMETER 2ft 6in (0.75m) or more

SPECIFIC GRAVITY .75

TYPICAL DRY WEIGHT 47lb/ft³ (750kg/m³)

POSSIBLE HEALTH RISKS Skin irritation, headache, sweating, respiratory problems, nausea, stomach cramps, fainting, drowsiness, weakness and blisters

Seasoning This is a fast-drying wood with a high shrinkage rate, so care needs to be taken to reduce the risk of splitting and distortion. You can wet-turn the work to completion, or use partially seasoned stock, but you must expect some movement. For minimal movement, rough-turn and set it aside to season before finish-turning.

Characteristics The heartwood varies greatly in colour, but is generally pinkish- or reddish-brown, with purple, orange or yellow streaks; it darkens on exposure. The yellow sapwood is not very distinct from the heartwood. The grain may be straight or irregular, with a fine or very fine texture and a low to medium lustre.

This is another timber that is becoming much scarcer due to there being many fewer trees so don't expect to see an abundance of large sizes available. However, predimensioned blanks of older stock are still available from some sources.

This is a hard, heavy timber that is highly prized. It has a moderate blunting effect on edge tools. It turns well with sharp tools and is capable of holding fine detail. This wood can be routed and carved satisfactorily, sands well, and will not present any problems other than the risk of heat-checking in endgrain. It can be glued easily and accepts finishes with ease.

Gonçalo alves

Astronium fraxinifolium and *A. graveolens*

OTHER NAMES Zorrowood, zebrawood, tigerwood, mura

GROWS Brazil, Paraguay and Uruguay

HEIGHT 120ft (37m)

TRUNK DIAMETER 2–3ft (0.6–0.9m)

SPECIFIC GRAVITY .95

TYPICAL DRY WEIGHT 59lb/ft³ (950kg/m³)

POSSIBLE HEALTH RISKS Dermatitis and irritation to skin and eyes

Seasoning Dry the wood slowly to avoid degrade; there can be a lot of warping and checking. Rough-turning and putting it aside to season is a must when making boxes, bowls or platters; consider coating with PVA to retard drying.

Characteristics The wide sapwood is grey or brownish-white, the heartwood light golden- to reddish-brown with irregular dark streaks or spots. It darkens quickly unless finishes with UV inhibitors in finishes are used. The grain is often interlocked, with harder and softer bands. It is quite oily. Available in large sizes, it is often used as a substitute for cocobolo (*Dalbergia retusa*).

This dense, hard, heavy wood produces a nice finish off the tool, but frequent sharpening is necessary. The interlocking grain may pluck out if you are not careful. It responds well to a final pass with a freshly honed scraper. The timber can be power carved and routed to add another dimension to your work. When sanding it tends to clog abrasives, and shows every score from the sanding process, so always work through the grades. The fine, sticky dust has a peppery smell and can be difficult to remove from clothing. To avoid heat-checking, do not use worn-out abrasive or apply undue pressure. I have found it accepts surface finishes and waxes and oils easily.

Seasoning It is slow-drying, with a risk of checking and splitting on the ends if not dried carefully. I prefer to rough-turn this timber and coat the endgrain areas with PVA to slow the drying. If you choose to turn a piece wet from start to finish, keep the wall thickness thin and even. With a maximum thickness of ⅛–¼in (3–6mm) I have not had any failures, but I have experienced checking at greater thicknesses. Movement during subsequent drying is visible, but not huge.

Characteristics The heartwood is a light creamy reddish-brown to red-brown, which contrasts with the light tan to brown sapwood. This wood has a fine texture with a fine even grain, but not as fine as pink ivory (*Berchemia zeyheri*). It cuts easily with sharp bevel-rubbing tools and produces a good finish off the tool. Sharp scrapers produce only a slightly inferior result, but of course do not leave a polished surface. It holds quite fine detail; I would not use it for cutting ultrafine hand-chased threads, but I have gone down to 10 and 12tpi without problems. This timber power carves and routs well, and I have not experienced any difficulties with gluing or applying oils, waxes or surface finishes.

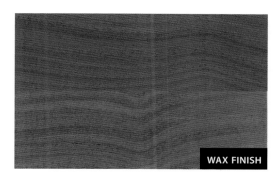

WAX FINISH

Brown ivory
Berchemia discolor,
syn. *Phyllogeiton discolor*

OTHER NAMES N'tacha, birdplum
GROWS Northeastern, southern and southwestern Africa
HEIGHT 16–66ft (5–20m)
TRUNK DIAMETER 3–6ft (0.3–0.6m)
SPECIFIC GRAVITY .99
TYPICAL DRY WEIGHT 62/ft³ (990kg/m³)
POSSIBLE HEALTH RISKS Not known

Seasoning This wood dries slowly with little degrade, but shrinkage can be high, which may result in end and surface checks. Honeycombing and cell collapse can occur in wet heartwood. There is a considerable movement in use, so dimensional stability is poor. It is advisable to rough-turn the work, allowing an extra ³⁄₈in (10mm) of wall thickness per 12in (300mm) diameter, before setting it aside to season. Alternatively, wet-turn the piece to completion. Use kiln-dried wood for turning furniture or joinery parts.

Characteristics The sapwood is whitish, pale yellow or light red-brown, the heartwood red-brown, but colours may vary. Yellow birch has a fine, even texture and a mostly straight, close grain. Wavy and curly grain can occur; such pieces are prized for their pleasing figure.

Sharp bevel-rubbing tools will give the best finish; scrapers will damage the surface. It can be carved and routed to create greater visual and tactile aspects. Careful sanding will produce a very fine finish, but keep the abrasive moving or you will sand away the soft areas, leaving the harder parts proud. Both penetrative and surface finishes will yield good results. This wood can also be stained or dyed.

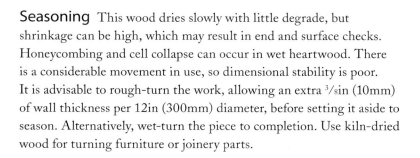

American yellow birch
Betula alleghaniensis

OTHER NAMES Hard birch, Canadian yellow birch, Quebec birch, swamp birch, betula wood
GROWS Eastern Canada and eastern USA
HEIGHT 70–100ft (21–30m)
TRUNK DIAMETER 2ft 6in (0.8m)
SPECIFIC GRAVITY .71
TYPICAL DRY WEIGHT 44lb/ft³ (710kg/m³)
POSSIBLE HEALTH RISKS Dermatitis and respiratory problems

Muhuhu

Brachylaena huillensis, syn. B. hutchinsii

OTHER NAMES Mkarambaki, muhugive, muhugwe

GROWS Eastern Africa

HEIGHT 80–90ft (24–27m)

TRUNK DIAMETER 2ft (0.6m)

SPECIFIC GRAVITY .93

TYPICAL DRY WEIGHT 58lb/ft³ (930kg/m³)

POSSIBLE HEALTH RISKS Dermatitis

Seasoning This dense wood needs to be dried slowly to minimize degrade. It has a tendency towards end splitting and surface checking. Partially seasoned stock can be turned to completion, but will move a little. I prefer rough-turning and coating the piece with PVA before seasoning further.

Characteristics The heartwood is a mid-tan colour when freshly cut, then mellows to a darker chestnut brown, often with dark streaks and a green tinge. The grain is closely interlocked, sometimes wavy or curly, with a fine, even texture. The sapwood is quite distinct, being grey-white. This aromatic wood has a scent similar to sandalwood.

Usually only small sections are available, typically predimensioned blanks rather than logs. Muhuhu cuts satisfactorily, and a fine finish is achievable with most tools, but it is prone to splintering off at the edges. It will also heat-check if excessive heat is generated during sanding. Power carving is possible, if you want to experiment. It sands well and is receptive to both surface and penetrative finishes.

WAX FINISH

Masasa

Brachystegia spiciformis

OTHER NAMES Msasa, lunda, n'sasa, zebrawood, bean-pod tree

GROWS Mozambique to Tanzania

HEIGHT 33–66ft (10–20m)

TRUNK DIAMETER 1–3 ft (0.3–0.9m)

SPECIFIC GRAVITY .97

TYPICAL DRY WEIGHT 61lb/ft³ (975kg/m³)

POSSIBLE HEALTH RISKS Not known

Seasoning Relatively slow-drying; checking and splitting on the ends of boards is very common. I have had no problems when rough-turning and setting it aside to dry before re-turning, or when turning from a bought blank to a finished, even-walled form. It moves a little; if you turn boxes, or need a predictable shape, rough-turn it and re-turn once dry and settled.

Characteristics The heartwood is typically an orangey red or brown, with a well-defined paler creamy-coloured sapwood. The grain is typically irregular and interlocked, and coarse in texture. It is a dense timber and one that can be cut satisfactorily with bevel-rubbing tools, but you are likely to experience small amounts of tearout on the interlocking grain. Scrapers do not produce a significantly worse surface than a bevel-rubbing tool. It takes reasonable detail but not fine threads, and responds well to carving – power carving is easiest – and routing, if you want to explore enhancing your turnings further. The wood sands and accepts finishes well.

Seasoning It dries slowly and is very likely to split and check, but is very stable when dry. Partially seasoned wood can be turned, but will move. It can also be rough-turned and set aside to season more fully before finish-turning.

Characteristics The heartwood ranges from grey-red to deep red, often with yellow and red stripes. The grain is straight or interlocked, with a very fine texture. It is not available in large sizes, so decorative and artistic work is usually undertaken with this wood.

The wood is very hard and blunts tool edges severely. It is easier to turn than to machine, but may contain silica, which will blunt tools rapidly. It cuts quite well with all sharp tools, especially with bevel-rubbing tools. It sands well, although the abrasive clogs readily and there is a risk of heat-checking on the endgrain. It can be brought to a high-gloss finish with oils and waxes or with surface finishes.

Satiné bloodwood
Brosimum rubescens, syn. B. paraense

OTHER NAMES Not known
GROWS Brazil
HEIGHT Small to medium-sized tree
TRUNK DIAMETER 1ft 8in (0.5m)
SPECIFIC GRAVITY 1.15
TYPICAL DRY WEIGHT 71lb/ft³ (1150kg/m³)
POSSIBLE HEALTH RISKS Not known

Seasoning This oily, resinous wood dries slowly; large sections never dry thoroughly. It can be turned part-seasoned or wet, but expect some movement or surface checking. Rough-turning and setting aside to season is usually successful: small surface checks can be removed during final turning, or filled with PVA and wood dust.

Characteristics Verawood self-lubricates like lignum vitae (*Guaiacum sanctum*). It is dense, hard, strong and abrasion-resistant. The heartwood varies from a soft green-brown to a brighter green, often with attractive darker streaks. The fine, sometimes interlocked grain holds fine detail and hand-chased threads well; it carves well with power tools. It gives off a pleasant smell when worked.

Scrapers may produce a finer finish than gouges or skews; either method produces some oily dust. Abrasives need frequent cleaning, but after careful toolwork only minimal sanding should be necessary. Verawood resists penetrative finishes, but oils and waxes can be used effectively. If surface finishes lift off or fail to take, wiping with solvent may help. If you use a power-buffing mop, loaded with a fine abrasive held in a wax compound, to polish the surface, the natural oils and resins themselves make a fine finish. Be careful not to generate too much heat – there is a risk of heat-checking.

Verawood
Bulnesia arborea

OTHER NAMES Guayacán, Maracaibo lignum vitae
GROWS Colombia and Venezuela
HEIGHT 40–50ft (12–15m)
TRUNK DIAMETER 2ft (0.6m)
SPECIFIC GRAVITY 1.0
TYPICAL DRY WEIGHT 62lb/ft³ (1000kg/m³)
POSSIBLE HEALTH RISKS Not known

Palo santo

Bulnesia sarmientoi

OTHER NAMES Argentine lignum vitae
GROWS Paraguay and Argentina
HEIGHT 30ft (9m)
TRUNK DIAMETER 1ft–1ft 4in (0.3–0.4m)
SPECIFIC GRAVITY 1.1
TYPICAL DRY WEIGHT 69lb/ft³ (1100kg/m³)
POSSIBLE HEALTH RISKS Not known

Seasoning This wood dries very slowly and is prone to checking. Rough-turning the piece then coating it with PVA before setting it aside to dry is recommended. Conversely, palo santo can be turned to completion, with an even wall thickness, from partially seasoned stock, but in this case it will move a bit.

Characteristics The heartwood is olive-green to brown with variegated stripes, mellowing quickly to a rich greenish-brown. It is oily to the touch, and fragrant. The sapwood is a narrow strip of off-white wood. Palo santo has a fine, even texture and an interwoven grain.

It is difficult to machine but easier to turn. It polishes well, but is resistant to some penetrative and surface finishes. Often sold as a substitute for lignum vitae (*Guaiacum sanctum*), it has many of the same characteristics: it turns and finishes in the same way, has a similar smell, but is not quite as dense – although it will take a hand-chased thread and carved detail. Abrasives are liable to clog, but if there is no sapwood present, wet sanding will produce a very fine finish; wipe over to remove any residual slurry before applying a final coat of finish.

Pernambuco

Caesalpinia echinata, syn. *Guilandina echinata*

OTHER NAMES Brazilwood, Bahia wood, Para wood, pau Brasil, Brazil ironwood, brasilete
GROWS Eastern Brazil
HEIGHT 25–40ft (8–12m)
TRUNK DIAMETER 1ft 8in–2ft 3in (0.5–0.7m)
SPECIFIC GRAVITY 1.2
TYPICAL DRY WEIGHT 75–80lb/ft³ (1200–1280kg/m³)
POSSIBLE HEALTH RISKS Irritation to eyes and skin; headaches, nausea and visual disturbance

Seasoning This wood is expensive, so dry it very slowly to avoid degradation and checking. I recommend rough-turning it and leaving it to season before finish-turning; this will give maximum stability. It can be turned to completion from partially seasoned stock, but is likely to distort slightly.

Characteristics The heartwood is bright orange-red, maturing to a deep red-brown. The sapwood is almost white. There can be a stripy or marbled figure, sometimes with pin knots. The grain may be straight or interlocked, with a fine, even texture and a natural lustre. The wood is mostly used for artistic or decorative work. This is a timber that we see very little of now, but if you do get hold of some you are in for a treat.

This hard, heavy wood blunts tool edges severely, but turns surprisingly well, with very few problems – endgrain heat-checking being the worst of these when sanding. It can hold quite fine detail and you can carve and rout it very easily. Often a fine finish can be achieved straight from the tool. It sands well and can be finished to a wonderful lustrous finish with either penetrative or surface finishes.

Seasoning This wood dries slowly and tends to have surface checks if dried in larger sections. I recommend rough-turning it and setting it aside to dry before finish-turning.

Characteristics This is a wonderful-looking wood. The heartwood is dark olive-brown or yellow-brown with dark brown or black lines; plainsawn surfaces have a figure reminiscent of partridge feathers. The narrow sapwood is yellow-white. The grain is straight to interlocked with a very fine, even texture. The samples I have are of a slightly oily nature, though this wood is not generally described as oily. It is not available in large sizes.

It is very dense, hard, and capable of holding very fine detail; it can be carved and routed with power tools. It turns well with freshly sharpened tools. Abrasives tend to clog when sanding, and care is needed to avoid heat-checking. If no sapwood is present it can be sanded wet rather than dry. It can be finished to a high polish with either penetrative or surface finishes.

Guayacán partridgewood
Caesalpinia paraguariensis, syn.
C. melanocarpa and *Acacia paraguariensis*
OTHER NAMES Guayacán, brown ebony
GROWS Paraguay
HEIGHT 30–50ft (10–15m)
TRUNK DIAMETER 2–3ft (0.6–0.9m)
SPECIFIC GRAVITY 1.25
TYPICAL DRY WEIGHT 78lb/ft³ (1250kg/m³)
POSSIBLE HEALTH RISKS Not known

Seasoning It dries rapidly with only slight end-checking. It can be turned wet or partially seasoned, though subsequent movement is erratic. If stability is required, rough-turn it and then set it aside to season before finish-turning.

Characteristics The heartwood is a creamy yellow-brown, with slightly lighter cream-coloured sapwood. The grain is straight or slightly interlocked, with a fine, even texture. It is capable of holding fine detail and can be carved with hand or power tools. This wood is not available in very large sections; usually it is sold as air-dried, predimensioned blanks and is used for small decorative or artistic work.

This wood turns, sands and finishes well, although it is prone to heat-checking on endgrain. It is often used as an alternative to European boxwood (*Buxus sempervirens*), because it works similarly and is not too dissimilar in looks, whether fresh-cut or aged; but it is not as dense as boxwood, and will not hold hand-chased threads. It does, however, carve and rout with ease. It is also available in larger sizes than boxwood.

Genero lemonwood
Calycophyllum multiflorum
OTHER NAMES Castelo boxwood, ivorywood, palo blanco
GROWS Central and South America
HEIGHT Small to medium tree
TRUNK DIAMETER Not known
SPECIFIC GRAVITY .82–.86
TYPICAL DRY WEIGHT 51–54lb/ft³ (820–860kg/m³)
POSSIBLE HEALTH RISKS Not known

Australian silky oak

Cardwellia sublimis

OTHER NAMES Northern silky oak, bull oak, Queensland silky oak

GROWS Queensland, Australia

HEIGHT 120ft (37m)

TRUNK DIAMETER 4ft (1.2m)

SPECIFIC GRAVITY .53

TYPICAL DRY WEIGHT 33lb/ft³ (530kg/m³)

POSSIBLE HEALTH RISKS Green wood may cause dermatitis

Seasoning This is a tricky one to season: wide boards may suffer cupping and checking or splits may occur if it is not dried slowly. Rough-turning and treating the endgrain sections with PVA to slow down the drying is recommended. It can also be wet-turned to an even thickness and left to move as it will.

Characteristics Silky oak is not a true oak. It is a soft pink to burnt orange or reddish-brown, maturing to a darker orange or red-brown. Large rays, shown off to the fullest on quartersawn stock, produce a clearly marked silver-grain figure. Figuring may also include delicate lace-type effects. It has a somewhat coarse but even texture, typically straight-grained with occasional interlocking grain, where the grain runs around the rays. You may encounter narrow ducts and gum lines.

This wood turns quite well and sharp tools will minimize grain pluckout on wet and dry timber alike. Scrapers need to be used sparingly to prevent tearout, especially on endgrain. Sharp edges may be prone to fracturing, but the timber can be carved and routed to a reasonable degree. Sanding is no problem and finishes of all kinds can be used with ease.

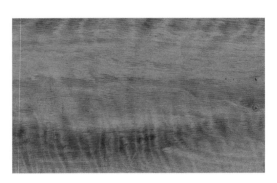

European hornbeam

Carpinus betulus

OTHER NAMES Not known

GROWS Europe, Turkey, Iran

HEIGHT 50–80ft (15–24m)

TRUNK DIAMETER 3–4ft (0.9–1.2m)

SPECIFIC GRAVITY .75

TYPICAL DRY WEIGHT 47lb/ft³ (750kg/m³)

POSSIBLE HEALTH RISKS Not known

Seasoning Hornbeam dries easily, with little degrade. It can be wet-turned to completion, worked partially seasoned, or rough-turned and seasoned before finish-turning, depending on your choice of project.

Characteristics This wood has a pleasant, subtle figure and colour variation. It is quite dense and hardwearing. The heartwood and sapwood look much alike: both are a dull creamy-white or milky colour, with occasional yellow-green streaking. Crossed or irregular grain is the norm, and it has a fine, even texture. Quartersawn surfaces may have a flecked appearance, produced by the broad medullary rays. It can also exhibit a mottled figure. It holds fine detail and is a good wood to use both for utilitarian and for decorative or artistic work.

It turns quite well, though endgrain tearout is a possibility when scrapers are used. It can be carved and routed. Sanding is satisfactory and the wood readily accepts both surface and penetrative finishes.

Seasoning It dries quickly, and this requires careful management: shrinkage, twisting and warping can be major problems if drying is too rapid. The wood can be wet-turned to completion and allowed to distort, or rough-turned and set aside to season before finish-turning. You might consider allowing an extra 5% wall thickness over the normal rough-turning norm to allow for the likely shrinkage and twisting. Kiln-dried wood is fine for utilitarian and joinery work.

Characteristics There is little difference between the four species of hickory available commercially. The sapwood, which is pale and clearly distinct from the heartwood, is sold as white hickory. The heartwood is mid-brown to red-brown, and sold as red hickory. The grain is usually straight but can be irregular or wavy, with a coarse texture.

It has a marked blunting effect on cutting edges, so tools will have to be sharpened regularly. It is satisfactory to turn, but the best finish is with bevel-rubbing tools. It can be carved. It is easy to sand and accepts finishes well. It is commonly used for furniture, joinery and utilitarian work, and for items requiring high-impact resistance.

Hickory
Carya spp., syn. *Hicoria* spp.

OTHER NAMES Pignut hickory (*C. glabra*), mockernut hickory (*C. tomentosa*), shellbark hickory (*C. laciniosa*), shagbark hickory, scalybark hickory (*C. ovata*)
GROWS Canada and USA
HEIGHT 50–100ft (15–30m)
TRUNK DIAMETER 2ft 6in (0.8m)
SPECIFIC GRAVITY .82
TYPICAL DRY WEIGHT 51lb/ft³ (820kg/m³)
POSSIBLE HEALTH RISKS Not known

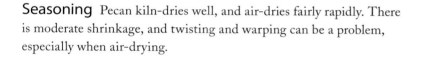

Seasoning Pecan kiln-dries well, and air-dries fairly rapidly. There is moderate shrinkage, and twisting and warping can be a problem, especially when air-drying.

Characteristics Pecan is available in large sizes, suitable for a wide range of projects, but it is noted chiefly for its strength and is used where durability and high-impact resistance are required: furniture, handles, flooring and so on. It can also be used for decorative and utilitarian turning. It is a pleasant wood to turn. The sapwood is a very light cream colour and the heartwood is a soft, mid-toned brown to pinkish-red, tinged with brown. The wood has a medium texture and can be somewhat brittle, so be careful of sharp edges or very fine detail.

Pecan cuts well with sharp bevel-rubbing tools, but scrapers, if not used sensitively, are liable to pluck or rough up the surface, especially on endgrain. My favoured method is to use bevel-rubbing tools and then go straight to abrasives to remove minor blemishes. It can be carved and routed satisfactorily with power tools. It will accept penetrative or surface finishes.

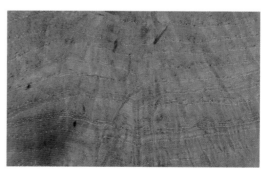

Pecan
Carya illinoinensis

OTHER NAMES Pecan nut
GROWS Canada and USA
HEIGHT 160ft (50m)
TRUNK DIAMETER 6ft (1.8m)
SPECIFIC GRAVITY .61
TYPICAL DRY WEIGHT 55lb/ft³ (881kg/m³)
POSSIBLE HEALTH RISKS Not known

Maracaibo boxwood

Casearia praecox, syn. *Gossypiospermum praecox*

OTHER NAMES Zapatero, palo blanco, agracejo; also Colombian, Venezuelan, West Indian boxwood
GROWS Venezuela, Colombia, Dominican Republic
HEIGHT Up to 30ft (10m)
TRUNK DIAMETER 8–16in (0.2–0.4m)
SPECIFIC GRAVITY .85
TYPICAL DRY WEIGHT 53lb/ft³ (850kg/m³)
POSSIBLE HEALTH RISKS Not known

Seasoning This wood dries slowly and is quite difficult to air-dry. Splitting and surface checking are common, and blue staining is possible if conditions are humid. Halve stock longitudinally or dimension it before drying to prevent splitting. It can be turned to completion from wet, partially seasoned or kilned stock, but, if accuracy is required, rough-turning and setting it aside to season is a must.

Characteristics The heartwood and sapwood look similar to each other, and can be anything from off-white to butter-yellow or lemon-yellow. The grain is mostly straight, the texture fine, uniform and compact. It can be used as a replacement for boxwood (*Buxus sempervirens*) in most circumstances but lacks the density of true boxwood. It holds very fine detail, but is certainly inferior to boxwood in its ability to hold a screw thread. Uses include inlay, stringing, chess pieces, bobbins, piano keys, woodwind instruments, carving and fine decorative turnings.

This wood cuts like a dream. Both bevel-rubbing tools and scrapers can give a good finish off the tool which requires very little sanding. As you would expect, it takes finishes readily and can be brought to a high polish if required.

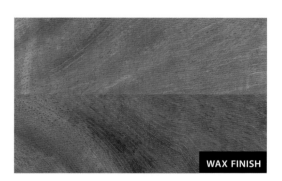

WAX FINISH

Mulumanhyama

Cassia abbreviata

OTHER NAMES Sjambok-pod, long-pod cassia
GROWS Eastern and southeastern Africa
HEIGHT 16–33ft (5-10m)
TRUNK DIAMETER 1–2 ft (0.3–0.6m)
SPECIFIC GRAVITY 1.02
TYPICAL DRY WEIGHT 64lb/ft³ (1025kg/m³)
POSSIBLE HEALTH RISKS Not known

Seasoning It is slow-drying, with checking and splitting on the ends of boards and blanks if the drying process is too fast. Rough-turning, coating the endgrain with PVA adhesive and setting aside to dry before re-turning it works fine; so does turning a blank from start to finish with a nice even wall. There is a bit of movement, so pick either method carefully to suit what you are making; but the pieces I have had, with varying moisture content, all seemed to behave reasonably well.

Characteristics The heartwood is a rich pinkish or reddish brown, through to a dark brown with some flecking or streaking. It is a dense, hard wood that has a medium texture and typically straight grain, occasionally wavy or interlocking. It is capable of holding reasonable detail, but ultrasharp edges serrate a little due to breakout; a very small flat or radius obviates the problem. It cuts well with gouges – skews are not bad either. Scrapers produce a reasonable cut, but not as good as gouges. It can be carved and routed, too. It sands easily and accepts finishes without any problems.

Seasoning Drying is slow and difficult, with a tendency to dry unevenly, resulting in checking, honeycombing and splits. It can be turned wet and allowed to move with very little difficulty, as long as the wall thickness is even. Rough-turning and coating the endgrain with PVA works well when you want stability of shape.

Characteristics The thin, white to creamy-brown sapwood contrasts well with the tan, grey-brown or reddish-brown heartwood. Aged heartwood timber can take on a deep, but quite cold-looking brown colour. Wormholes are common. Typically it has straight grain, but it can be spiral-grained. American chestnut is fairly coarse in texture. Some liken this wood to oak in appearance.

There is nothing to dislike about this timber. It turns well, can hold reasonable detail and can be carved and routed if you want to be adventurous. As usual, scrapers are not as effective as bevel rubbing-tools such as gouges and skews. It sands well and accepts surface and penetrative finishes without issue, too.

As with oaks, ashes, olive and other chestnuts, this timber has tannin in it and, when wet, will leave a blue stain on iron and steel.

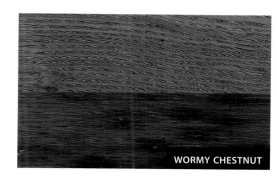

WORMY CHESTNUT

American chestnut
Castanea dentata

OTHER NAMES Chestnut, wormy chestnut
GROWS Eastern USA and southern Ontario, Canada
HEIGHT 20ft (6m)
TRUNK DIAMETER Prior to the chestnut blight of 1904, trees could grow to 60–100ft (18–30m) with trunk diameters of 2–4ft (0.6–1.2m)
SPECIFIC GRAVITY .48
TYPICAL DRY WEIGHT 30lb/ft³ (480kg/m³)
POSSIBLE HEALTH RISKS Not known

Seasoning To reduce the risk of honeycombing and cell collapse, air-dry first, then kiln-dry. If turning wet or partially seasoned wood, expect some movement. To minimize this, rough-turn and set aside to season, coating with PVA to guard against surface checking.

Characteristics The wood is hard, heavy, somewhat oily, and can be brittle. The heartwood is a mid-chocolate to reddish-chocolate, with darker streaks. The sapwood is creamy-white or yellowish. The wood darkens considerably with age. The texture is medium to coarse, the grain usually straight but sometimes interlocked. Quartersawn wood may be attractively striped.

It cuts cleanly in most instances. Bevel-rubbing tools leave a reasonable finish. Scrapers do not cut so well, and the surface will need some sanding; endgrain tearout is likely if interlocking grain is present. Keep tools sharp and make slow, deliberate cuts. Be careful when turning beads, or near the edges of work: it can splinter or break out. It can be carved and routed, but avoid fine edges. Oily, sticky dust is produced during turning. Abrasives clog quickly and there is a risk of heat-checking on the endgrain. Both penetrative and surface finishes can be used, but grain-filling may be needed.

Blackbean
Castanospermum australe

OTHER NAMES Beantree, Moreton Bay bean, Moreton Bay chestnut
GROWS Eastern Australia
HEIGHT 120ft (37m)
TRUNK DIAMETER 3–4ft (0.9–1.2m)
SPECIFIC GRAVITY .70
TYPICAL DRY WEIGHT 44lb/ft³ (700kg/m³)
POSSIBLE HEALTH RISKS Dermatitis; irritation to nose, eyes, throat, armpits and genitals

Cedar of Lebanon

Cedrus libani

OTHER NAMES True cedar

GROWS Middle East, UK, USA

HEIGHT 80ft (24m)

TRUNK DIAMETER 3ft (0.9m)

SPECIFIC GRAVITY .56

TYPICAL DRY WEIGHT 35lb/ft³ (560kg/m³)

POSSIBLE HEALTH RISKS Respiratory problems and rhinitis

Seasoning This softwood dries easily with a slight tendency to warp; highly figured areas may move a lot. It can be turned wet or partially seasoned, but for accurate work rough-turning is best.

Characteristics The heartwood ranges from a light toffee brown to greenish-orange or yellow. The latewood is darker and denser than the earlywood. The sapwood is thin, and whitish or yellow-grey in colour. This soft, light timber has a medium to fine texture and mostly straight grain. Bark inclusions and large knots are often found, and the edges of the annual rings can be rippled or wavy. The resinous wood has a strong, incense-like scent. Large sizes are available.

Cedar cuts well with bevel-rubbing tools, producing ribbon-like shavings, though old wood may be dusty. Endgrain or cross grain around knots may pull out if you use scrapers in conventional mode.

Cedar can be carved and routed. It sands well and accepts both surface and penetrative finishes. It will polish to a wonderful silky sheen. Knots can be very hard and resinous, and may clog abrasives. Swirling grain around the knots may form stunning patterns. The downside is that shakes or splits may occur in these areas.

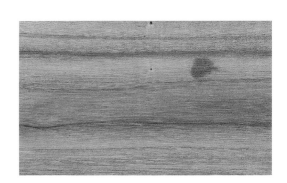

American hackberry

Celtis occidentalis

OTHER NAMES Common hackberry, bastard elm, sugarberry, nettletree, hoop ash

GROWS Canada and eastern USA

HEIGHT 80ft (25m)

TRUNK DIAMETER 1ft 6in–3ft (0.5–0.9m), sometimes more

SPECIFIC GRAVITY .64

TYPICAL DRY WEIGHT 40lb/ft³ (640kg/m³)

POSSIBLE HEALTH RISKS Not known

Seasoning Hackberry dries readily with minimal degrade, but there is a risk of buckling because of curvature in the trunk. It exhibits some movement during drying.

Characteristics Hackberry is a member of the elm family, and closely related to sugarberry (*C. laevigata*). The sapwood, which is very wide and makes up most of the timber content of the tree, is yellow-grey or green-grey to light brown. The small area of heartwood, if present, is a greenish yellow-grey to soft grey-brown, sometimes with lighter streaks of greenish-yellow. The wood is susceptible to blue staining and has irregular grain, sometimes straight and sometimes interlocked, with a fine, uniform texture. It is capable of holding fine detail. Hackberry is used for functional and utilitarian work, furniture and decorative turnings.

Once seasoned, it cuts well with bevel-rubbing tools – less well with scrapers, but any blemishes are easily removed with abrasive. It sands well using dry or wet methods, and accepts finishes and stains readily.

Seasoning Putumuju dries at a moderate rate and does not usually warp, split or check. Shrinkage is minimal. It can be turned wet to completion, but where accuracy of shape is required, rough-turning and setting it aside to dry is recommended. On figured pieces it may be necessary to even out the drying process by coating the rough-turned blank with PVA.

Characteristics The heartwood is variegated yellow to orange, sometimes tinged with a rainbow of colours. Sadly, it changes quickly to a mid orange-brown with some variegated stripes. The sapwood is yellow and distinct from the heartwood. The grain may be straight or irregular. It is quite fine-grained, will hold fine detail, and can be carved with hand or power tools.

Putumuju is a lovely wood to turn, wet or seasoned. Its only real shortcoming is that it is not available in larger sizes. It cuts well with all tools, but the best finish is obtained from bevel-rubbing tools. Scrapers give good results, especially when shear-scraping, but a little more sanding will be needed.

It sands well, but watch out for heat-checking on endgrain. A high polish can be achieved with either surface or penetrative finishes.

Putumuju
Centrolobium spp.

OTHER NAMES Canarywood, araribá, porcupinewood
GROWS Southern Brazil, Ecuador, Panama
HEIGHT 100ft (30m)
TRUNK DIAMETER 2ft 6in–4ft (0.75–1.2m)
SPECIFIC GRAVITY .75–1.00, according to species
TYPICAL DRY WEIGHT 47–62lb/ft³ (750–1000kg/m³)
POSSIBLE HEALTH RISKS Not known

Seasoning Greenheart dries slowly and degrade can be considerable, especially in thick wood, with end-splitting, checking and lengthening of existing shakes.

Characteristics This is a dense, hard, very heavy wood. The heartwood can range from a light yellow-green, through dark green with tinges of brown or yellowish-brown, to dark brown or black; it may have some dark streaking as well. The grain is straight to roey, sometimes interlocked, with a fine, uniform texture. It is capable of holding fine detail. The sapwood, which looks similar to the heartwood, is pale greenish-yellow.

Interlocking grain makes this a tricky wood to work with. Bevel-rubbing tools are the best option to achieve a reasonable finish off the tool; then go straight to abrasives to remove any minor blemishes. Using scrapers will result in a lot of tearout. Whichever tools are used, there is a tendency for sharp edges to break away, flake or splinter. Abrasives will clog quickly, but a fine finish can be achieved. Greenheart resists some surface finishes; penetrative finishes such as oil do not penetrate far, but do polish up nicely. Be careful of splinters, which turn septic very quickly; the dust is particularly unpleasant, too.

Greenheart
Chlorocardium rodiei, syn. *Ocotea rodiei* and *Nectandra rodiei*

OTHER NAMES Demerara, viruviru; yellow, brown, black, white greenheart
GROWS Guyana, Surinam, Brazil, Venezuela, some Caribbean islands
HEIGHT 75–125ft (23–38m)
TRUNK DIAMETER 3ft (0.9m)
SPECIFIC GRAVITY 1.03
TYPICAL DRY WEIGHT 64lb/ft³ (1030kg/m³)
POSSIBLE HEALTH RISKS Cardiac and intestinal disorders, throat irritation; splinters are toxic

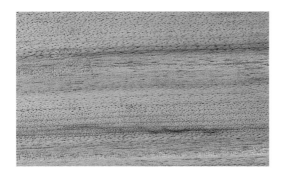

Camphor or camphor laurel

Cinnamomum camphora

OTHER NAMES Camphortree, kusonoki, ohez, kalingag, dalchini, kayu

GROWS Japan, Taiwan, China, Australia; cultivated in southern USA

HEIGHT 60–100ft (18–30m) or more

TRUNK DIAMETER 2–4ft (0.6–1.2m)

SPECIFIC GRAVITY .35–.50

TYPICAL DRY WEIGHT 26–38lb/ft³ (416–609kg/m³)

POSSIBLE HEALTH RISKS Not known

Seasoning Air-dries well, with some shrinkage, occasionally with slight warping. The wood is stable once dried.

Characteristics This tree is classified as a weed in Australia; it is so invasive that there is large-scale clearance under way to give native timbers a chance to grow. The lightweight wood has a medium to fine texture. The heartwood and sapwood are both light creamy-tan to light tan, with darker streaks of greenish-pink, red or brown. The grain is usually straight but sometimes interlocked or wavy, with a high natural lustre. It sometimes shows mottled or roe figure. Large sizes are available, so many types of project are possible.

This is a soft, light wood, easy to work; it carves and routs well, is easy to sand and can be taken to a silky-smooth finish with a high lustre. It can be glued but might resist adhesion at times. It accepts oils, waxes, sanding sealers and lacquers without difficulty. I much prefer a matt or satin finish on this wood, but experiment to find out what you like. The wood has a distinctive smell – clothes boxes used to be made from it to keep moths out. I find the smell pleasant but others certainly might not; it does, however, fade with time – as does the colour.

WAX FINISH

Leadwood

Combretum imberbe

OTHER NAMES Mhama, nangali, monzo, motswiri

GROWS South Africa to Tanzania

HEIGHT 23–50ft (7–15m)

TRUNK DIAMETER 1–3ft (0.3–0.9m)

SPECIFIC GRAVITY 1.23

TYPICAL DRY WEIGHT 70.5lb/ft³ (1130kg/m³)

POSSIBLE HEALTH RISKS Not known

Seasoning The wood moves a little and I have encountered some checking on thicker sections. Rough-turning works well: I coat the endgrain with PVA and set it aside to dry and settle before finish-turning it. Do this if you want to create nicely fitting lids on anything. You can turn to completion in one go, as long as the wall thickness is even – but do expect a small amount of movement.

Characteristics The heartwood ranges from red-tinged brown to charcoal and purplish brown; the sapwood is creamy yellow. It is as dense as its name implies, somewhat oily, and has a uniform, fine grain. It blunts cutting edges quickly but takes fine detail and can be used for chasing coarser threads. It can be power-carved and routed. Bevel-rubbing tools give a lovely finish as long as they are sharp, though the wood produces only small shavings and oily dust when turned. A scraper will give a great finish off the tool. Leadwood sands satisfactorily but clogs abrasives – and do be careful not to cause heat checks on the endgrain. It has accepted all the surface finishes and waxes and oils I have used on it without problem, and it turns a very deep, dark colour, which gets darker over time, too. It is a timber that works well in segmented and laminated work, providing a good alternative to ebony and other dark timbers.

Seasoning Surface checking and end-splitting are common during seasoning. Bocote can be wet-turned but, because it is only available in small sizes, it is more commonly turned to completion from partially seasoned stock, or rough-turned and then left to season. Coating with PVA after rough-turning will reduce the likelihood of splitting.

Characteristics This dense, oily wood has a medium to fine texture. The heartwood ranges from soft red-brown to deep brown with darker streaks. The sapwood is a pale creamy-white tinged with grey.

It cuts very well with bevel-rubbing tools, but only tolerably well with scrapers, even in shear-scraping mode. The dust is sticky and clinging, with a strong but not unpleasant smell.

It is capable of holding reasonable detail – $^1/_{16}$in (1.5mm) beads – provided they are cleanly cut and no cracks are present. Bocote can be carved or routed quite easily, too. Coves, beads and V-cuts create an interesting visual element by visually misaligning the coloured streaks.

Carving and routing can be easily be done on this timber. It is a timber often used in laminated and segmented wotk, but you may have to dewax the surfaces to be glued to ensure full adhesive bonds.

The wood sands satisfactorily, but will clog abrasives and heat-check if you are not careful. It can be taken to a high polish with either surface finishes or oils and waxes.

Bocote
Cordia gerascanthus, C. elaeagnoides, C. alliodora

OTHER NAMES Mexican rosewood, grand palisander, lauro pardo, lauro negro, Ecuador laurel, princewood, Spanish elm, anacanuite
GROWS Mexico
HEIGHT 70–100ft (21–30m)
TRUNK DIAMETER Not known
SPECIFIC GRAVITY .85 but varies widely
TYPICAL DRY WEIGHT 53lb/ft³ (850kg/m³)
POSSIBLE HEALTH RISKS Not known

Seasoning Some end-splitting and surface checking can occur, but usually it is well behaved. It responds well both to rough-turning and setting aside to dry, and to turning from start to finish with a nice thin, even wall. There is some movement as it dries, so if you want a predictable shape, rough-turn it first.

Characteristics The silvery cream-yellow sapwood is distinct from the heartwood, which ranges from light tan or burnt caramel to a much darker and deeper reddish brown. It has a coarse to medium texture with an interlocked and wavy grain. It can be cut satisfactorily with gouges and skews, but small amounts of tearing and pullout are likely on the interlocking grain. Scrapers, used delicately, produce only a slightly worse surface. It can just about hold detail such as beads down to about $^5/_{64}$in (2mm) without major breakout, but you have to go very gently, and slightly radius or flatten the edges of these features. Mango can be carved and routed, with the same caveat about fine edges. It sands reasonably well, but abrasives clog because of its slight oiliness. Mango accepts surface and penetrative finishes without difficulty.

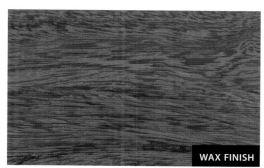

WAX FINISH

Wild mango
Cordyla africana

OTHER NAMES Mutondo
GROWS South Africa to Tanzania
HEIGHT 75–90ft (23–27m)
TRUNK DIAMETER 2–3ft (0.6–0.9m)
SPECIFIC GRAVITY .81
TYPICAL DRY WEIGHT 51lb/ft³ (810kg/m³)
POSSIBLE HEALTH RISKS Not known

OIL FINISH

Cypress

Cupressus spp.

OTHER NAMES Mexican cypress (*C. lusitanica*)
GROWS Southern and central USA, South America, southern and eastern Africa, Australia, New Zealand
HEIGHT 70–100ft (21–30m)
TRUNK DIAMETER 3ft (1m)
SPECIFIC GRAVITY .48
TYPICAL DRY WEIGHT 30lb/ft³ (480kg/m³)
POSSIBLE HEALTH RISKS Not known

Seasoning Cypress dries quickly with little degrade. For furniture or architectural work you can use kiln-dried stock that has been acclimatized in the workshop for a bit. For decorative or artistic work, it can either be wet-turned to completion, using a thin, even wall thickness, or rough-turned and set aside to season before finish-turning.

Characteristics This is a soft, light softwood. The heartwood is pale creamy-yellow to pinkish-brown, the sapwood a bit lighter. There are sometimes streaks of resin. The grain is quite straight, with a fine, even texture; cultivated trees may have more knots.

It is best to go straight from chisel or gouge to using abrasives; it does not finish well from the scraper. Cypress can be a bit brittle, so do not leave sharp edges that may break out. Knots are prone to tearout. Abrasives may clog, and care must be taken, especially with power sanding, not to linger and create hollows. Cypress takes penetrative or surface finishes well.

This comparatively inexpensive wood is excellent to practise on. You can see immediately if the tools are sharp and the cutting approach angle is correct – if not, the grain will tear out.

Rimu

Dacrydium cupressinum

OTHER NAMES Red pine
GROWS New Zealand (supply is strictly regulated by legislation)
HEIGHT 80–100ft (24–30m)
TRUNK DIAMETER 6ft 6in (2m)
SPECIFIC GRAVITY .53
TYPICAL DRY WEIGHT 33lb/ft³ (530kg/m³)
POSSIBLE HEALTH RISKS Dust may irritate eyes and nose

Seasoning Rimu kiln-dries and air-dries reasonably well, but may surface-check. It can be rough-turned and set aside to season further, but the movement is so small that I have found no need to do this except for precision items such as lidded boxes. If the wood is very wet, expect movement; either turn it wet to completion with a thin wall thickness, or rough-turn and set aside to season.

Characteristics The wood is a medium yellowish-tan or reddish-tan, sometimes with an orange-yellow tint. The irregular darker streaks fade on exposure to light. The wood is straight-grained with a fine, even, uniform texture. The heartwood can exhibit an attractive figure, caused by various-coloured pigments in the wood; these tend to fade, but will remain vibrant for longer if the finish contains UV inhibitors.

It cuts very well with skews and gouges, leaving a silky-smooth surface straight off the tool. After profiling, go straight to abrasives; scrapers are likely to tear out the endgrain, and shear-scraping is only slightly better. Rimu carves, routs and sands very well and readily accepts both surface and penetrative finishes; a few coats may be necessary to ensure even coverage.

Seasoning This wood can split when being air-dried, I find, but kiln-dries well with little degrade. It is a wood best rough-turned and set aside to season before finish-turning; you can coat the piece with PVA if you wish. Partially seasoned pieces can be turned, but unless they are turned thin they are likely to check; there will be some movement.

Characteristics The basic colour is a rich purple-brown, but parts may be almost black or purplish-black, with streaks of deep, rich violet red, rich violet-brown and black and, occasionally, a creamy-red tinged with yellow. It is quite oily, with a fine, uniform texture that holds detail well. The creamy-white sapwood contrasts starkly with the heartwood; it is usually removed before the wood is exported but, when present, it can be used to good visual effect. It is an expensive wood, and veneer companies and cabinetmakers tend to snaffle large quantities of it. It is only available in small sizes, either as pre-dimensioned blanks or as sections of trunk, so small or medium-sized decorative work is the norm. It turns well with all tools. It rarely exhibits interlocking grain, but when it does, grain tearout is likely with all but the sharpest tools. This wood sands well, but will clog abrasives. It readily accepts penetrative finishes, but may be resistant to some surface finishes.

Brazilian kingwood

Dalbergia cearensis

OTHER NAMES Violete, violetta, violet wood
GROWS South America, mostly Brazil
HEIGHT 50–100ft (15–30m)
TRUNK DIAMETER 1-2ft (0.3–0.6m)
SPECIFIC GRAVITY 1.2
TYPICAL DRY WEIGHT 75lb/ft³ (1200kg/m³)
POSSIBLE HEALTH RISKS Eye and skin irritation

Seasoning Brazilian rosewood is slow to dry, and liable to check and split. It is not available in large sizes, and is usually supplied air-dried in small predimensioned blanks that are best rough-turned and set aside to stabilize before finishing. It can be worked partially seasoned, but may check and will certainly move.

Characteristics This is an amazing wood to look at, and is mostly used for decorative or artistic work and in furniture restoration. It is dense, heavy and hard, with a waxy or oily feel. The heartwood is a reddish, dark chocolate-brown to rich purplish-brown colour with purplish-black and golden-brown streaks. The sapwood is fairly wide and creamy or greyish-white. The scarcity of this timber now makes this a wood that one rarely encounters but it does crop up from time to time as new or salvaged timber.

The grain is generally straight but sometimes wavy, with an even, fine texture. Brazilian rosewood is able to hold fine detail and can be carved and routed readily. The wood turns satisfactorily with all tools, though bevel-rubbing tools may become gummed up with a wax-like resin that needs to be cleaned off every so often. Abrasives also clog readily, and the wood is prone to heat-checking. It resists some surface finishes but readily accepts waxes and oils; these do not penetrate far and create a wonderful finish.

Brazilian rosewood

Dalbergia nigra

OTHER NAMES Rio rosewood, Bahia rosewood, palisander, jacarandá, jacarandá da Bahia, jacarandá do Brasil
GROWS Southeastern Brazil
HEIGHT Up to 38m (125ft)
TRUNK DIAMETER 3–4ft (1–1.2m)
SPECIFIC GRAVITY .85
TYPICAL DRY WEIGHT 53lb/ft³ (850kg/m³)
POSSIBLE HEALTH RISKS Dust may cause dermatitis, eye irritation and respiratory problems

Honduras rosewood

Dalbergia stevensonii

OTHER NAMES Nogaed, palisandro de Honduras
GROWS Belize (formerly British Honduras)
HEIGHT 50–100ft (15–30m)
TRUNK DIAMETER 3ft (0.9m)
SPECIFIC GRAVITY .96
TYPICAL DRY WEIGHT 60lb/ft³ (960kg/m³)
POSSIBLE HEALTH RISKS Dermatitis and asthma

Seasoning The wood air-dries very slowly with a risk of splitting, but can be kiln-dried with little degrade. For restoration work, kiln-dried wood is sufficient; for decorative or artistic work, rough-turn the piece, coat with PVA and set aside to season.

Characteristics This is a beautiful wood with a sumptuous appearance. The heartwood ranges from light pinkish- or reddish-brown to deep reddish- or violet-brown, with lighter and darker irregular bands. The grain is usually straight but can be wavy. It has a medium to fine texture. The sapwood is a pale cream when newly cut, but quickly darkens to yellow on exposure to light. Honduras rosewood is much prized by cabinetmakers and veneer companies, and is always expensive. Turners use it mostly for smallish decorative or artistic pieces. The colour contrast between sapwood and heartwood can be used to good effect.

The wood cuts best with bevel-rubbing tools, but a good finish can be obtained using a scraper. Some dust is produced when turning. Abrasives clog quickly, and the wood will heat-check if you are not careful. Wet sanding works well and produces a finer finish than dry sanding, as long as the sapwood is not present to cause colour contamination. It can be carved and routed, and will take surface and penetrative finishes well.

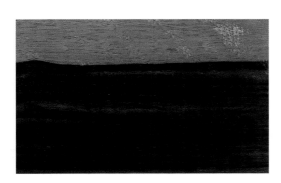

Macassar ebony

Diospyros celebica

OTHER NAMES Coromandel, calamander wood, Indian ebony; *D. tomentosa*, *D. marmorata*, *D. melanoxylon* and *D. ebenum* are related species
GROWS India, Sri Lanka, Philippines, Indonesia
HEIGHT 50ft (15m)
TRUNK DIAMETER 1ft–1ft 6in (0.3–0.45m)
SPECIFIC GRAVITY 1.09
TYPICAL DRY WEIGHT 68lb/ft³ (1090kg/m³)
POSSIBLE HEALTH RISKS Dermatitis, conjunctivitis, mucous membrane irritation; possible skin sensitizer

Seasoning The wood should be seasoned slowly. Deep, long checks or hairline shakes can develop in the wood, and fast drying will result in end-splits and surface checking. It is advisable to rough-turn the pieces and leave them to dry further before use, if accuracy and stability are required.

Characteristics Macassar ebony is a strikingly beautiful wood that is very heavy, very dense and very hard. It is close-grained, and the grain is usually straight but can occasionally be wavy or irregular. The wood has a fine, even texture with a metallic sheen. The heartwood is black or sometimes grey, with streaks running through it that range from light biscuit through light brown or reddish-brown to deep brown. The sapwood contrasts well with the heartwood and is a creamy biscuit-brown colour.

This is a very brittle wood that can be difficult to work: the grain is liable to tear out and the edges may splinter off. It blunts cutting edges quickly and can produce a lot of dust but holds quite fine detail. Use sharp tools and a gentle cut to minimize grain tearout, but great care needs to be taken when using a scraper. Routing and power carving are possible. Sand carefully to avoid heat-checking and you will likely encounter clogging of abrasives due to natural oils in the wood. If glueing up sections you might need to dewax the surface first. I have not encountered any problems using surface finishes, waxes or oils.

Seasoning Air-drying is quick, with occasional surface checking. Part-seasoned wood can be turned to completion, maintaining an even wall thickness to avoid splitting. Work requiring accuracy must be rough-turned, coated with PVA and left to season.

Characteristics African ebonies are normally available only in short billets or smallish predimensioned pieces of heartwood. *D. crassiflora* is the blackest, but may still have some silver or grey in it. Other ebony species can have black and rich brown stripes in the heartwood. All species are hard and dense, and the grain ranges from straight to interlocked, with a very fine, even texture. Cutting edges blunt quickly.

A fine finish can be produced off the tools and, unusually, scrapers can sometimes produce a better finish than bevel-rubbing tools. If the grain is interlocking, some tearout may occur; very sharp tools will minimize this, but not stop it completely. It is somewhat brittle, so can splinter or fracture on or near sharp edges. It can be power-carved to good effect. Noxious dust can be produced during turning. Sanding is OK if care is taken to avoid heat-checking, and the wood can be finished with surface or penetrative finishes. The pale sapwood, if free from checks, can be effective as a contrast to the dark heartwood.

African ebony
Diospyros crassiflora

OTHER NAMES Cameroon, Gabon, Madagascar, Nigerian ebony
GROWS Cameroon, Ghana, Nigeria, Congo
HEIGHT 50–60ft (15–18m)
TRUNK DIAMETER 2ft (0.6m)
SPECIFIC GRAVITY 1.03
TYPICAL DRY WEIGHT 64lb/ft³ (1030kg/m³)
POSSIBLE HEALTH RISKS Dust may cause acute dermatitis, skin inflammation, conjunctivitis and sneezing

Seasoning This wood can be difficult to dry, suffering from considerable shrinkage, end and surface checks, and brown chemical staining. It moves significantly in service. Persimmon is a wood that I find turns well when wet – keep an even wall thickness and allow it to move as it likes – but I have had quite a high failure rate with rough-turning and setting it aside to season. I have tried varying the wall thickness – both thicker and thinner than I normally use – and the results are unpredictable.

Characteristics The heartwood forms only a small central core, and may be black or a rich red-brown. The sapwood, which makes up the majority of the timber, is creamy-white when freshly cut, darkening to yellow-brown or grey-brown on exposure, with brown or grey spots. The grain is quite close and straight, with a fine and even texture, and is capable of holding fine detail.

The wood turns well with any tools, as long as they are sharp, but bevel-rubbing tools produce a better finish than scrapers. Sanding is good, but heat-checking is likely if too much heat is generated. It will accept any finish of your choice.

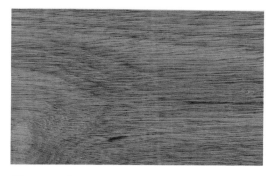

Persimmon
Diospyros virginiana

OTHER NAMES American ebony, bara-bara, boa-wood, butterwood, possum wood, Virginia date palm, white ebony
GROWS USA
HEIGHT 80–120ft (24–37m)
TRUNK DIAMETER 1–2ft (0.3–0.6m)
SPECIFIC GRAVITY .83
TYPICAL DRY WEIGHT 52lb/ft³ (830kg/m³)
POSSIBLE HEALTH RISKS Heartwood may cause dermatitis

Queensland walnut

Endiandra palmerstonii

OTHER NAMES Australian walnut, black walnut, oriental wood, walnut bean, Australian laurel
GROWS Queensland, Australia
HEIGHT 120–140ft (37–43m)
TRUNK DIAMETER 6ft (1.8m)
SPECIFIC GRAVITY .68
TYPICAL DRY WEIGHT 42lb/ft³ (680kg/m³)
POSSIBLE HEALTH RISKS Not known

Seasoning This wood dries quickly, but is prone to end splits. Kiln-drying works, but on thin stock warping can occur. Splitting risk is much reduced in quartersawn timber. Wet-turned work moves a little and rough-turned bowls move a bit, too, but not enough to require extra wall thickness on rough-turned work. I do, however, coat the endgrain with PVA to slow the drying process.

Characteristics The sapwood is a creamy yellow to pale yellow and contrasts highly with the heartwood, which is a deep brown with stripes of black or a beautiful, deep, variegated reddish-brown. The timber often has interlocking irregular grain that may be wavy. It has a medium, even, uniform texture. It produces a nice figure on quartersawn surfaces.

I can't seem to get much of this handsome wood, so it is a real treat when I do. The interlocking grain can be tricky with anything but very sharp tools. Scrapers work, but not as nicely as gouges and skews. The wood can be very abrasive, so frequent sharpening is required. It can be routed and power-carved easily, and sanding is not a problem, although the heartwood dust will contaminate the sapwood, if present. I have not had any problems when applying surface finishes or waxes and oils.

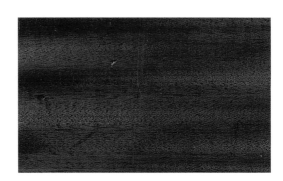

Sapele

Entandrophragma cylindricum

OTHER NAMES Sapelewood, sapele mahogany, sapelli, scented mahogany, aboudikro, penkra
GROWS Western, central and eastern Africa to Uganda
HEIGHT Up to 150ft (45m)
TRUNK DIAMETER 4–6ft (1.2–1.8m)
SPECIFIC GRAVITY .62
TYPICAL DRY WEIGHT 39lb/ft³ (620kg/m³)
POSSIBLE HEALTH RISKS Skin irritation and sneezing

Seasoning Sapele dries quickly, is prone to distortion and may surface-check a little. Kiln-dried timber is fine for most projects, but rough-turning and setting it aside to season works well also.

Characteristics The heartwood is reddish-yellow when first cut, darkening to a mid- to deep red or rich red-brown on exposure. The sapwood is cream to pale yellow but is rarely used. The grain is usually interlocked and wavy, which can create a fiddleback or mottle figure. It sometimes exhibits a very striking striped or roe figure on the quartercut surface. Sapele is a moderately hard and strong timber of medium density, with a fine and even texture. Used extensively in joinery and cabinetmaking, it offers many opportunities for turners to create components for these trades, as well as to explore its potential for artistic work. Since it is available in large sizes, there is plenty of scope to experiment.

It generally behaves itself during turning but the interlocking grain areas are prone to grain tearout with all tools. You may find it best to skip the scraper stage and go straight from gouges or skews to abrasives. Sapele can be sanded with either dry or wet sanding methods, and can be taken to a high polish with either surface or penetrative finishes.

Seasoning Degrade is minimal, provided the wood is dried at a moderate rate; if dried too fast, it may twist. It can be turned from a partially seasoned state. Kiln-dried stock is usually sufficient when turning for joinery or cabinetmaking, but for greater accuracy it can be rough-turned and set aside to season.

Characteristics The sapwood is light brown, up to 2in (50mm) thick and clearly distinct from the heartwood. The latter is pinkish-brown, darkening to a deep red-brown or chocolate-brown on exposure. The grain is usually interlocked, with a medium texture. Quartersawn surfaces may have a ribbon figure or stripe, which can cause this wood to be mistaken for sapele (*E. cylindricum*). There can be other figuring such as rippling, but this is not so common.

Utile has a moderate blunting effect on edge tools but, as long as you maintain a good keen edge on your tools, it will cut well. Small chips with quite a lot of dust will be produced with bevel-rubbing tools, but a good finish off the tool is possible. Scrapers will cause grain tearout, and shear-scraping is not much better; instead, go straight to abrasive to remove minor blemishes left from the gouge or skew. It sands well and will readily accept finishes of all descriptions.

Utile

Entandrophragma utile

OTHER NAMES Assié, sipo, abebay, efuodwe, liboyo, kisi-kosi, afau-konkonti
GROWS Western, central and eastern Africa
HEIGHT 150–200ft (45–60m)
TRUNK DIAMETER 2ft 8in–6ft (0.8–1.8m)
SPECIFIC GRAVITY .66
TYPICAL DRY WEIGHT 41lb/ft³ (660kg/m³)
POSSIBLE HEALTH RISKS Skin irritation

Seasoning The roots are boiled after harvesting to prevent splitting and to retain colour. They can be turned to completion straight away, but the wall thickness must be thin and even to minimize the risk of cracking. Alternatively, the burr can be rough-turned and set aside to season; coating with PVA reduces cracking and checking. Leave the wet root structure too long, though, and it can rot in the centre.

Characteristics The roots are mid-brown with a reddish-orange tinge, with some lighter and darker patches. They can have a fantastic swirling, twisting grain figure, or a more mottled, tightly swirled pattern – each piece is unique. Dyes can enhance the contrast in the figuring phenomenally.

These roots are wonderful to turn and carve, especially when wet or partially seasoned. The wood cuts very easily with all tools, but the best cuts are made with gouges and skews. It sands and polishes well. Old wood can be dusty and a bit brittle. The biggest drawback is the irregular shape and size: you need to be careful in your selection to make sure that you can obtain the required profile. I find them very effective for hollow-form projects: the irregular shapes may give rise to natural-edged voids that have great visual appeal. Watch out for any embedded stones: if you do not remove them straight away they can whizz off the rotating workpiece at high speed.

OIL FINISH

Briar burr (burl)

Erica arborea

OTHER NAMES Tree heath
GROWS Southwestern Europe
HEIGHT AND DIAMETER Not known; sold as root burrs for turning, typically 8 x 8 x 6in (200 x 200 x 150mm)
SPECIFIC GRAVITY 0.75
TYPICAL DRY WEIGHT 4kg for a piece 8 x 8 x 6in (200 x 200 x 150mm)
POSSIBLE HEALTH RISKS Not known

Australian eucalyptus burrs

Timbers from Australia are becoming increasingly popular with turners around the world. The burrs ('burls' in Australian and US usage) listed here all have similar characteristics. Burrs are usually sold just as they have been cut off the tree, as a carbuncle-like piece that has one flat face; the other surfaces are all natural-edged, sometimes with bark still attached. Other pieces are supplied with the bark sandblasted off. Through-cut slabs or slices can also be bought. Most of these burrs, I find, are best turned as they come – usually part-seasoned – without further drying. My experience has mostly been with red mallee, York gum, yellow box and coolibah, which are slow-growing and quite dry when bought anyway, though they do have some moisture in them – the pieces I had were at 15% moisture content when bought.

If you are going to cut up the burr to make boxes and the like, then rough-turning and setting the piece aside to season works well. You may find that you need to coat the piece with PVA to even out the stabilizing process.

Since the working qualities of these timbers are mostly very similar, only red mallee (*Eucalyptus oleosa*, *E. socialis*) has been described in detail; it is a representative example of the harder, denser eucalyptus burrs.

POSSIBLE HEALTH RISKS Some species may cause contact dermatitis or nose and throat irritation. As with all woods, do take precautions to minimize exposure to dust

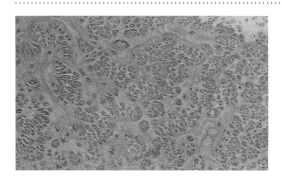

Brown mallee
Eucalyptus spp.

GROWS Southeastern Australia

TYPICAL BURR SIZE 13–15lb (6–7kg)

CHARACTERISTICS Brown mallee burr is dense, hard, heavy and oily. The heartwood is tan-coloured and the sapwood is a creamy grey-white. The burr figuring commonly consists of various-sized clusters of tightly packed pippy knots or 'eyes', and the grain is tight and interlocked. There is much colour variation from piece to piece.

Being oily, it is reasonably easy to cut with bevel-rubbing tools, producing some nice shavings as well as chips. It scrapes well with minimal grain tearout, provided sensitive cuts are made with sharp tools. Tearout may occur, but is not as pronounced as in some other species. It clogs abrasives quite quickly, so regular cleaning of them is necessary. Being dense and oily, it accepts hand-chased threads reasonably well.

OIL FINISH

Ridge-fruited mallee
Eucalyptus angulosa and *E. incrassata*

GROWS Western Australia and South Australia

TYPICAL BURR SIZE 13–15lb (6–7kg)

CHARACTERISTICS Ridge-fruited mallee burr is dense, hard and heavy, with irregular or interlocking grain. The heartwood is a rich red with hints of orange, tan and violet-brown. The sapwood is pinkish-cream. The burr figuring is best described as dramatic, and it often has big whorls and streaks in various hues of the heartwood colour. This wood has the same working qualities as red mallee (*E. oleosa*, *E. socialis*).

GROWS From Northern Territory to Western Australia and Queensland

TYPICAL BURR SIZE 18–26lb (8–12kg)

CHARACTERISTICS Coolibah is the hardest of the burrs discussed on these pages, and is reputed to be one of the hardest woods available. It can replace lignum vitae (*Guaiacum sanctum* or *G. officinale*) in some situations. Coolibah works in much the same way as red mallee (*E. oleosa*, *E. socialis*), but owing to its hardness it is a bit more difficult to work and slower to cut, producing chips and frequently some dust as well. Because of the irregular, interlocking grain it is very likely to suffer from tearout. The heartwood is a rich milk-chocolate colour, which contrasts well with the creamy-tan sapwood. The figuring tends to consist of wavy, swirling whorls, interspersed with pips or 'eyes' that look like elongated bubbles; it can have darker, irregular flecks running through it.

OIL FINISH

Coolibah
Eucalyptus coolabah, syn. *E. microtheca*
OTHER NAMES Also spelt **coolabah**

GROWS Goldfields region of Western Australia

TYPICAL BURR SIZE 13–15lb (6–7kg)

CHARACTERISTICS York gum burr is extremely hard and dense, which is due in part to the conditions in which it grows. It works in the same manner as red mallee (*E. oleosa*, *E. socialis*). The heartwood is a greyish- or reddish-tan colour and the sapwood creamy-tan, but the colour varies somewhat from one piece to another. The burr figuring is a loose pippy formation with some wavy or twisted swirling patterns. It is a fantastic wood to look at, but moderately difficult to work. York gum and many other species are sometimes marketed under the general name of Goldfield burrs.

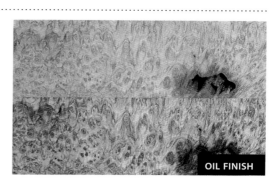

OIL FINISH

York gum
Eucalyptus loxophleba

GROWS Victoria and New South Wales

TYPICAL BURR SIZE 18–20lb (8–9kg)

CHARACTERISTICS Yellow box burr has a very attractive figure. It is dense and cuts well. It has a slightly oily nature, and is close-grained. It typically has gum pockets irregularly placed amongst whorls, or swirling or wavy grain. The sapwood is grey-brown, a little darker than the heartwood, which is a yellowish-tan colour with a reddish-orange tinge. It has a higher moisture content than other burrs listed here, so care is needed when drying: part-turn the piece and seal with PVA to even out the drying process, then set it aside to season further. You can turn it from partially seasoned stock, but expect more movement than one gets with the other eucalyptus species. It turns well, and shavings are produced when cutting this wood. It sands and finishes well also.

OIL FINISH

Yellow box
Eucalyptus melliodora

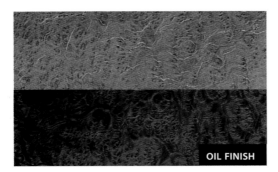

OIL FINISH

Western grey box

Eucalyptus microcarpa

GROWS Southern Australia

TYPICAL BURR SIZE 13–15lb (6–7kg)

CHARACTERISTICS Western grey box is very similar to brown mallee in working quality. It has more pips or knots than swirling grain. The sapwood is greyish-white and the heartwood a mid-orange-tan; a distinct narrow grey line separates the two. This is a visually stunning burr that will respond well to a bit of love and care in working it.

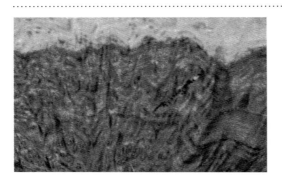

Red mallee

Eucalyptus oleosa and *E. socialis*

OTHER NAMES Oil mallee, giant mallee

GROWS Western Australia

TYPICAL BURR SIZE 13–15lb (6–7kg)

CHARACTERISTICS Red mallee burrs are dense, hard, heavy, close-grained and slightly oily. The wood has a greyish-cream sapwood, which is distinct from the reddish-tan or brown heartwood. The burr figuring – which is often a beautiful, swirling whorl pattern – has various orange or reddish-tan hues in it. Depending on how it is cut, the figuring can show as dramatic striations.

There is a lot of interlocking grain, which means that tools produce chips rather than shavings. Grain tearout is a distinct possibility around the figured areas. Because of its hardness, this timber belongs to that rare group of woods where you may find it easier to scrape than to use a gouge or other bevel-rubbing tool. If a scraper is used sensitively, it is possible to get a smooth surface finish with minimal tearout. This is particularly true of burrs that are very old and dry; these may produce a lot of dust during turning, and often resist cutting well with a gouge. As with many other Australian burrs, cutting edges do not last long, so frequent sharpening will be necessary.

For artistic or decorative work, or for natural-edged pieces, this burr can be used in large slabs. When it dries fully, the surface of the timber tends to take on a 'hammered' texture, more so than brown mallee. Though many might frown, this wood can be power-carved and routed.

It is a difficult wood to sand, as it often clogs the abrasive and is so dense that any anomalies take an age to wear away; get as good a finish off the tool as you can before sanding. Do not be tempted to skip grades, but work through them all to achieve a very fine finish. Red mallee can be finished with oils, waxes or surface finishes as you require. I find that the wood darkens a little with age, but the fantastic figuring will still be visible. This is not an easy wood to turn, but the effort will be well rewarded.

GROWS Central and southern tablelands, New South Wales, Victoria

TYPICAL BURR SIZE 26–33lb (12–15kg)

CHARACTERISTICS I love working with burrs and figured wood of all varieties, and this is one of the nicest you are likely to encounter. Red box burr is harder than yellow box (E. melliodora) burr. It is a tight, pippy, 'eyed' burr, but this may be combined with other formations such as wavy or swirling patterns. It has a warm brownish-red heartwood and a softer, lighter-coloured sapwood which contrasts well with the richer heartwood.

Its turning qualities are a hybrid between those of red mallee (*E. oleosa*, *E. socialis*) and yellow box.

OIL FINISH

Red box
Eucalyptus polyanthemos

GROWS Western Australia

TYPICAL BURR SIZE 26–31lb (12–14kg)

CHARACTERISTICS Salmon gum burr is what is termed a 'resin-gum burl', which means that there are gum pockets in the wood. These show as voids or fissures that may have a lining of resin, or be completely filled with resin. The resin appears black to the eye but, when a light is shone on it, it can be a very deep red or amber. It is hard, and blunts tool edges quickly. The resin pockets and various sizes of fissures will fill up with sanding dust and finishing material, so they need to be carefully cleaned out to create a consistent, clean-looking finish. The burr itself is a deep, rich red-brown colour that has a twisted, swirling grain formation. It sometimes has darker flecks running through it.

Apart from the gum pockets, it behaves for the most part in a similar way to red mallee (*E. oleosa*, *E. socialis*).

Salmon gum
Eucalyptus salmonophloia

GROWS Western Australia

TYPICAL BURR SIZE 26–31lb (12–14kg)

CHARACTERISTICS Gimlet burr has light creamy-golden sapwood and rich reddish-brown heartwood irregularly interspersed with darker patches. Swirls and twisting patterns are common, flecked with little pockets of resin gum. It works in much the same way as red mallee (*E. oleosa*, *E. socialis*), but being less oily it does not cut quite as cleanly. The wood is dense, hard and heavy, like all the eucalyptus burrs mentioned here. The grain is fine and even in texture but extremely erratic – some parts interlocked, others twisted – which is typical of many burrs.

Rather than using proprietary finishes out of the can, you could tint a plain oil or surface finish by adding powdered dyes or artists' oil colours to it. With any of the burrs mentioned here, these tinted finishes can be used to highlight and enhance the figuring. You could try staining or dyeing the wood directly, but these timbers are so dense that, in my experience, the finish is bound to be very patchy as a result of uneven penetration.

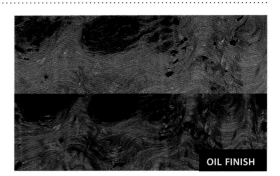

OIL FINISH

Gimlet
Eucalyptus salubris
OTHER NAMES Gimlet gum

END OF BURRS SECTION

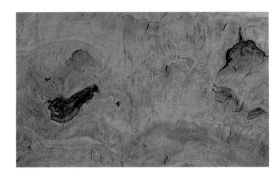

River red gum

Eucalyptus camaldulensis, syn. E. rostrata

OTHER NAMES Red river gum, Murray red gum, red gum, river gum, Queensland blue gum

GROWS Australia

HEIGHT 65ft (20m) but can reach up to 115ft (35m)

TRUNK DIAMETER 6ft (2m)

SPECIFIC GRAVITY .82

TYPICAL DRY WEIGHT 51lb/ft³ (825kg/m³)

POSSIBLE HEALTH RISKS Not known

Seasoning This wood dries well, provided much care is taken, but there are sometimes problems with longitudinal shrinkage and distortion caused by gum pockets. If stabilized wood is required, then rough-turning followed by further drying will help. When rough-turning highly figured pieces, allow an extra ¼–½in (6–13mm) of wall thickness per 12in (300mm) overall diameter.

Characteristics The heartwood can range from vibrant pink through soft red or orange to a reddish-brown, and is distinct from the paler sapwood. It mellows quickly to a mid-brown colour unless a finish with a UV inhibitor is used. Veins of gum can be present. Burrs vary in figure from tight clusters of knots to, more commonly, swirling grain.

The wood is medium-dense and is capable of holding quite reasonable fine detail. Any gum pockets or interlocking grain do not normally present a problem to the turner who works with sharp tools and takes delicate finishing cuts, but some pluckout may occur when scraping. If using a scraper, very gentle cuts or shear-scraping are recommended. The wood carves and routs well and great fun can be had combining power or hand carving with the turned forms.

Rose gum

Eucalyptus grandis

OTHER NAMES Flooded gum, scrub gum

GROWS New South Wales and Queensland, Australia. Also plantation-grown in Brazil, South Africa and Malaysia

HEIGHT 140–170ft (45–55m)

TRUNK DIAMETER 3–6ft (1–2m)

SPECIFIC GRAVITY .80

TYPICAL DRY WEIGHT 50lb/ft³ (800kg/m³)

POSSIBLE HEALTH RISKS Not known

Seasoning This wood responds well to kiln- and air-drying as long as care is taken during the early stages. If done too quickly, surface checking and cell collapse is likely.

Characteristics The sapwood, though paler, is not always easy to distinguish from the heartwood, which ranges in colour from a soft creamy pink to a rosy burnt orange or red-brown. Typically it has a uniform, moderately coarse-textured grain that is usually straight but occasionally interlocking.

It is highly prized as a timber for furniture, construction, boats and suchlike. From a turner's perspective, this is a nice timber to work. Like a blank canvas, it can hold reasonably fine detail – coves, beads and V-cuts – without fracturing out; and it carves and routs well, too. It is one of those timbers that rarely cause the turner any problems, apart from minor endgrain tearout, which is easily removed by sanding. It sands easily and also accepts surface and penetrative finishes well.

Seasoning Australian red mahogany is slow to dry and does not suffer much degrade in the process. Once dry it is also relatively stable. It can be turned wet to a fine, even wall thickness and left to dry with minimal risk of splitting. Rough-turning also works. I have not needed to place PVA on the endgrain areas to retard the moisture loss, but it can be done to minimize the risk of checking and splitting.

Characteristics This is not a true mahogany, but its rich colouring resembles that of some true mahoganies. The sapwood, a soft creamy colour, is distinct from the heartwood, which is often a rich, deep dark red. It has a slightly interlocked grain that may yield a ripple figure, and a medium to coarse, even texture. This hard, dense timber will hold reasonable detail. Despite its hardness and density, it is a good wood to turn. Wet timber will result in a good finish off the tool, although minor tearout occurs when scrapers are used. Turning the wood dry also presents no problems, but there are very few long shavings produced. Instead, you are more likely to encounter short shavings, chippy short bits of wood and some dust. It can be power-carved and routed, and I haven't encountered any problems with the application of oils, waxes or surfaces finishes.

Australian red mahogany

Eucalyptus pellita and E. resinifera

OTHER NAMES Red mahogany eucalyptus, red mahogany, red stringybark, red messmate

GROWS Eastern Australia

HEIGHT 150ft (45m)

TRUNK DIAMETER 3–5ft (1–1.5m)

SPECIFIC GRAVITY .96

TYPICAL DRY WEIGHT 60lb/ft³ (960kg/m³)

POSSIBLE HEALTH RISKS Not known

Seasoning This wood may be a bit tricky to dry and season. I find it acceptable to turn as long as you slow things down, otherwise you will likely encounter surface checking. Rough-turning the piece and coating the ends with PVA will help, not only with drying and stabilizing the timber, but also with slowing the drying rate down. If you are not worried about the shape, wet turn it to completion with a thin, even wall thickness.

Characteristics The pale pink sapwood is a bit lighter in colour than the heartwood, which ranges from light to darkish pink through to a dark reddish brown.

Typically it has a straight grain that will occasionally be interlocked; this produces nice figuring. You also may encounter gum pockets. The texture is moderately coarse. Don't let its hardness put you off. Turning it with gouges, scrapers or skews will not result in any major damage, though slight pullout may occur on endgrain. It can hold reasonable detail and takes well to power carving and routing. Very short shavings are produced when cutting this wood – slightly longer if wet-turning – with some dust and small chips. I have been able to use oils, waxes and surface finishes to good effect.

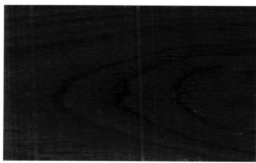

Sydney blue gum

Eucalyptus saligna

OTHER NAMES Blue gum

GROWS New South Wales and southern Queensland. Introduced to USA, New Zealand, South Africa, parts of Asia and Hawaii

HEIGHT 160ft (50m)

TRUNK DIAMETER 6ft (2m)

SPECIFIC GRAVITY .90

TYPICAL DRY WEIGHT 56lb/ft³ (900kg/m³)

POSSIBLE HEALTH RISKS Contact dermatitis; nose and throat irritation

American beech

Fagus grandifolia

OTHER NAMES Beech

GROWS Eastern Canada and USA

HEIGHT 150ft (45m)

TRUNK DIAMETER 4ft (1.2m)

SPECIFIC GRAVITY .74

TYPICAL DRY WEIGHT 46lb/ft³ (740kg/m³)

POSSIBLE HEALTH RISKS Dermatitis, eye irritation, decrease in lung function and rare incidence of nasal cancer

Seasoning Care is needed in drying, because the wood dries rapidly and tends to split, warp and surface-check. There can be a substantial amount of shrinkage, and some discolouration. American beech can be wet-turned, or rough-turned and set aside to season further. Joinery and cabinetmaking parts can be turned satisfactorily from kilned stock.

Characteristics The narrow sapwood is off-white with a pink tinge, while the heartwood is light to dark reddish-brown. American beech tends to be slightly darker and less consistent than European beech (*F. sylvatica*). It occasionally forms burrs and ripple figure, but otherwise it is a somewhat bland timber. It is available in large sizes and has a close, uniform texture. The grain is usually straight, but occasionally interlocked. These qualities make it an excellent choice for turned components in joinery and cabinetmaking, for artistic work, and – because it has no smell or taste – domestic utilitarian ware.

Apart from some endgrain tearout, usually when using scrapers in conventional cutting mode, this wood is a pleasure to work with. It cuts very cleanly with gouges and skews, and may require only a very light sanding to remove blemishes. It holds reasonably fine detail and is a good candidate for carving and routing. It sands and polishes well and can be brought to a high polish if needed.

Silver ash

Flindersia bourjotiana and *F. schottiana,*
syn. *F. pubescens*

OTHER NAMES Queensland silver ash, white ash (*F. bourjotiana*); Australian maple, northern silver ash, silkwood maple

GROWS New South Wales and Queensland, Australia; Papua New Guinea

HEIGHT 115ft (35m)

TRUNK DIAMETER 3ft (1m)

SPECIFIC GRAVITY .64 (*F. bourjotiana*)

TYPICAL DRY WEIGHT 35lb/ft³ (560kg/m³)

POSSIBLE HEALTH RISKS Skin irritation, sneezing

Seasoning Silver ash can usually be air- or kiln-dried with little degrade – maybe a little warping. Wet-turning to a thin wall thickness and letting it move works well; movement is slight in any case, except maybe on figured timber. Rough-turning works well where dimensional accuracy and stability are required: lidded boxes, vessels with joints in them and suchlike.

Characteristics These two *Flindersia* species have similar working characteristics and colouring. The heartwood ranges from a creamy grey-white to pale orange-tinted grey-brown; the sapwood is not clearly differentiated from the heartwood. Silver ash has a mainly straight grain with a uniform, medium texture. When interlocked or wavy grain is present, figuring may be found, but it is not that common. It has a lustrous, silky appearance that is highly valued.

Turning silver ash presents no major issues, except that scrapers are liable to pluck out the endgrain a little. It is a nice wood to carve and rout. I have used oils, waxes and surface finishes without encountering any problems.

CONSERVATION STATUS (see icons, left)
1 *F. bourjotiana* no information; **2** *F. schottiana* some concern

Seasoning There is a risk of movement and distortion when drying. Wet-turning to a thin wall thickness and letting it move works well. Rough-turning it and setting it aside (I coat the endgrain with PVA) seems to work fine within the accepted wall thickness guidelines.

Characteristics This is not a true maple but is highly prized for its working qualities and for its lustrous silky appearance. It has a creamy, straw-white coloured sapwood and the heartwood ranges from a mid pinkish-tan colour to pink-tinged brown. It darkens on exposure to a warm, mid reddish-brown. The wood usually has interlocked curly grain of medium uniform texture. A wide range of figuring is quite common: bird's-eye, mottled, band-like stripes, ripple or fiddleback.

It is a nice timber to turn, though the high incidence of figuring means that one is never quite sure how the product will look until it is finished. Gouges and skews give a fine finish, with only occasional tearout where there is interlocking grain. Scrapers give variable results depending on how they are used. This timber is a good choice if you want to carve or rout decorative effects. It also sands well and accepts oil, waxes and surface finishes without any problems. It can be fumed with ammonia to deepen the already rich colouring.

CONSERVATION STATUS (see icons, right)
1 *F. brayleyana* no information; **2** *F. pimenteliana* endangered

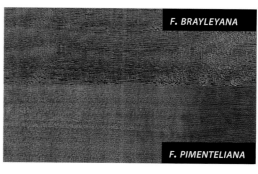

Queensland maple
Flindersia brayleyana and formerly *F. pimenteliana,* which is now endangered

OTHER NAMES Australian maple, flindersia, maple silkwood, silkwood; sometimes marketed as silver ash (see previous entry)
GROWS Northern Queensland, Australia; Papua New Guinea
HEIGHT 100ft (30m) or more
TRUNK DIAMETER 3–4ft (0.9–1.2m) or more
SPECIFIC GRAVITY .55
TYPICAL DRY WEIGHT 34lb/ft³ (550kg/m³), but can be heavier
POSSIBLE HEALTH RISKS Dermatitis

Seasoning End-coating helps prevent shakes and splits. Thick pieces never really dry; rough-turning followed by further seasoning is best, but it can be turned wet or part-seasoned if accuracy is not required.

Characteristics The heartwood is greenish-brown, sometimes nearly black. The grain is irregular and strongly interlocked, with a uniform, fine texture; it can hold very fine detail. About a third of its weight is guaiac gum, which makes it feel oily or waxy, and can stick to blades and cutting edges. The sapwood is cream or pale yellow. Fresh-cut wood or dust has a very distinctive smell.

This exceptionally dense, heavy and hard wood is excellent for mallet heads. For thread chasing, it is nearly as good as boxwood (*Buxus sempervirens*) or African blackwood (*Dalbergia melanoxylon*). It is usually only available in small sizes; old bowling balls are a possible source. A gouge will mostly produce small chips and oily, sticky dust. Sometimes a better finish can be achieved with a freshly honed scraper.

It takes a long time to sand out blemishes, so get as good a finish as you can straight from the tool. To avoid heat-checking, wet sanding is best, using oil or wax as the lubricant – but when sapwood is present there is a risk of colour contamination. The wood resists some surface finishes; a wipe over with cellulose thinners may help. It polishes readily with oils and waxes, to a highly lustrous finish.

Lignum vitae
Guaiacum sanctum and *G. officinale*

OTHER NAMES Holywood (*G. sanctum*), ironwood, palo santo, guayacán, guayacán negro
GROWS Florida, Central America, Caribbean
HEIGHT 23ft (7m)
TRUNK DIAMETER 1ft 8in (0.5m)
SPECIFIC GRAVITY 1.23
TYPICAL DRY WEIGHT 77lb/ft³ (1230kg/m³)
POSSIBLE HEALTH RISKS Dermatitis

Ovangkol

Guibourtia ehie

OTHER NAMES Ovengkol, amazaque, amazakoué, anokye, ehie, shedua, hyeduanini
GROWS Gabon, Ghana, Ivory Coast, Nigeria
HEIGHT 100–150ft (30–45m)
TRUNK DIAMETER 2–3ft (0.6–0.9m)
SPECIFIC GRAVITY .80
TYPICAL DRY WEIGHT 50lb/ft³ (800kg/m³)
POSSIBLE HEALTH RISKS Not known

Seasoning It seasons quickly with little degrade, but is difficult to kiln-dry. It can be wet-turned, but is more commonly turned partially seasoned or kilned. It moves only a little. It can be rough-turned and set aside to season; coating with PVA minimizes the risk of splits.

Characteristics The heartwood ranges from a golden honey-brown to dark reddish-brown, with greyish or deep violet-black stripes. The grain is straight or interlocked, with a moderately coarse texture. It sometimes has an attractive figure, ripple, roey or mottled, especially on quartersawn surfaces. The creamy-white sapwood is about 4in (100mm) thick. Ovangkol is available in reasonable sizes.

It turns satisfactorily, but endgrain and figured areas may tear out; sharp bevel-rubbing tools will help. Scrapers in shear-scraping or conventional mode do not produce as good a finish, but may help in smoothing uneven surfaces. There is a risk of splintering at the edges. Fully seasoned wood produces a fair amount of dust, so I typically use bevel-rubbing tools to get as good a finish as I can, then go straight to abrasives. The shavings will stain metal and hands. The wood can be routed, but with power carving it can be difficult to get a decent cut and finish. The wood sands well wet or dry, but avoid the wet method if sapwood is present. It takes surface or penetrative finishes well.

Holly

Ilex aquifolium and *I. opaca*

OTHER NAMES European holly (*I. aquifolium*), American holly (*I. opaca*). There are many different species of holly worldwide
GROWS Europe and western Asia (I. *aquifolium*), USA (*I. opaca*)
HEIGHT 40–70ft (12–21m)
TRUNK DIAMETER 1–2ft (0.3–0.6m)
SPECIFIC GRAVITY .80
TYPICAL DRY WEIGHT 50lb/ft³ (800kg/m³)
POSSIBLE HEALTH RISKS Not known

Seasoning This wood is best cut in the winter to minimize discoloration. It is highly likely to split if dried in the round; it dries best when cut into small stock and weighted down. When rough-turning, allow an extra 5% of wall thickness to compensate for the large movement, and coat with PVA before leaving it to season slowly; allow plenty of airflow, or blue staining is likely.

Characteristics Holly is hard, heavy and dense. The sapwood is slightly paler than the heartwood, and both range from creamy-white to ivory (the wood can be bleached to make it whiter). The close grain is able to hold very fine detail. It is not usually available in large sizes.

Holly is great for wet-turning: it distorts a lot, and some fantastic shapes are possible. When seasoned, irregular grain can cause problems, but usually it is well behaved. Tearout can be minimized by using a freshly honed gouge. Conventional scraping often causes damage, so gentle cuts in shear-scraping mode are recommended. It can be carved, textured and routed easily and holds reasonable detail.

A fine finish can be achieved with wet sanding. It will take both penetrative and surface finishes, but both will have a darkening effect. Finishes with UV inhibitors will minimize darkening with age.

Seasoning Butternut dries slowly with minimal shrinkage or degrade, and is fairly stable in use. It needs to be air-dried thoroughly before kilning. Alternatively, it can be wet-turned to completion or rough-turned and set aside to season further.

Characteristics This is a very light, soft timber. The heartwood is light reddish-brown, often featuring darker reddish-brown streaks. The sapwood is usually about 1in (25mm) wide and can range from off-white to a light, creamy grey-brown. Butternut has straight grain, with a medium to coarse, but soft texture and the lustre of satin. Ripple or mottled figure is occasionally present. Fungal stain colouring can add another dimension to what is otherwise a relatively bland-looking wood. It is not available in very big sizes, but is great for small decorative or utilitarian work. It is brilliant to carve with hand or power tools, and also to rout. It is a firm favourite of carvers, but its potential in turning is often overlooked.

The soft timber is easy to work with sharp bevel-rubbing tools, but it is best to skip scrapers and go straight to abrasives. Butternut sands well and finishes well with surface or penetrative finishes, but can be a little 'hungry', so it may require a few coats to achieve an even coverage.

Butternut
Juglans cinerea

OTHER NAMES White walnut, oilnut, nogal, nogal blanco, nuez meca
GROWS Canada and USA
HEIGHT 40–70ft (12–21m)
TRUNK DIAMETER 1–2ft (0.3–0.6m)
SPECIFIC GRAVITY 1.03
TYPICAL DRY WEIGHT 64lb/ft³ (1030kg/m³)
POSSIBLE HEALTH RISKS Skin and eye irritation

Seasoning Slow seasoning is needed to prevent end-splitting and fine surface checking. It can be turned to completion wet, partially seasoned or kiln-dried. Alternatively, it can be rough-turned and set aside for further seasoning. If the work in hand does not demand great accuracy, work straight from the piece you have.

Characteristics The heartwood is light pink, mid-red or violet-red, but darkens to a dull orange-red or mid-brown with age. There may be small knots. The narrow sapwood is light cream. Pencil cedar has fine, even, straight grain and a fine texture. Though not a true cedar, it has a cedar-like scent, which can be quite heady in confined spaces. It is not available in large sizes and is usually bought as through-cut boards or predimensioned blanks. It can be used for joinery, cabinetmaking, decorative and utilitarian turning, but because of the scent it is not recommended for items that may come into contact with food. This is a wood that can be carved and routed well.

It cuts well with sharp bevel-rubbing tools, giving a very good finish. Scrapers are likely to cause torn grain, so use gouges and skews, then go straight to abrasive. It sands well with wet or dry methods. It readily takes both surface and penetrative finishes, but oil finishes impart a wonderful, warm yellow colour, further enhancing what is already a beautifully coloured wood.

Virginian pencil cedar
Juniperus virginiana

OTHER NAMES Pencil cedar, red cedar, eastern red cedar, juniper, savin
GROWS Canada and USA
HEIGHT 40–60ft (12–18m)
TRUNK DIAMETER 1–2ft (0.3–0.6m)
SPECIFIC GRAVITY .53
TYPICAL DRY WEIGHT 33lb/ft³ (530kg/m³)
POSSIBLE HEALTH RISKS Not known

African mahogany

Khaya ivorensis and related species

OTHER NAMES Akuk, bandoro, bisselon, eri kiree, ogwango, undianunu, n'gollon, zaminguila, oganwo, acajou. Related species: *K. anthotheca, K. grandifoliola, K. senegalensis, K. nyasica*

GROWS Tropical areas of western, central and eastern Africa

HEIGHT 110–140ft (33–43m)

TRUNK DIAMETER 6ft (1.8m)

SPECIFIC GRAVITY .53

TYPICAL DRY WEIGHT 33lb/ft³ (530kg/m³)

POSSIBLE HEALTH RISKS Dermatitis, respiratory problems, rhinitis and nasal cancer

Seasoning Dries very quickly and hardly degrades, but any reaction or tension wood will cause distortion. Kiln-drying and air-drying are both acceptable, but for most purposes rough-turning followed by further seasoning is recommended.

Characteristics African mahogany is unrelated to American or true mahogany (*Swietenia macrophylla*). When freshly cut it is a light pinkish-brown, but on exposure to light it darkens to a deep red, often with a purple tinge. It darkens with age to an almost uniform mid-brown.

The interlocked grain produces striped or roey figure on quartersawn surfaces, and crotch and swirl figures are often present. The texture may be fine or coarse, with a high, golden lustre. The sapwood is usually creamy-white to yellow, but sometimes it resembles the heartwood. The wood is prone to thunder shakes, especially in figured logs. A medium-dense wood, available in large sizes, it is suited to architectural work as well as artistic and decorative pieces.

Sharp gouges and skews produce nice curly shavings with very little dust. The endgrain can tear out a little if too much pressure is used. The variable grain can make the cut a little woolly, especially when scraping. The wood carves and routs well, but best results are obtained with power tools. It sands easily with both wet and dry methods, but wet-sand only if no sapwood is present. It readily takes both penetrative and surface finishes and can be polished or buffed to a high lustre.

Laburnum

Laburnum anagyroides

OTHER NAMES Golden chain

GROWS Central and southern Europe

HEIGHT 20–30ft (6–9m)

TRUNK DIAMETER 1ft (0.3m)

SPECIFIC GRAVITY .82

TYPICAL DRY WEIGHT 52lb/ft³ (820kg/m³)

POSSIBLE HEALTH RISKS Seeds are highly toxic to humans and animals

Seasoning Dry slowly to prevent end-checking and splitting. Partially seasoned or wet wood can be turned to completion, or it can be rough-turned, coated with PVA and set aside to season. Trees and boughs are hard to season whole, so part-turning is recommended.

Characteristics The heartwood is bright yellow-brown with a green tinge when freshly cut, but darkens to a rich golden-brown, then deep purplish- or red-brown, and eventually a deep, rich dark brown. The sapwood is narrow and creamy-white. Laburnum usually has straight grain, a fairly fine texture and a lustrous surface. It is hard and dense. It has a pleasing growth-ring figure when flatsawn, and a fleck pattern when quartersawn. It holds quite fine detail and can be carved with hand or power tools. Not available in very big sizes, it is usually bought as a whole trunk or bough, or as predimensioned blanks.

The finest finish off the tool is achieved with skews and gouges. Scrapers can cause tearout; if you must use them, shear-scraping is best. The wood carves and routs well. The high contrast between the sap and heartwood makes this an excellent choice for natural-edge work. The wood sands well wet or dry, but avoid the wet method if sapwood is present. There may be some heat-checking if too much heat is generated. A high finish can be obtained with oils or surface finishes. Oil darkens the wood, but imparts a warm glow when burnished.

Seasoning A very stable timber, favoured for boatbuilding due to its stability and low shrinkage. It dries readily but tends to suffer slight surface checking. It can be turned wet or partially seasoned, or can be rough-turned and set aside for further seasoning.

Characteristics This handsome softwood has pale, narrow sapwood, not very distinct from the heartwood, which is light cream to buttery brown. Huon pine has straight grain, with fine, closely spaced growth rings, giving it a fine and even texture. It is quite a light, soft wood with fair strength. It is oily when freshly worked, and this essential oil, methyl eugenol, helps it to resist decay and attack by lyctus borers. The oil has a pleasant smell and helps the wood to cut cleanly. It can be used for decorative and utilitarian pieces, and carves and routs well. However, since logging is controlled for environmental reasons, it is difficult to get hold of and usually commands a very high price.

This is an easy wood to work with gouges and skews; skip the scrapers and go straight to abrasives. It sands satisfactorily but can clog abrasives and is vulnerable to heat-checking. It can be sanded wet or dry. It accepts most finishes well but, due to its oil content, it may resist some surface finishes.

Huon pine
Lagarostrobos franklinii, syn. Dacrydium franklinii

OTHER NAMES White pine, Macquarie pine
GROWS Southwestern Tasmania
HEIGHT 65–125ft (20–38m)
TRUNK DIAMETER 3ft 3in–6ft (1–1.8m)
SPECIFIC GRAVITY .52
TYPICAL DRY WEIGHT 32lb/ft³ (520kg/m³)
POSSIBLE HEALTH RISKS Not known

Seasoning Thick pieces may tend to warp during the early stages of drying, but it can generally be air- or kiln-dried without problems – though splitting may occur if it is dried too fast. Architectural, joinery or cabinetmaking turnery can be done with kiln-dried wood, but if you need accuracy then rough-turning and setting it aside to season is a must. If you can obtain boughs, sections of trunk, or partially seasoned pieces, these can be turned wet or partially seasoned to completion.

Characteristics The heartwood is mid-brown with red tints, and may have dark streaks. The sapwood is wide, and creamy-yellow with a hint of red. The grain is often irregular and interlocked, and may exhibit a ribbon stripe. The texture is uniform, and this attractive wood has a lustre like satin. Many pieces have a fine figure. You may find the heartwood sold as redgum or figured redgum; the sapwood may be sold separately as sapgum.

This timber is especially easy to work and only slightly affects the cutting edges of your tools, but it cuts best with bevel-rubbing tools. It is a nice wood to carve and rout as well as turn. It sands well with the dry sanding method; wet sanding should only be undertaken if no sapwood is present. It will accept any finish of your choice. Try it – you won't be disappointed.

American red gum
Liquidambar styraciflua

OTHER NAMES Gum, sweetgum, sapgum, redgum, star-leafed gum, alligator tree, alligator wood, liquidambar, hazel pine, bilsted, satin walnut
GROWS USA
HEIGHT 80–120ft (24–36m)
TRUNK DIAMETER 2–3ft (0.6–0.9m)
SPECIFIC GRAVITY .56
TYPICAL DRY WEIGHT 35lb/ft³ (560kg/m³)
POSSIBLE HEALTH RISKS Dermatitis

American tulipwood

Liriodendron tulipifera

OTHER NAMES Yellow poplar, white poplar, tulip poplar, tulip tree, whitewood, canary whitewood, canoe wood, saddletree. Unrelated to Brazilian tulipwood (*Dalbergia decipularis*)
GROWS Throughout eastern USA
HEIGHT 80–120ft (24–37m)
TRUNK DIAMETER 2–3ft (0.6–0.9m)
SPECIFIC GRAVITY .51
TYPICAL DRY WEIGHT 31lb/ft³ (510kg/m³)
POSSIBLE HEALTH RISKS Dermatitis

Seasoning This timber air-dries and kiln-dries very well, normally without degrade. If dried too slowly, sapwood stains and mould can develop. It can be wet-turned successfully, or set aside to season after rough-turning. But for the majority of projects you can get away with working kiln-dried or partially seasoned wood to completion.

Characteristics The sapwood is off-white, often with streaks, while the heartwood varies from pale yellow-brown to olive-green-brown, and may be streaked with blue-green, red-purple or brown-black. The light green colour of fresh-cut heartwood tends to darken to a mid green-brown on exposure to light. The grain is straight and texture is medium to fine. This wood is widely used in joinery, where it is usually painted or stained. It can be used for decorative work, and it carves and routs well, but it is a bland wood without much inherent visual appeal. Since it takes paint, stain or spray lacquer well, you could consider using colour in your work, perhaps together with carving.

It works satisfactorily with bevel-rubbing tools. Scrapers will more likely than not tear out the grain. It sands well, though many textbooks suggest otherwise; I have been able to achieve a very fine finish by sanding through the grades down to 400 grit or finer. It takes finishes well, but may require a few coats to ensure even coverage.

African walnut

Lovoa trichilioides

OTHER NAMES Benin walnut, Nigerian golden walnut, Ghana walnut, alona wood, bibolo, congowood, eyan, lovoa, nivero noy
GROWS Tropical west Africa
HEIGHT 150ft (45m)
TRUNK DIAMETER 4ft (1.2m)
SPECIFIC GRAVITY .56
TYPICAL DRY WEIGHT 35lb/ft³ (560kg/m³)
POSSIBLE HEALTH RISKS Irritation to mucous membranes and alimentary tract; nasal cancer

Seasoning It dries readily with little degrade whether kiln- or air-dried, though there may be some distortion and existing shakes are likely to extend. Heart shakes are common. Movement is usually slight, but sometimes it may shrink quite a bit. The wood is best rough-turned and then seasoned further. The sections usually available are boards or predimensioned blanks, either part-seasoned or kiln-dried. Part-seasoned blanks can be turned to completion, but will distort a little.

Characteristics This is not a true walnut. The sapwood, separated from the heartwood by a narrow transition zone, is a creamy-tan colour. The heartwood is a rich honey-brown with dark purplish-black gum lines. The grain is usually interlocked but can be straight, and has a fine texture with distinct growth rings. Quartersawn surfaces can exhibit a ribbon figure with alternating areas of darker and lighter wood. It is used in joinery, cabinetmaking and decorative turning.

The wood cuts well with most tools, but produces much dust. Scrapers usually tear the grain, but if they are very sharp and a light touch is used, you may get away with only a little sanding. It can be carved, preferably with power tools, and can be routed, too. It sands reasonably well, though a little clogging is likely. It takes finishes readily and can be polished to a high gloss if needed; for a super-smooth finish, the grain will need filling.

Seasoning This wood dries slowly and tends to suffer surface checks. It can be turned partially seasoned to completion, but will move, sometimes quite a lot. For lidded boxes or other precise work, rough-turning and setting aside to season is a must; coating rough-turned pieces with PVA will minimize checking.

Characteristics The heartwood ranges from light pink-brown to violet-brown, streaked with lighter and darker tones of brown and reddish-brown. The sapwood is narrow, and pale cream in colour. The grain texture is fine and uniform, occasionally interlocking.

It holds reasonably fine detail, but blunts cutting edges quickly. It is difficult to saw, but far easier to work on the lathe. Sharp tools and a delicate cut are necessary to minimize grain damage. Scrapers do not, on the whole, create as good a finish as bevel-rubbing tools, but with a freshly honed edge in shear-scraping mode you can achieve a surface that needs only the lightest touch with abrasives to clean it up. It can be carved and routed to good effect. When turning or sanding, take care not to generate too much heat, or heat-checking may occur. A fair amount of dust may be created, so take sensible precautions to limit exposure to it. The wood finishes well with oils and waxes.

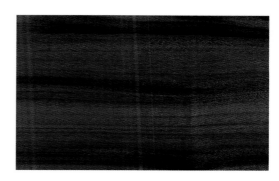

Santos rosewood
Machaerium scleroxylon

OTHER NAMES Not known
GROWS Bolivia
HEIGHT Medium-sized tree
TRUNK DIAMETER 1ft 8in (0.5m)
SPECIFIC GRAVITY .85
TYPICAL DRY WEIGHT 53lb/ft³ (850kg/m³)
POSSIBLE HEALTH RISKS Dust can cause skin and nasal irritation

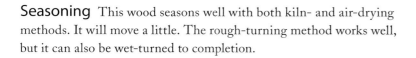

Seasoning This wood seasons well with both kiln- and air-drying methods. It will move a little. The rough-turning method works well, but it can also be wet-turned to completion.

Characteristics Osage-orange is dense, very hard and resilient. The heartwood varies from greenish-yellow or golden-yellow to bright orange with darker streaks, darkening in time to a uniform brown. The sapwood is light yellow. The grain is usually close and straight, but can be interlocking or irregular; the texture is somewhat coarse.

This wood can be problematic to use, but the results are worth the effort. It has a severe blunting effect on tools, so frequent sharpening is necessary. It cuts more easily wet or partially seasoned than fully seasoned, but interlocking grain is highly likely to tear out if you use anything but the most delicate of cuts with a sharp gouge. Scraping will exacerbate the problem. If the grain is straight, however, scrapers can be used to remove any surface undulations, either in conventional or in shear-scraping mode. The wood is suitable for carving, preferably with power tools, though it does not hold very fine detail. It can be somewhat brittle, and splintering may occur at the edges.

It sands and finishes easily and readily accepts penetrative or surface finishes. It can be easily glued when creating segmented items.

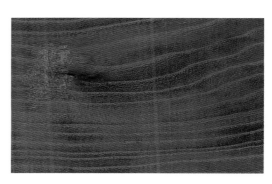

Osage-orange
Maclura pomifera

OTHER NAMES Bow wood, bodare, bodark, bois d'arc, hedge, hedge apple, horse apple, naranjo chino, mock-orange, osage
GROWS USA
HEIGHT 50ft (15m)
TRUNK DIAMETER 2ft (0.6m)
SPECIFIC GRAVITY .76
TYPICAL DRY WEIGHT 48lb/ft³ (760kg/m³)
POSSIBLE HEALTH RISKS Not known

Magnolia

Magnolia grandiflora

OTHER NAMES Evergreen magnolia, southern magnolia, mountain magnolia, sweet magnolia, cucumber wood, black lin, bat tree, big laurel, bullbay

GROWS USA; cultivated in UK

HEIGHT 60–80ft (18–24m)

TRUNK DIAMETER 2–3ft (0.6–0.9m)

SPECIFIC GRAVITY .56

TYPICAL DRY WEIGHT 35lb/ft³ (560kg/m³)

POSSIBLE HEALTH RISKS Not known

Seasoning When kiln-dried, magnolia suffers little degrade. Air-drying makes it shrink excessively, warp and check, and this tendency to distort can be exploited to good effect by wet-turning to a thin, even wall thickness. Turning partially seasoned wood will also result in movement. It can be rough-turned and set aside for further drying; but allow an extra ¼in (6mm) or so of wall thickness per 12in (300mm) diameter to take account of the increased movement.

Characteristics The sapwood is a pale yellow-white. The heartwood is a light creamy-green tinged with tan, although it can be a little darker, bordering on mid-brown, often with dark reddish-violet streaks caused by mineral deposits. The grain is straight, with a regular fine, close texture. Magnolia can be used for utilitarian and decorative turning. It can be carved with hand or power tools and routed if you fancy some doing something a little different.

This wood turns well with skews and gouges, but conventional scraping will result in grain tearout; shear-scraping is a little better, but not much. It is best to use the skew or gouge, depending on the type of work being undertaken, and then go straight to abrasives to remove any blemishes. It sands well, but be careful to keep the abrasive moving to avoid creating hollows. It takes surface or penetrative finishes well.

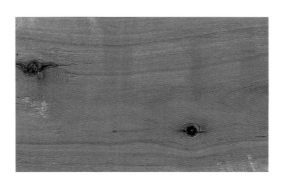

Apple

Malus sylvestris, syn. *M. pumila, Pyrus malus*

OTHER NAMES None. Crab apple (various *Malus* spp.) provides similar wood

GROWS Temperate zones worldwide and cooler areas of tropical regions

HEIGHT 25–50ft (8–15m)

TRUNK DIAMETER 1–2ft (0.3–0.6m)

SPECIFIC GRAVITY .70

TYPICAL DRY WEIGHT 43lb/ft³ (700kg/m³)

POSSIBLE HEALTH RISKS Not known

Seasoning Apple dries slowly, and air-drying is likely to result in distortion. It can be kiln-dried with little degrade. It can be turned wet or partially seasoned to completion; the bark is thin and will stay in place if you want to include it on natural-edge work. Or you could rough-turn it and set it aside to season.

Characteristics The heartwood is between pink, beige and orange in colour. The grain is usually straight, occasionally irregular or interlocking, with a fine, even texture. It can hold fine detail, and can be carved with hand or power tools. I have on occasion been able to cut threads of 10 and 12tpi (threads per inch), but not always. Experiment with this and the other fruitwoods and find out what they can do. As with many fruitwoods, the roots are great to turn, if they are big enough; but they must be dried carefully so as not to split. The colour of the root timber varies from reddish-tan or orange to a dark reddish-brown.

Like other fruitwoods, this is a pleasure to turn. It responds well to all tools as long as the grain is straight and even. If there is irregular grain present, then scrapers may cause tearout. Its versatility is worth exploring to the full to maximize the visual and tactile aspects of your work. It sands and finishes well.

Seasoning Mango is best kiln-dried swiftly after felling, as it is prone to fungal staining if air-dried. On the other hand, the colours in the fungal-stained wood can be very pleasant. It is a great wood for wet-turning to completion; or, if accuracy is required, it can be rough-turned and set aside to season further. Kiln-dried stock is fine for joinery or furniture turnings.

Characteristics Mango is usually a soft buttery-brown to light tan, with dark wavy flecks where the pores are exposed, giving a marbled look. There may be long bands of light creamy-red running through the wood. The texture is fine to medium, and the grain is sometimes wavy. It can hold very fine detail, and is nice to carve and rout. Sadly, because the trees are grown only for their fruit, the wood is rarely available outside the areas where it grows. I would love to get my hands on some more of it. It can be used for decorative and utilitarian turning.

It cuts well with all tools, although a better finish is achieved with bevel-rubbing tools. The only time that grain tearout seems to occur is when interlocking grain is present, which is not common. The wood sands well, accepts finishes readily and can be finished to a high polish.

Mango
Mangifera indica

OTHER NAMES Manga, mangue, manako, mangot

GROWS India, China, southeast Asia, West Indies, USA (Florida, Hawaii), Mexico, Peru, Brazil, South Africa

HEIGHT 65–100ft (20–30m)

TRUNK DIAMETER 3ft (1m)

SPECIFIC GRAVITY .51

TYPICAL DRY WEIGHT 32lb/ft³ (510kg/m³)

POSSIBLE HEALTH RISKS Not known

Seasoning This wood is usually air-dried locally; once cut, dried and debarked, it is considered to be reasonably safe to work with. The blanks I have had were kiln-dried. I rough-turned them, coated them with PVA and set them aside to season. There was not much movement, and no splitting or end-checking.

Characteristics This is a hard, dense, very attractive wood. I must admit that the health warnings on this wood worried me, but the working of it was fine and I suffered no reactions. I have only used the wood for decorative pieces. The heartwood is deep reddish- or purplish-brown. The sapwood is generally a creamy honey-brown with occasional soft red and green hues, and is clearly distinct from the heartwood. There is often a beautiful grain pattern, and the texture is fine and uniform.

The wood works fine with very sharp tools, but produces dust that some people may react to. Scrapers and dull tools can cause endgrain tearout, but freshly honed scrapers work fine on most occasions. Sanding is fine and it takes finishes readily.

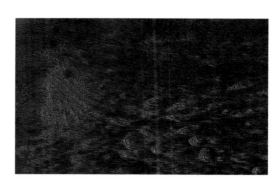

Honduras walnut
Metopium brownei

OTHER NAMES Chechem, cachin, chechen, coral sumac, poison wood, black poison wood

GROWS Cuba, Jamaica, northern Guatemala, Belize, Mexico, Dominican Republic

HEIGHT up to 50ft (15m)

TRUNK DIAMETER Not known

SPECIFIC GRAVITY .64

TYPICAL DRY WEIGHT 40lb/ft³ (640kg/m³)

POSSIBLE HEALTH RISKS Black, caustic sap from freshly felled wood causes a reaction akin to that of poison ivy

Zebrano

Microberlinia brazzavillensis

OTHER NAMES Zebrawood, African zebrawood, zingana

GROWS West Africa, mainly Cameroon and Gabon

HEIGHT 150ft (45m)

TRUNK DIAMETER 4–5ft (1.2–1.5m)

SPECIFIC GRAVITY .74

TYPICAL DRY WEIGHT 46lb/ft³ (740kg/m³)

POSSIBLE HEALTH RISKS Irritation to eyes and skin

Seasoning Kiln-drying and air-drying can be used, but splitting, checking and distortion are possible if dried too quickly. Trunk and branch wood can be wet-turned to completion, in which case some movement will occur; but you will most likely be working from part-seasoned blanks with variable moisture content. If accuracy is required, rough-turn the piece and set it aside to season further, coating with PVA to retard moisture loss. Part-seasoned pieces have a musty smell.

Characteristics Zebrano is available in large sizes, usually as through-cut boards or predimensioned blanks. The heartwood is mainly straw to pale buff-brown, with random streaks of dark brown or purplish-black. The sapwood is pale and rather featureless. The grain is usually interlocked and variable. The texture is coarse and uneven, and the wood is hard, moderately heavy and strong. Not the easiest of woods to turn, it cuts well with very sharp gouges or skews, but scrapers make the surface woolly. It can be routed, but carving of any other sort is hard. Fine detail is hard to maintain. Segmented turners like to use zebrano to contrast with plainer timbers.

It sands well dry, but watch out for heat-checks. Wet sanding makes the surface murky because of colour contamination. It takes surface or penetrative finishes well, but the grain may need filling. The related species *M. bisulcata* is critically endangered and should not be used.

WAX FINISH

Panga panga

Millettia stuhlmannii

OTHER NAMES Partridgewood, jambiré, messara

GROWS East Africa

HEIGHT 60ft (18m)

TRUNK DIAMETER 1ft 8in–2ft (0.5–0.6m)

SPECIFIC GRAVITY .80

TYPICAL DRY WEIGHT 55lb/ft³ (880kg/m³)

POSSIBLE HEALTH RISKS Not known

Seasoning It dries slowly but care is needed to avoid surface checking. It is usually supplied partially seasoned, and rough-turning works a treat; seal the endgrain with PVA if you want, then set it aside to dry before finish-turning.

You can turn wet or partially seasoned wood to finished thickness and then let it dry and move as it wants. I have not encountered any problems with either method.

Characteristics The clearly demarcated sapwood is a pale creamy yellow to pale yellow. The heartwood is a rich, deep chocolate-brown with very dark streaks running though it. Typically only the heartwood is bought, but occasionally sapwood is present.

The wood is dense, and small chips are to be expected rather than shavings. A scraper will pluck out the grain a little. No matter what tool one uses, a fair amount of dust is produced. The wood tends to splinter at fine edges so minute chamfers and radiuses are necessary to 'soften' the sharp edges to minimize fracturing. It power-carves and routs satisfactorily and I have not experienced any problems with applying oils, waxes or lacquers or other surface finishes.

Seasoning Opepe dries well if quartersawn, but when flatsawn it is likely to check, split and distort. It is usually supplied in par-seasoned boards or predimensioned blanks, either through-cut or square-edged, so the wood can be turned to completion as it is, but will move and may split or check if not turned thin. It may be rough-turned, coated with PVA to minimize checking or splitting, and set aside to season further.

Characteristics The heartwood is a uniform honey-yellow when freshly cut, maturing on exposure to orange-brown or red-brown with a distinctive coppery lustre. The sapwood is a creamy grey-white and about 2in (50mm) thick. The grain is usually interlocked or irregular, with a coarse to medium texture. Ribbon or rope figures may give a striking appearance to quartersawn surfaces. It can be used for joinery, furniture and decorative turning.

The irregular and interlocking grain can prove tricky to work. Very sharp gouges – or skews, for spindle work – used with a slow, deliberate cut give the best finish off the tool and will result in minimal grain tearout. All other tools can and probably will lift the grain and cause tearout. It sands satisfactorily, but be careful of endgrain heat checks. It takes finishes readily and can be brought to a high polish if needed. Some grain filling may be required if you need an ultrasmooth finish.

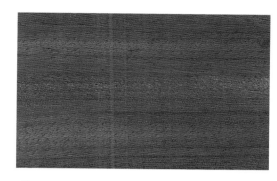

Opepe
Nauclea diderrichii, syn. *Sarcocephalus diderrichii*

OTHER NAMES Akondoc, aloma, badi, bilinga, kusia, kusiaba, linzi, n'gulu, maza
GROWS Equatorial west Africa
HEIGHT 160ft (50m)
TRUNK DIAMETER 5ft (1.5m)
SPECIFIC GRAVITY .74
TYPICAL DRY WEIGHT 46lb/ft³ (740kg/m³)
POSSIBLE HEALTH RISKS Dermatitis, irritation of mucous membranes, dizziness, visual disturbance, nosebleeds and blood spitting

---

Seasoning The outer, lighter wood dries easily, but the heartwood needs careful drying to avoid surface checking, internal honeycombing and cell collapse. The wood's movement can be used to good effect when wet-turning to completion. Kiln-dried wood is fine for joinery or furniture applications. Alternatively, rough-turn, leaving an extra ½–1in (13–25mm) or so of wall thickness per 12in (300mm) diameter to allow for movement. Coat with PVA to even out the drying process.

Characteristics The main heartwood, known as red myrtle, is pinkish-tan to sumptuous red-brown, with a paler outer zone between this and the narrow, pale cream sapwood. The grain is usually straight but may be slightly interlocked, and is sometimes slightly wavy, which results in some nice figure on quartersawn stock. The texture is fine, even and lustrous. It is not a true myrtle or beech. This dense hardwood has a moderate blunting effect on edge tools, and can be used for turning utilitarian or decorative items. This is a good candidate for power carving and routing.

This wood cuts well wet, partially seasoned or fully seasoned. Bevel-rubbing tools give a slightly better cut than scrapers, but freshly honed scrapers should cause no more than minor blemishes on the endgrain. It sands and finishes well, but watch out for heat-checks on endgrain.

Tasmanian myrtle
Nothofagus cunninghamii

OTHER NAMES Tasmanian beech, myrtle beech, mountain beech, Australian nothofagus
GROWS Tasmania and Victoria, Australia
HEIGHT 100–130ft (30–40m) or taller
TRUNK DIAMETER 3–5ft (0.9–1.5m)
SPECIFIC GRAVITY .72
TYPICAL DRY WEIGHT 45lb/ft³ (720kg/m³)
POSSIBLE HEALTH RISKS Irritation to mucous membranes

Blackgum

Nyssa sylvatica

OTHER NAMES Tupelo, black tupelo, tupelo gum, yellow gum tree, sour gum, wild pear tree, stinkwood

GROWS USA, from Maine to Michigan, Illinois to Texas

HEIGHT 60–120ft (18–37m)

TRUNK DIAMETER 2–4ft (0.6–1.2m)

SPECIFIC GRAVITY .46

TYPICAL DRY WEIGHT 29lb/ft³ (460kg/m³)

POSSIBLE HEALTH RISKS Not known

Seasoning Drying needs great care to prevent warping and twisting. There can be a lot of movement, which makes this an excellent timber to experiment with wet-turning, using a thin, even wall thickness. If stability is an issue, rough-turn and set aside to season.

Characteristics This lightweight wood is very tough and capable of holding reasonably fine detail. It is suitable for furniture and joinery applications and for decorative and functional turning. Its heartwood ranges from a pale creamy grey-brown or yellowish-tan to soft brown. The wide sapwood is paler, sometimes a creamy buff-brown. The grain is close and interlocked, the texture uniform.

The interlocking grain can be a problem for skews and scrapers (less so for gouges), and may result in tearout. Sharp tools traversed slowly across the work will usually be sufficient. Scrapers will not create as good a finish but can, with care, give a surface that requires only a small amount of sanding. I have had some success with power carving, and with chip-carving as accent decoration, though it wasn't easy. It routs satisfactorily with a slow traverse rate. The wood sands and finishes well, though oils darken the surface quite a lot. If you wish to maintain the creamy colour of the wood, use a surface finish such as lacquer containing UV inhibitors.

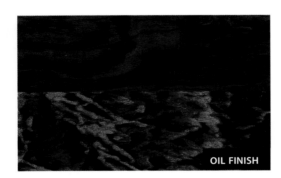

OIL FINISH

Imbuia

Ocotea porosa, syn. *Phoebe porosa*

OTHER NAMES Amarela, Brazilian walnut, imbuya, canella imbuia, embuia

GROWS Southern Brazil

HEIGHT 130ft (40m)

TRUNK DIAMETER 6ft (1.8m)

SPECIFIC GRAVITY .66

TYPICAL DRY WEIGHT 41lb/ft³ (660kg/m³)

POSSIBLE HEALTH RISKS Sawdust can be an irritant to the nose, eyes and skin

Seasoning Imbuia dries quickly. It is prone to warp unless care is taken, and thicker stock has a tendency to honeycomb and cell collapse. Movement in use is medium to small. If you plan to rough-turn a piece and set it aside to season, consider coating the endgrain or the whole item with thinned-down PVA to slow the drying process.

Characteristics The heartwood ranges from yellow-green through orange to chocolate-brown, with variegated streaks. The grain is usually straight, but often curly or wavy with a fine ribbon figure. This reasonably hard, heavy, dense wood has a medium to fine texture and is naturally lustrous. It may have quilted, burry (burled) or blistered figuring, and clusters of pippy burr. Imbuia resembles American walnut (*Juglans nigra*) but has a finer texture. It mellows quickly to a mid-brown or deep brown, but the grain pattern remains distinct.

It can hold quite fine detail. Seasoned wood cuts well with bevel-rubbing tools, producing small shavings with some dust. Freshly honed scrapers give a nice surface finish. Interlocking grain can be dealt with by delicate cuts with a sharp gouge or scraper. Burr and quilted forms, however, present an increased risk of tearout.

Natural oils make the dust a little sticky, so abrasives must be cleaned regularly. The wood can be power-carved and routed, and all types of finishes can give good results.

Seasoning The wood is slow to dry, with a tendency to check and split, and may honeycomb if dried too quickly. Kiln-drying is best. It is great for wet-turning, but can also be turned partially seasoned if some movement is acceptable. This wood can be rough-turned, coated with PVA and set aside to season further.

Characteristics The heartwood is generally buff-brown, with irregular darker streaks ranging from mid-brown to purplish-black, resulting in a marbled look. This is an oily wood, but not so much as European olive (*O. europaea*). The grain is usually straight but sometimes interlocked, with a fine and even texture. The sapwood is creamy-yellow. The shavings can stain hands and steel. It is used for decorative and utilitarian turning, and for furniture and joinery components; it can also be carved.

There is only a minor risk of tearout on interlocking grain; otherwise it produces a fine finish off the tool. It can take fine detail and coarse threads can be cut on it. It can be carved and routed. It sands well, but beware of heat-checking. It may prove resistant to some surface finishes, in which case you should wipe it over with a solvent such as cellulose thinners or methylated spirit (denatured alcohol) before applying the finish. There are no problems with oils and waxes, and the surface can be taken to a high polish.

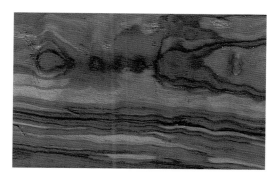

East African olive
Olea hochstetteri and *O. welwitschii*

OTHER NAMES Olive, olivewood, ironwood, loliondo, musharagi, olmasi
GROWS Cameroon, Congo, Ethiopia, Guinea, Ivory Coast, Kenya, Sierra Leone, Sudan, Tanzania, Uganda, Zambia
HEIGHT 80–100ft (24–30m)
TRUNK DIAMETER 2–3ft (0.6–0.9m)
SPECIFIC GRAVITY .89
TYPICAL DRY WEIGHT 55lb/ft³ (890kg/m³)
POSSIBLE HEALTH RISKS Dust may irritate skin, eyes, nose and lungs

Seasoning Very difficult: the wood is prone to cracks and checks that are often not visible on the surface. It can be turned partially seasoned as long as the wall thickness is even. It seems to be quite stable and does not move or shrink much. Rough-turning works well, if you want more accuracy in the shape.

Characteristics The heartwood can vary from a beautiful rich, honeyed golden-orange to dark reddish-brown, almost purplish-black, mottled with a golden orange-red. The narrow sapwood is a pale creamy-yellow. Sadly, the wood darkens quickly on exposure to light, becoming a more uniform, deep brown colour. It is brittle and extremely hard, with a high lustre. It appears to be available only in small sizes as sections of trunk or bough, which often contain splits or wormholes, or as predimensioned blanks. Small decorative work is ideal for this wood. It power-carves and routs well.

This is a tough wood that requires very sharp tools, traversed slowly across the wood, to achieve a good cut. On some pieces it is easier to achieve a good finish with scrapers than with bevel-rubbing tools. Some dust is produced when turning, and this has a strong, unpleasant, peppery smell. The wood can heat-check when sanding, so be careful. It can be sanded dry or wet, but only sand wet if no sapwood is present. This wood can be finished with both surface and penetrative finishes.

Desert ironwood
Olneya tesota

OTHER NAMES Ironwood, Arizona ironwood, Sonora ironwood, palo de hierro, tesota
GROWS Mexico, USA (Colorado, southwest Arizona, southern California)
HEIGHT 18–25ft (5.5–7.5m)
TRUNK DIAMETER 1ft 6in (0.46m)
SPECIFIC GRAVITY .86
TYPICAL DRY WEIGHT 54lb/ft³ (860kg/m³)
POSSIBLE HEALTH RISKS Not known, but the dust is particularly unpleasant

167

Lancewood

Oxandra lanceolata

OTHER NAMES Yaya, asta, haya prieta, bois de lance

GROWS Caribbean and Amazon

HEIGHT 50ft (15m)

TRUNK DIAMETER 1ft 6in (0.46m)

SPECIFIC GRAVITY .81

TYPICAL DRY WEIGHT 51lb/ft³ (810kg/m³)

POSSIBLE HEALTH RISKS Not known

Seasoning This wood is fairly difficult to dry and has a high shrinkage rate. If the endgrain is not sealed the wood will check badly. It can be turned to completion when wet or partially seasoned, in which case some movement will occur; or it can be rough-turned, coated with PVA and set aside to season further – but dry it slowly.

Characteristics The heartwood is dark silvery-brown in colour. The creamy butter-yellow sapwood is the part of the wood that is typically encountered, unless you are able to obtain sections of the trunk or boughs where heartwood is present. The grain is usually straight and has a fine texture. It is only available in small sections, so the turner is restricted to small decorative work.

This is a hard but lovely wood to work with, though sadly it is quite bland to look at. It cuts well with all tools, can be carved and routed with ease and holds reasonably fine detail. Lancewood also sands easily and readily accepts finishes of all kinds. This sounds too good to be true, but if you have the opportunity to try this wood I think you will like it.

White peroba

Paratecoma peroba

OTHER NAMES Ipé peroba, peroba branca, peroba de campos, peroba manchada, golden peroba, peroba amarella

GROWS Brazil

HEIGHT 90–130ft (27–40m)

TRUNK DIAMETER 5ft (1.5m)

SPECIFIC GRAVITY .75

TYPICAL DRY WEIGHT 47lb/ft³ (750kg/m³)

POSSIBLE HEALTH RISKS The dust may cause dermatitis, nasal irritation and asthma; splinters may become septic

Seasoning This wood usually dries quickly with few problems other than slight splitting and, due to variable grain, maybe a bit of twisting if you buy whole boards. The wood can be turned from start to finish with a nice even wall thickness; you are likely to encounter a bit of movement, but not a massive amount. I prefer to rough-turn pieces and then set them aside for a while before finish-turning them.

Characteristics The sapwood is white to creamy-yellow and the heartwood varies from a soft, light olive to a darker olive tinged with green or red, with occasional faint variegated streaks. The grain has a fine, uniform texture and may occasionally be interlocking or wavy.

This wood does not present the turner with any problems. It is nice to turn, though scrapers might pull the endgrain a little. It carves, routs and sands well and takes oils, waxes and surfaces finishes with no fuss.

Seasoning The wood can be air-dried in 30–60 days, and kiln-dried in 30–60 hours. It can be rough-turned and re-turned when dry; if turned wet to completion, movement is only slight.

Characteristics Paulownia is a fast-growing tree. It is an important plantation-grown timber. The sapwood is a light silverish colour tinged with white. The heartwood ranges from a pale reddish-tinged brown to a colder grey- or tan-tinged brown. It is soft and straight-grained with a coarse texture. Despite its light weight it is capable of holding reasonable detail and can be carved and routed well.

This wood is a delight to turn. Bevel-rubbing tools produce a fine finish off the tool, but use scrapers only if you have to – and if you do, expect to do a lot of sanding. It sands well, and oils and waxes are easy to use. Some people recommend sealing the wood with a sanding sealer or something similar prior to putting a surface finish on. This certainly works, but I have not found it necessary.

Paulownia
Paulownia fortunei, P. tomentosa

OTHER NAMES Kiri, Chinese empress tree, dragon tree, princess tree, foxglove tree
GROWS Native to China, Indochina, Japan and Korea; plantation-grown in many countries
HEIGHT 130ft (40m); plantation-grown trees are shorter
TRUNK DIAMETER 6ft (2m) maximum
SPECIFIC GRAVITY .27
TYPICAL DRY WEIGHT 20lb/ft³ (320kg/m³)
POSSIBLE HEALTH RISKS Not known

Seasoning This wood can be kiln- or air-dried, but tends to warp during drying. It can be turned wet or partially seasoned to completion – in which case it will shrink and move – or rough-turned and set aside to season further.

Characteristics The heartwood ranges from pink to light, creamy reddish-brown, while the wide sapwood is a milky off-white colour. The grain varies according to where the tree has grown, but is generally straight with a medium figuring. It has medium lustre and texture. The wood can be used for decorative or utilitarian work. It is only available in small to medium sizes. It turns very well, carves well and is capable of holding quite fine detail.

Scrapers do not cut as cleanly as bevel-rubbing tools; even in shear-scraping mode they are likely to create a woolly surface or tear out the endgrain a little. This is not a problem, since the finish that can be achieved with bevel-rubbing tools is so good that you can go straight to abrasives afterwards to remove any minor blemishes. Avocado sands and finishes well.

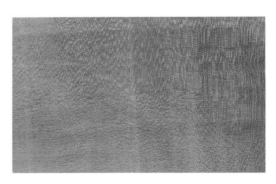

Avocado
Persea americana, syn. P. edulis, Laurus persea

OTHER NAMES Persea, alligator pear, apricot (Virgin Islands); many other names in different countries
GROWS Mexico, Guatemala, Honduras, USA (Hawaii, Florida and California)
HEIGHT 30–60ft (9–18m)
TRUNK DIAMETER 2ft 6in (0.76m)
SPECIFIC GRAVITY .53
TYPICAL DRY WEIGHT 33lb/ft³ (530kg/m³)
POSSIBLE HEALTH RISKS Not known

Celery-top pine

Phyllocladus aspleniifolius, syn.
P. rhomboidalis

OTHER NAMES Not known
GROWS Tasmania, Australia
HEIGHT 100ft (30m)
TRUNK DIAMETER 3ft (1m)
SPECIFIC GRAVITY .64
TYPICAL DRY WEIGHT 40lb/ft³ (640kg/m³)
POSSIBLE HEALTH RISKS Not known

Seasoning This timber dries well with little degrade. If you are turning for joinery or cabinetmaking applications, you can get away with using kiln-dried sections. Partially seasoned wood can be turned, but will move and, if the walls are too thick, they may check. If you require accuracy and stability you will need to season the wood further; one option is to rough-turn and set the piece aside to dry more.

Characteristics This is not a true pine. The heartwood colour varies from a creamy pale yellow to a soft tan. The narrow sapwood is typically the same colour and not distinct from the heartwood. It has a straight grain with a fine, even texture. The growth rings are clearly defined and closely spaced. The wood turns, carves and routs well and can be used for both decorative and utilitarian work.

This is a lovely clean wood to work with. It cuts well with skews and gouges, but does not respond well to scrapers no matter how they are used. After using the bevel-rubbing tools, go straight to abrasives. It readily accepts either surface or penetrative finishes.

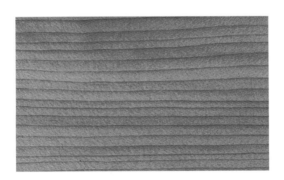

Sitka spruce

Picea sitchensis

OTHER NAMES Silver spruce, tideland spruce, Menzies spruce, coast spruce, yellow spruce
GROWS Western parts of North America, from northern Canada to Alaska
HEIGHT 125–200ft (38–60m)
TRUNK DIAMETER 3–6ft (0.9–1.8m)
SPECIFIC GRAVITY .43
TYPICAL DRY WEIGHT 27lb/ft³ (430kg/m³)
POSSIBLE HEALTH RISKS Respiratory irritation, bronchial asthma, rhinitis and dermatitis

Seasoning This wood dries easily using both air-drying and kilning methods, though if larger sections are dried too fast there may be twisting and cupping. Young wood may have checks, splits and raised grain. Movement is medium to small. Trunk, boughs or part-seasoned sections can be turned green and allowed to distort. Turnings for joinery or cabinetmaking can use kiln-dried wood, but if you require more stability, rough-turn the piece and set it aside to season further.

Characteristics Available in large sizes, this softwood has creamy-whitish to light pink-brown heartwood with a violet tinge, which darkens to a pink-tinged silver-brown. The sapwood is pale buttery-yellow and looks similar to the heartwood. The grain is usually straight, close and free of knots and defects, though wood from young trees may contain a significant proportion of spiral grain. The texture is fine, even and silky, especially in older-growth wood.

It is easy to work with sharp bevel-rubbing tools, which will leave a fine, silky surface. Scrapers tear the grain, so go from bevel-rubbing tools straight to abrasive. Sitka spruce can be carved and routed, and this is commonly done on turnings for furniture.

Sitka spruce has a slight resinous odour, and the resin can clog abrasives. It readily takes finishes of all descriptions. Softwoods are often overlooked by turners, except for architectural or joinery work. This is sad, because utilitarian ware and decorative work offer many worthwhile possibilities, and the results can look great.

Seasoning Honey mesquite dries well, but small checks and splits can develop during air-drying. Partially seasoned or air-dried sections can be turned to completion, and rarely move much; but for absolute stability, rough-turn the piece and set it aside to season. This is one of the most dimensionally stable woods you are ever likely to encounter.

Characteristics The heartwood is a rich, deep honey-brown to dark copper-brown, with darker wavy lines. The texture is fine or medium, with straight or wavy open grain; occasionally the grain is irregular. It often exhibits beautiful figuring and produces stunning burrs (burls). The sapwood is up to 1in (25mm) thick and pale creamy-white. This is a hard, tough, heavy wood, good for turning furniture and joinery parts as well as utilitarian and decorative wares.

Sharp tools are essential for a good finish. Old, dry wood produces a lot of dust, and endgrain tearout is likely when using scrapers. Freshly seasoned wood is much more pleasant and easy to work, with tearout likely only if the grain is irregular. Scrapers sometimes produce a finer surface than gouges or skews. It can hold reasonably fine detail and can be power-carved and routed if you want to do something different.

It may be resistant to some surface finishes but it readily accepts oils, followed by waxes, and can be power-buffed to a fine polish.

Honey mesquite
Prosopis juliflora and *P. glandulosa*

OTHER NAMES Honey locust, ironwood, Texas ironwood, algarroba, honeypod
GROWS North and South America
HEIGHT 20–40ft (6–13m)
TRUNK DIAMETER Up to 1ft 8in (0.5m)
SPECIFIC GRAVITY .80
TYPICAL DRY WEIGHT 50lb/ft³ (800kg/m³)
POSSIBLE HEALTH RISKS Respiratory irritation and dermatitis

Seasoning Drying is quick and easy, because of the low moisture content of the heartwood. Staining from extractives, ring failure and honeycombing occur occasionally. Partially seasoned timber is fine for many kinds of utilitarian or decorative work, but for joinery or furniture components kiln-drying is advisable. It rarely needs rough-turning, except for precision items such as boxes.

Characteristics The sapwood can be creamy-yellow or pinkish-white, and varies in thickness. The heartwood is variable in colour, and shows a very strong contrast between earlywood and latewood in the annual rings: summerwood is orange-brown or red-brown, while the softer springwood is a soft yellow-orange. The grain is normally straight but can be uneven, and is sometimes wavy or curly. Wood with narrow growth rings has a more uniform texture. It is a great wood for furniture or joinery, but also very suitable for decorative and utilitarian wares. It's a shame that many turners don't fully explore softwoods.

Sharp bevel-rubbing tools are essential for a good finish. Scrapers, or tools which are less than sharp, will result in tearout or a woolly surface. This wood can be carved and routed – an option that is rarely explored on turned work.

It sands well, but the abrasive is liable to clog and, because the wood is soft, sanding may create hollows if you do not keep moving. It accepts surface finishes and oils and waxes well, but may require many coats of a surface finish to avoid patchiness.

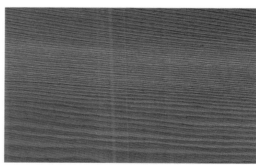

Douglas fir
Pseudotsuga menziesii

OTHER NAMES Blue Douglas fir, Oregon pine, British Columbian pine; also Colorado, Oregon, Rocky Mountain Douglas fir
GROWS Canada and USA; also introduced to New Zealand, Australia and parts of Europe
HEIGHT 80–200ft (24–60m) or more
TRUNK DIAMETER 2–5ft (0.6–1.5m)
SPECIFIC GRAVITY .53
TYPICAL DRY WEIGHT 33lb/ft³ (530kg/m³)
POSSIBLE HEALTH RISKS, Dermatitis, nasal cancer, rhinitis, respiratory problems; splinters may become septic

WAX FINISH

Muninga

Pterocarpus angolensis

OTHER NAMES Mninga, bloodwood, brown African padauk, mukwa, kiaat, kajat, ambila

GROWS Angola, Botswana, Namibia, Zimbabwe, Zambia, South Africa, Tanzania, Congo

HEIGHT 40–60ft (12–18m)

TRUNK DIAMETER 1ft 4in–2ft 6in (0.4–0.75m) or wider

SPECIFIC GRAVITY .62

TYPICAL DRY WEIGHT 39lb/ft³ (620kg/m³)

POSSIBLE HEALTH RISKS Sawdust can cause dermatitis, nasal irritation and bronchial asthma

Seasoning The wood dries easily with almost no degrade. Projects requiring precision and stability need rough-turning, but most items can be turned from partially seasoned stock. Furniture and joinery parts and decorative turning are all suitable uses.

Characteristics This is a dense, heavy and hard wood. The greyish-yellow sapwood is distinct from the heartwood, which ranges from a soft, honeyed golden-brown through a rich reddish-chocolate colour to a deep red or violet-brown with dark purple-brown or reddish irregular streaks. The grain can be straight or interlocking, with a medium texture. It sometimes exhibits mottled, striped or wavy figuring. Occasionally there are small white spots in the wood.

This attractive wood is not one of the easiest to work. A fair amount of dust is produced. The edges are brittle and can break out. Tearout is likely on endgrain or interlocking grain: use scrapers very carefully and with a freshly honed edge. Bevel-rubbing tools give the best finish, but need a slow, deliberate, delicate cut with a freshly sharpened tool. Power carving and routing give good results. Natural-edge work shows off the contrast between heartwood and sapwood to the fullest.

The wood sands well, but you should wet-sand only if there is no sapwood present. It readily accepts surface or penetrative finishes, and can be taken to a very high polish. The results are well worth the care that needs to be taken when working with this wood.

Andaman padauk

Pterocarpus dalbergioides

OTHER NAMES Padauk, Andaman redwood, maidon, vermilion wood

GROWS Andaman Islands

HEIGHT 80–120ft (25–37m)

TRUNK DIAMETER 3–5ft (0.9–1.5m)

SPECIFIC GRAVITY .77

TYPICAL DRY WEIGHT 48lb/ft³ (770kg/m³)

POSSIBLE HEALTH RISKS Sawdust may cause itching, swollen eyelids, nasal irritation and vomiting

Seasoning It can be air- or kiln-dried with little danger of degrade, but may occasionally warp or split. It is available in large sizes, in boards or predimensioned blanks. Projects can be turned to completion from wet or part-seasoned pieces, but will move a little; or they can be rough-turned and set aside to stabilize further.

Characteristics With its rich, luxuriant colours, this is the prima donna of all the padauks. It is also the slowest to lose its fresh-cut vibrancy. The heartwood ranges from a deep, honeyed orange-red to a darker, rich red-brown, with darker streaks of red, brown, violet or black. It ages to a deep, rich red-brown. The narrow sapwood is off-white or yellow-grey. Natural-edge work will show off the sapwood–heartwood contrast to the fullest. The wood has a waxy or oily feel, but not as much as olive (*Olea europaea*) or cocobolo (*Dalbergia retusa*). The irregular, interlocked or wavy grain produces a ribbon, roe or curly figure. It has a fairly coarse, uniform texture.

The interlocking, irregular grain can be a problem, but slow, deliberate cuts with freshly sharpened edges should give good results. Bevel-rubbing tools produce the best surface. Scrapers have to be sharp minimize grain tearout. A lot of fine, sticky dust may be produced. Power carving and routing present no problems. It sands satisfactorily – though it will readily clog abrasives – and accepts finishes well.

Seasoning Dries quite slowly with hardly any degrade; red wood takes longer than yellow. Very stable in use. Responds well to wet-turning, but does not move excessively; burrs, however, move unpredictably. Can be rough-turned and set aside for further seasoning. When using burr wood, coat the rough-turned piece with PVA.

Characteristics Heartwood ranges from light yellow through golden-yellow to brick red, darkening quickly on exposure. Sapwood is a light straw colour. Amboyna from Cagayan in the Philippines is typically harder, heavier and has a darker, blood-red colour. The figure can be mottled, fiddleback, curly or rippled. Quartersawn wood can have a ribbon figure, and flame may appear on flatsawn surfaces. The burr form is highly sought-after and commands extremely high prices. The shavings are reported to turn water fluorescent blue.

Endgrain tearout is likely unless you are turning the piece wet. Scraping works reasonably well, but be careful of the endgrain. Burr timber tends not to tear out, although the tightly clustered knots may cause problems in old, dry wood, which produces a lot of dust. Freshly seasoned amboyna burr works more easily than plain wood; turned wet, it distorts to create wonderful 'organic' shapes. Amboyna can hold quite fine detail, and carves and routs well.

Abrasives clog quite quickly; sand gently to avoid heat-checking. Amboyna takes finishes well and can be brought to a high lustre.

Amboyna
Pterocarpus indicus

OTHER NAMES Philippines or Solomons padauk, Papua New Guinea rosewood, yaya sa, narra, red narra, yellow narra, sena, angsena
GROWS East Indies
HEIGHT 130ft (40m)
TRUNK DIAMETER 3ft (1m)
SPECIFIC GRAVITY .66
TYPICAL DRY WEIGHT 41lb/ft³ (660kg/m³)
POSSIBLE HEALTH RISKS Dermatitis, asthma and nausea

Seasoning Dries with almost no degrade, apart from a risk of surface checking. Turning to completion from wet or part-seasoned wood is an option, as is rough-turning and setting it aside to season, depending on the project.

Characteristics Burma padauk is hard, heavy and dense. The heartwood ranges from a light, soft orange-red to deep, rich coppery-red, sometimes with dark lines when freshly cut. It changes colour considerably on exposure, becoming a rich, honeyed orange-brown. The narrow sapwood is a creamy off-white. The grain is usually interlocked, with a moderately coarse to medium texture. When quartersawn, it may display a ribbon-striped figure.

This wood should be worked in the same way as Andaman padauk (*P. dalbergioides*). However, Burma padauk can be a bit brittle and there is a risk of the edges fracturing or splintering if a heavy-handed cut is made, so be careful and make slow, deliberate cuts. This wood also produces a fine, sticky dust during turning. Like the Andaman padauk, it carves and routs well. It sands and finishes well, but suffers from quite a lot of colour degrade over time.

Burma padauk
Pterocarpus macrocarpus

OTHER NAMES Pradoo, mai pradoo, pterocarpus
GROWS Myanmar (Burma), Laos, Philippines, Thailand, Vietnam
HEIGHT 80ft (24m)
TRUNK DIAMETER 2–3ft (0.6–0.9m) or more
SPECIFIC GRAVITY .85
TYPICAL DRY WEIGHT 53lb/ft³ (850kg/m³)
POSSIBLE HEALTH RISKS Dermatitis, asthma and nasal irritation

STEAMED

Pear

Pyrus communis

OTHER NAMES Common pear, pearwood, peartree, wild pear, choke pear
GROWS UK and mainland Europe, western Asia and USA
HEIGHT 30–40ft (9–12m)
TRUNK DIAMETER 1–2ft (0.3–0.6m)
SPECIFIC GRAVITY .70
TYPICAL DRY WEIGHT 44lb/ft³ (700kg/m³)
POSSIBLE HEALTH RISKS Not known

Seasoning This wood is slow-drying and may warp if not weighted down. Gentle kiln-drying is recommended; air-drying will most likely result in splitting. It is stable once dry. Pear can either be rough-turned and set aside to season further, or wet-turned to completion. Wet-turned pieces can sometimes distort quite a lot.

Characteristics The heartwood can range from light pinkish-cream through soft orange-red to pale pinkish-brown; steaming produces a more intense pink. Steamed pear eventually mellows to a soft coffee-brown; unsteamed wood ages to a creamy coffee colour. This dense wood has a very fine, even texture and can hold intricate detail; it is used for the endgrain blocks used in wood engraving, and for netsuke. The grain is usually straight. On quartersawn surfaces a mottled figure may sometimes be present. It rarely forms burrs. The roots are sometimes large enough to turn but suffer badly from splitting and cell collapse during drying. This is a wonderful wood to turn, wet or dry. It generally cuts best with gouge or skew; abrasive may not be needed. Scrapers produce an acceptable surface with a little endgrain tearout on dry wood and some woolliness on the endgrain of wet wood.

Dry sanding without due care may cause heat-checks. Pear readily accepts both surface and penetrative finishes and is a favourite choice for ebonizing.

American red oak

Quercus rubra

OTHER NAMES Red oak, northern red oak, grey oak, Canadian red oak; also sold with southern red oak or Spanish oak (*Q. falcata*) as 'red oak'
GROWS Eastern Canada and USA; also Iran, Europe and UK
HEIGHT 60–90ft (18–27m)
TRUNK DIAMETER 3ft (1m)
SPECIFIC GRAVITY .77
TYPICAL DRY WEIGHT 48lb/ft³ (770kg/m³)
POSSIBLE HEALTH RISKS Asthma, sneezing, eye and nose irritation, nasal cancer

Seasoning The wood dries slowly and is quite difficult to season. Endgrain checking, ring failure, honeycombing and iron stains are distinctly possible. The project being tackled will dictate whether wet, partially or fully seasoned wood is required. Rough-turning is recommended if you want accuracy and minimal future movement.

Characteristics The heartwood has a tan to mid-reddish-brown colour. Red oak is not dissimilar to white oak (*Q. alba* and other species), but is a little more pinkish-red in colour and has smaller rays, which results in a less pronounced figure. The grain is usually straight and open, but can vary. It generally has a coarse texture, but this also varies. The sapwood is off-white to light brown. This hard, heavy wood has a slight blunting effect on saws, but a bigger effect on turning tools, so frequent sharpening is necessary. It is available in large sizes, suitable for a wide range of projects.

It behaves and cuts in the same manner as *Q. alba*, although I find the latter nicer to work. If a very smooth surface finish is required, the grain will have to be filled before the application of a surface or penetrative finish – it takes both readily.

Seasoning The wood of this garden tree is not sold commercially, but can sometimes be had from tree surgeons. It is easy to air-dry, and not prone to cracks or other defects. Once dried, the sticky exudation from between bark and wood ceases. If left in the round, there is a risk of end-splitting, so sealing the ends after dimensioning is a must. Pieces can be wet-turned to completion, or rough-turned and set aside to season.

Characteristics This lovely wood has the greenest colour of any timber I know. The heartwood is a greenish orange-brown or honey-yellow; the dramatically contrasting sapwood is narrow and creamy-white. The wood is light, soft and brittle, with visible growth rings and ring pores. Sadly, it fades to a deeper brown, but retains the green tinge.

The wood cuts best wet or partially seasoned; use sharp bevel-rubbing tools followed by abrasive. Dry wood can be dusty, and is prone to tearout, especially with scrapers. The central pith is soft, but it is hard to avoid using it since the wood only comes in small sizes. Put a few drops of cyanoacrylate (superglue) on it; once this is hard, the pith can safely be turned.

When sanding, keep the abrasive moving: if you linger, hollows will form. The wood shows every scratch, so sand carefully and do not skip grades. It will heat-check if too much heat is generated. It readily takes surface and penetrative finishes, and can be brought to a high polish.

Staghorn sumac
Rhus typhina

OTHER NAMES Sumac, hairy sumac, velvet sumac, American sumac, vinegar tree; the name may also be spelt **sumach**
GROWS USA, UK and parts of mainland Europe
HEIGHT Up to 40ft (12m)
TRUNK DIAMETER 1ft (0.3m)
SPECIFIC GRAVITY .45
TYPICAL DRY WEIGHT 34lb/ft³ (545kg/m³)
POSSIBLE HEALTH RISKS Not known

Seasoning Primavera dries easily with little degrade, but there may be some warping and checking. For joinery or furniture parts, it can be turned to completion from kiln-dried wood. It can be worked from wet or partially seasoned stock, but expect a small amount of movement. It responds well to rough-turning and setting aside to season before finish-turning.

Characteristics This pleasant-looking timber is used a lot in joinery and cabinetmaking, but it is also a delightful wood for decorative turning. It can be carved as well. It starts off a soft buttery-cream colour, darkening on exposure to a reddish honey colour with streaks of pink, orange, red and various shades of brown. It can have straight, interlocked or wavy grain, and may have a good ribbon, mottle, roey or narrow fiddleback figure. The wood has a medium to coarse texture.

It is a light wood that cuts well with gouges and skews, but not so well with scrapers, which can tear out the grain, especially when it is interlocking or wavy. The wood is quite soft, holds quite fine detail, can be routed and carved. It is easy to sand and finish, though grain-filling may be needed if you require a very smooth surface.

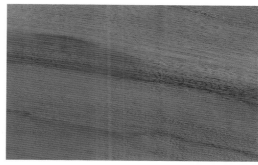

Primavera
Roseodendron donnell-smithii, syn. *Tabebuia donnell-smithii*

OTHER NAMES Duranga, San Juan, palo blanco, cortez, cortez blanco, roble
GROWS Central America
HEIGHT 75–100ft (23–30m)
TRUNK DIAMETER 2–3ft (0.6–0.9m) or more
SPECIFIC GRAVITY .45
TYPICAL DRY WEIGHT 28lb/ft³ (450kg/m³)
POSSIBLE HEALTH RISKS Not known

Willow

Salix spp.

OTHER NAMES Black willow, swamp willow, Gooding willow, Dudley willow (*S. nigra*); white or common willow (*S. alba*); cricket-bat willow (*S. alba* var. *coerulea*); crack willow (*S. fragilis*)

GROWS Europe, western and central Asia North Africa, North America

HEIGHT 70–90ft (21–27m)

TRUNK DIAMETER 3–4ft (0.9–1.2m)

SPECIFIC GRAVITY .45

TYPICAL DRY WEIGHT 28lb/ft³ (450kg/m³)

POSSIBLE HEALTH RISKS Sensitizer. Those who are allergic to aspirin may be allergic to willow

Seasoning This wood may warp during seasoning if care is not taken. Crack willow (*S. fragilis*) can split badly when drying. All species are liable to retain pockets of moisture. The wood can be turned to completion when wet or partially seasoned; expect a fair amount of movement, which can be exploited to good effect. Seasoned wood, especially when kiln-dried, can be turned with only a little movement – unless it is highly figured, in which case a lot of distortion may occur. For accurate work I favour rough-turning and setting aside to season, leaving extra wall thickness to allow for movement.

Characteristics This is quite a lightweight timber. Willow in general has a creamy-white sapwood with a creamy, pink-tinged heartwood. Black willow's heartwood varies from reddish-tan to silvery-brown, and the sapwood is creamy-red or light fawn. The grain is usually straight, but can be interlocked, and the wood has a uniform texture. It can at times exhibit a wonderful mottled figuring.

Willow turns rather like poplar (*Populus* spp.). It is light in weight and marks readily. It cuts best with very sharp gouges and skews, used with a delicate, slow cut; even so, a woolly surface may result, especially on wet wood. After shaping with these tools, go straight to abrasives to remove minor blemishes. Scrapers will create a woolly surface that requires a lot of abrasive work to get clean. Willow can be carved and routed satisfactorily when dry. It sands and finishes well.

American sassafras

Sassafras officinale and *S. albidum*

OTHER NAMES Red sassafras, saxifrax tree, black ash golden elm, cinnamon wood, aguetree

GROWS Eastern USA

HEIGHT 40–90ft (12–27m)

TRUNK DIAMETER 2–5ft (0.6–1.5m)

SPECIFIC GRAVITY .45

TYPICAL DRY WEIGHT 28lb/ft³ (450kg/m³)

POSSIBLE HEALTH RISKS Skin and respiratory irritation; possibly carcinogenic

Seasoning It requires care in drying as it tends to check slightly, but it can be kiln- or air-dried. It can be turned to completion from wet or partially seasoned stock if movement is acceptable, or rough-turned and set aside to season further for precision items such as boxes. Kilned stock is fine for joinery or furniture parts.

Characteristics This is a very pleasant, aromatic timber. The heartwood is light brown when freshly cut, darkening to a matt, coppery red-brown. The narrow sapwood is yellowish-white. The wood has a coarse texture and the grain is generally straight, but it can be a bit brittle. It is quite a soft timber. The grain figuring is often compared to that of white ash (*Fraxinus americana*), and it has quite a pleasant smell. It can be used for cabinetmaking, joinery, decorative and utilitarian turning.

This is a pleasant wood to turn. I would recommend using bevel-rubbing tools first, then skipping scrapers – which will tear the grain – and going straight to abrasives to remove any blemishes. The wood is capable of holding reasonable detail and can be carved and routed if you would like to explore these elements. Do keep the abrasive moving, to avoid creating unwanted hollows. The wood sands and finishes well, readily accepting surface and penetrative finishes.

Seasoning Tamboti seasons well if dried slowly. I have only been able to obtain air-dried pieces, some of which were quite wet and required further seasoning. It can be turned wet or partially seasoned to completion, and moves only a little. It also responds well to rough-turning and setting aside to season, but because of its oil content this takes a fair while – longer than ash or oak (*Fraxinus, Quercus* spp.), for instance. Coat the rough-turned piece with PVA to even out the drying and minimize splitting – I had a few failures before I tried this.

Characteristics This beautiful wood is heavy, dense and richly coloured. The heartwood has bands of light and dark reddish, honeyed browns. The narrow sapwood is a light, creamy butter colour – a truly lovely mix. The grain is generally straight but can be interlocked and wavy. It is capable of holding quite fine detail.

I only use this wood for decorative items and find that it cuts well with all tools, but there is a fair amount of oily dust produced during the cut and when sanding, so good extraction is a must. A good finish straight off the tool is possible, provided very sharp tools are used with a slow, deliberate cut. Frequent sharpening will be necessary. It sands satisfactorily, but clogs the abrasive quickly and is prone to heat-checking. It finishes well.

Tamboti
Spirostachys africana,
syn. *Excoecaria africana*

OTHER NAMES Tambooti, African sandalwood
GROWS Southern and eastern Africa
HEIGHT 50ft (15m)
TRUNK DIAMETER 2ft (0.6m)
SPECIFIC GRAVITY .80
TYPICAL DRY WEIGHT 50lb/ft³ (800kg/m³)
POSSIBLE HEALTH RISKS Bark exudes a sticky sap that is highly irritant to skin and eyes, but this is removed when timber is dimensioned. Wood can cause severe skin irritation. It taints food when used as a cooking fuel

---

Seasoning This wood is difficult to season without checking: if left in the round, it will split badly. It is best to cut along the centre of the log, seal the ends with sealant or PVA and leave it to season. Alternatively the wood can be turned wet, using a thin, even wall thickness; or rough-turned and set aside to season, again using PVA to retard moisture loss. Even so, there will be a high failure rate, so I prefer to turn wet or part-seasoned wood to completion.

Characteristics A member of the olive family (*Oleaceae*), lilac is a shrub that grows to the size of a small tree. It is not sold commercially, but may be obtained from someone who is removing it from the garden. The narrow sapwood is pale cream with visible growth rings, very pleasant to look at and to work. The heartwood is a creamy, buttery colour with pinkish-violet streaks; it has a fine, uniform grain and texture. The central pith can be soft; you may need to avoid it altogether, or you could stabilize it with cyanoacrylate (superglue). Lilac carves well and is easy to work with bevel-rubbing tools; less so with scrapers. It sands satisfactorily, but watch out for heat-checking. It accepts finishes readily. The wood has a sweet, pleasant smell reminiscent of the tree's fragrant flowers. Sadly, the sizes available limit its use to small items.

Lilac
Syringa vulgaris

OTHER NAMES Not known
GROWS Europe, Asia, northern USA
HEIGHT 10–15ft (3–4.5m) on average
TRUNK DIAMETER 3–6in (75–150mm)
SPECIFIC GRAVITY .72
TYPICAL DRY WEIGHT 45lb/ft³ (720kg/m³)
POSSIBLE HEALTH RISKS Not known

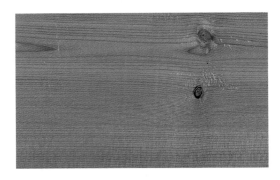

Pacific yew

Taxus brevifolia

OTHER NAMES Yew, western yew

GROWS Western North America from southern Alaska to California

HEIGHT 20–40ft (6–12m)

TRUNK DIAMETER 12–15in (0.3–0.4m)

SPECIFIC GRAVITY .62

TYPICAL DRY WEIGHT 39lb/ft³ (620kg/m³)

POSSIBLE HEALTH RISKS Avoid inhaling dust: this has been shown to cause swelling, and skin or nasal sensitivity in some people

Seasoning Slow drying is essential to reduce the risk of serious shakes. Endgrain should be sealed; this applies to boards as well as rough-turned pieces. The wood responds well to turning from either a wet or a part-seasoned state; it can also be rough-turned. The bark is thin and can be incorporated into the design.

Characteristics The heartwood goes from a light orange to orange-brown or red-brown, and is clearly distinct from the narrow, creamy off-white sapwood. It has a close, fine grain and an even texture, and is capable of holding fine detail. This wood can form wonderful burrs (burls) which vary in figure from small clusters of pips to areas of swirling grain, showing a variety of colours from orange-tan to reds, purples and browns. It can be used for furniture and joinery components as well as decorative or utilitarian wares. Like European yew (*T. baccata*), it may be inadvisable for items in contact with food.

It is easier and more pleasant to work than European yew: it usually has straighter grain and is less prone to endgrain tearout. A good finish is achieved with bevel-rubbing tools, but scrapers give variable results. Old wood produces a fair amount of dust. Routing and power-carving techniques work on this wood. It can heat-check when sanding on endgrain, so be careful; otherwise it sands well as long as you don't skip grades, and takes finishes readily.

Teak

Tectona grandis

OTHER NAMES Burma teak

GROWS India, Myanmar (Burma), Thailand, Vietnam; plantations in other tropical countries

HEIGHT up to 150ft (45m)

TRUNK DIAMETER 6–8ft (1.8–2.4m)

SPECIFIC GRAVITY .65

TYPICAL DRY WEIGHT 40lb/ft³ (650kg/m³)

POSSIBLE HEALTH RISKS Dermatitis, conjunctivitis, irritation to nose and throat, swelling of the scrotum, nausea and over-sensitivity to light

Seasoning Teak kiln-dries and air-dries well. Furniture or joinery parts can be made from kiln-dried stock. Part-seasoned material can be used, but items that need to maintain their shape are best rough-turned and set aside to season.

Characteristics The heartwood is honey-brown or reddish-brown, sometimes with dark markings, and darkens considerably on exposure. The sapwood is a pale, creamy yellow-brown, and can be narrow or medium width. The grain is usually straight but sometimes wavy or interlocking, giving an attractive figure.

The texture is rather coarse and uneven, and it has an oily or waxy feel. Straight-grained wood carves well. Silica deposits, visible as white or grey flecks, can have a severe blunting effect on tools.

Teak will cut well and produce a fine surface on one project, and on another it will rip the edges off tools as though you were rubbing them on cement. Wavy or irregular grain can tear out easily. That said, in the main it is relatively easy to work with sharp tools. Scrapers will not produce as clean a surface as gouges or skews. Lots of fine, oily, noxious dust is produced, more when working with very dry or old wood. It can be routed and carved. When sanded, it heat-checks on endgrain if too much heat is produced, and it readily clogs abrasives. The wood's oily nature means that some surface finishes do not bond well; wiping over with solvent first should help. It can be finished with oils and waxes.

Seasoning The wood is liable to surface checks, splits and warping. Slow drying reduces degrade. It can be turned to completion partially seasoned, but will move. It may be worked kiln-dry for joinery or cabinetmaking purposes, but rough-turning is also an option.

Characteristics The pinkish sapwood is clearly differentiated from the heartwood, which varies from reddish light or mid-brown with fine dark streaks, to a dark burnt umber with darker bands or streaks. The grain is usually fairly straight, but often interlocked or irregular. The texture is coarse to medium. Quartersawn timber can have an attractive figure. It is harder and denser than teak (*Tectona grandis*). It produces a dirty dust which may contain minute splinters. It is brittle and prone to chipping at the edges; it blunts tools severely, and interlocking grain is very likely to tear out. Partially seasoned wood cuts a little more easily, with less dust, than kiln-dried wood; however, it will move more once turned – not much more, but too much for boxes or platters.

Many writers claim that it is easy to turn, but that is not my experience. The best cuts are made with sharp bevel-rubbing tools, but it does scrape satisfactorily if a very light touch is used. It routs well and can be carved successfully with power-carving tools – hand tools take much longer. Abrasives clog quite quickly but a good finish can be obtained. Oils add some extra warmth to the colour.

Indian laurel

Terminalia alata, T. coriacea, T. crenulata, T. elliptica, syn. *T. tomentosa*

OTHER NAMES Taukkyan, asna, cay, hanta, neang, mutti, sain
GROWS India, Myanmar (Burma), Bangladesh and Pakistan
HEIGHT 100ft (30m)
TRUNK DIAMETER 3ft (1m)
SPECIFIC GRAVITY .86
TYPICAL DRY WEIGHT 53lb/ft³ (860kg/m³)
POSSIBLE HEALTH RISKS Dust can be an irritant

Seasoning The wood dries rapidly and can distort. Slow kilning minimizes degrade, but it can also be turned to completion wet or from partially seasoned stock; conversely it can be rough-turned and set aside to season further.

Characteristics European lime is denser than basswood, and holds finer detail; but for turning purposes there is little to choose between them. Lime is probably better known as a carving timber, for which it is superb. Though plain to look at, its subtle colour and figure are very effective when a clean, fresh look is required so as not to overwhelm the form. The wood is initially a soft, creamy pale yellow or uniform off-white to pinkish-tan, but ages eventually to a uniform light golden-brown. The grain is usually straight but sometimes irregular, with a fine and uniform texture; generally there is little or no figure, but it can display a ripple or mottled figure at times. Lime can also form burrs (burls); those I have encountered were of a tight, pippy cluster formation. The sapwood looks similar to the heartwood.

This wood cuts well with sharp skews and gouges; less so with scrapers, which can create a woolly surface unless you slow down the rate of traverse and make a shear cut. It can be turned wet or dry readily. It holds fine detail, but marks easily. Lime sands well, but be careful not to sand hollows in the work or destroy fine detail. It accepts finishes of all types well.

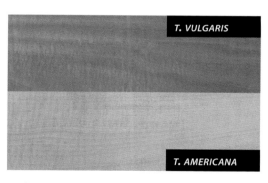

T. VULGARIS

T. AMERICANA

Lime and basswood

Tilia vulgaris and *T. americana*

OTHER NAMES Linden (*T. vulgaris*); American lime, American whitewood, American linden (*T. americana*)
GROWS Europe, including UK (*T. vulgaris*); eastern Canada and USA (*T. americana*)
HEIGHT 80–100ft (25–30m)
TRUNK DIAMETER Up to 4ft (1.2m)
SPECIFIC GRAVITY .54 (*T. vulgaris*); .41 (*T. americana*)
TYPICAL DRY WEIGHT 34lb/ft³ (540kg/m³) (*T. vulgaris*); 26lb/ft³ (410kg/m³) (*T. americana*)
POSSIBLE HEALTH RISKS Not known

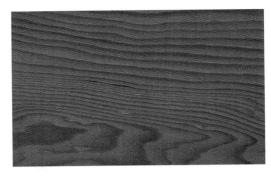

Western hemlock

Tsuga heterophylla

OTHER NAMES Pacific hemlock, British
Columbian hemlock, west coast hemlock,
hemlock spruce, Alaska pine
GROWS Western Canada and USA, UK, China
and Japan
HEIGHT 100–150ft (30–46m)
TRUNK DIAMETER 3–4ft (0.9–1.2m)
SPECIFIC GRAVITY .50
TYPICAL DRY WEIGHT 31lb/ft³ (500kg/m³)
POSSIBLE HEALTH RISKS Bronchial problems,
rhinitis, dermatitis, eczema, possibly nasal cancer

Seasoning Hemlock dries slowly but well. Possible problems include
shakes, uneven moisture content, iron stains and warping; when kiln-
dried, there may be fine surface checks. Kiln-dried timber is fine for
most of the projects this wood is used for: furniture and joinery parts,
or utilitarian work.

Characteristics Hemlock is a softwood. The sapwood is around
3–5in (75–125mm) thick and looks similar to the heartwood, which
is creamy-tan to pale golden-brown. Latewood areas are darker and
exhibit hues of pinkish-orange, violet or rose-tan.

An attractive bold growth-ring figure is likely to be present on
plainsawn surfaces. There may also be dark streaks caused by maggots,
known as 'bird pecks'. The grain is normally straight and even, with a
medium to fine texture.

The wood cuts cleanly with very sharp gouges and skews. Do not be
tempted to use scrapers unless you are willing to accept a torn surface,
or are prepared to spend a lot of time sanding. After turning with
bevel-rubbing tools, go straight to abrasives to remove minor blemishes.

Hemlock is typically used for stair spindles, table legs and other
spindle-turning projects, but can be explored more fully for faceplate
work. It routs well, can be carved satisfactorily if the detail is not too
fine, and sands and finishes well.

American elm

Ulmus americana

OTHER NAMES Elm, American white elm,
Florida elm, soft elm, water elm. There are six
species of elm in North America with similar
characteristics
GROWS Canada and USA
HEIGHT 100ft (30m)
TRUNK DIAMETER 2–4ft (0.6–1.2m)
SPECIFIC GRAVITY .56
TYPICAL DRY WEIGHT 35lb/ft³ (560kg/m³)
POSSIBLE HEALTH RISKS Dermatitis; dust is an
irritant to nose and eyes

Seasoning It may warp or twist during seasoning, sometimes
severely if dried too quickly; ring failure can also occur, but splitting is
unlikely. If drying in a kiln, keep temperatures low. Depending on the
project, it can be turned to completion using wet, part-seasoned or kiln-
dried wood. Rough-turning and setting aside to dry is recommended
for projects where accuracy is needed.

Characteristics This is a pleasant wood to look at and to work.
It is not as showy in colour or figuring as English or wych elm
(*U. procera, U. glabra*), but has a more subtle, mellow appearance
which I find attractive. The heartwood is light silver-brown, tan or
mid-brown, with hints of red. The wide sapwood is a light silvery-
brown or reddish-brown. The grain can be straight or irregular and
occasionally exhibits figuring. The texture is coarse. American elm
is great for joinery and furniture, as well as utilitarian and decorative
turned items.

Its working qualities are much the same as for English elm, though
it is a little softer and scrapers can leave a woolly surface. It can be
turned wet or dry without any major problems. Carving and routing are
options to explore when working with dry timber. Some surface finishes
may require multiple coats to ensure an even appearance. Oils and
waxes, however, seem to work fine.

Seasoning This wood dries fairly rapidly and successfully, but can distort unless it is dried with closely spaced stickering. It can be turned to completion using wet or part-seasoned stock. Kiln-dried stock will be fine for most joinery and cabinetmaking situations, but rough-turning and setting it aside to season further is essential when very stable timber is required.

Characteristics This is a very pretty species of elm. The heartwood is light to mid-umber, with a greenish tinge or green streaking. The amount of green varies considerably, as does the colour. The sapwood is pale and distinct from the heartwood when freshly cut. The grain of the wood is usually straight, with a medium texture; it is usually finer and straighter than English elm (*U. procera*). The tree sometimes forms burrs, and the wood can also exhibit an attractive figure if the grain is crossed or interlocking.

The wood responds to turning in the same way as English elm. It can be turned wet or dry easily and holds reasonable detail. Carving and routing are possibilities worth considering.

Applying surface and penetrative finishes should not present you with any problems.

Wych elm
Ulmus glabra

OTHER NAMES Elm, mountain elm, white elm, Scots elm, Scotch elm, Irish leamhan
GROWS UK (north and west), Ireland, Europe, western Asia
HEIGHT 130ft (40m)
TRUNK DIAMETER 5ft (1.5m)
SPECIFIC GRAVITY .67
TYPICAL DRY WEIGHT 42lb/ft³ (670kg/m³)
POSSIBLE HEALTH RISKS Dermatitis, nasal cancer; dust can be an irritant

Seasoning The wood dries rapidly, with a likelihood of distortion, checks, splits and cell collapse. When rough-turning, allow an extra ¼in (6mm) of wall thickness per 12in (300mm) diameter, especially when using burrs. Alternatively, turn it to completion while wet, choosing a shape that will be enhanced by subsequent movement.

Characteristics The heartwood is soft tan to reddish-brown, ageing to a rich, deep reddish-brown; the sapwood is not used. Elm is a medium to lightweight wood, somewhat coarse in texture, with prominent annual rings; it has a wonderful pattern of irregular and cross grain and an attractive speckled or feathery texture. It carves well.

It is available in large sections. However, following the severe outbreak of Dutch elm disease in the 1970s, the supply of mature trees is now very limited. Elm burrs are highly prized and expensive.

Slow, deliberate cuts with sharp tools will cope with the contorted grain. There is a moderate risk of endgrain tearout. Skew chisels may have trouble with the grain; gouges cut well. Scrapers may 'pull' the endgrain or cross grain; shear-scraping is the better option.

Elm sands well by dry or wet methods, and accepts both surface and penetrative finishes. The grain can be filled if desired with a proprietary grain filler, or a coat of sanding sealer followed by successive coats of a surface finish such as cellulose, cut back between coats.

English elm
Ulmus procera

OTHER NAMES Elm, nave elm, red elm
GROWS Northern Europe including UK
HEIGHT 80ft (24m)
TRUNK DIAMETER 3ft (0.9m)
SPECIFIC GRAVITY .55
TYPICAL DRY WEIGHT 34lb/ft³ (550kg/m³)
POSSIBLE HEALTH RISKS Dermatitis, irritation to nose and throat, nasal cancer

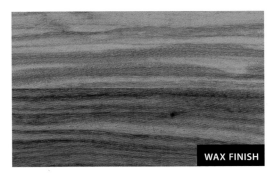

WAX FINISH

Xylia

Xylia torreana

OTHER NAMES Hairy sand ash, Zambesi ash, n'calala, n'cala

GROWS Southeast and southern Africa

HEIGHT 20–50ft (6–15m)

TRUNK DIAMETER 1–2 ft (0.3–0.6m)

SPECIFIC GRAVITY 1.10

TYPICAL DRY WEIGHT 63lb/ft³ (1010kg/m³)

POSSIBLE HEALTH RISKS Not known

Seasoning Checking and splitting are likely on the ends of boards and blanks – even when end-sealed – if dried too fast. Either rough-turn – coating the endgrain with PVA to slow the moisture loss – and set aside to dry before re-turning, or turn from start to finish with a nice thin, even wall. In the latter case there may be significant movement, but not enough to create wildly warped 'organic' forms.

Characteristics This attractive timber has creamy-yellow to creamy-tan sapwood, and heartwood that varies in the same piece from light orangey or red-brown, russet, deep reddish brown, and even deep blackish red-brown, with distinct lighter curly bands. It has a medium-fine to fine texture with interlocked grain. This is a nice wood to turn, as long as you keep your tools sharp; it takes quite fine detail and doesn't present any major issues with either bevel-rubbing tools or scrapers, although the latter will slightly fluff up the endgrain or interlocking grain if the wood is damp when turned. Any grain plucking on dry wood is minute and easily sanded out. It is nice to carve and rout, and I have had no problems with gluing it, or applying penetrative or surface finishes.

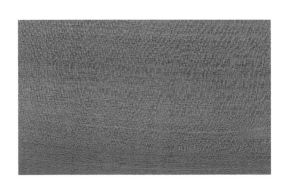

West Indian satinwood

Zanthoxylum flavum, syn. *Fagara flava*

OTHER NAMES Jamaican satinwood, aceitillo, espinillo, yellow sanders, yellow wood, yellowheart

GROWS Caribbean, and southern Florida, USA

HEIGHT 40ft (12m)

TRUNK DIAMETER 1ft 3in–1ft 8in (0.4–0.5m)

SPECIFIC GRAVITY .73

TYPICAL DRY WEIGHT 45lb/ft³ (730kg/m³)

POSSIBLE HEALTH RISKS Dermatitis

Seasoning This is a slow-drying wood. I have only been able to obtain air-dried sections, which moved a little when turned, just enough to be noticeable on bowls, platters and boxes. No movement occurred on items that were rough-turned and allowed to season, but some developed surface checks. Coating rough-turned pieces with PVA greatly reduces surface checking.

Characteristics The sapwood darkens from the bark until it merges with the heartwood, which is a light buttery colour at first, darkening to a pale orange or honeyed tan. The grain is typically interlocked or irregular, with a fine, even texture and a high lustre. There may be a roey or mottle figure.

This dense, heavy wood has a moderate blunting effect on tools. It can hold fine detail, but parts of it may be brittle, so take care with the edges of work as well as features such as beads, fillets and coves. It cuts well with sharp tools and a slow, deliberate cut. Scrapers should be freshly sharpened and used only with very light cuts to minimize tearout, which is likely on endgrain. The wood can be power-carved and routed to good effect, but be careful when sanding: it is prone to heat-checking, but apart from that it sands well. A fine dust is produced which has quite a pleasant smell. It readily accepts both surface and penetrative finishes, and can be taken to a high polish if required.

Further Reading

The Australian Timber Buyer's Guide
(Rozelle, NSW: Skills Publishing, 1994)
ISBN 0 646 18096 7

Bishop, Peter, *100 Woods: A Guide to Popular Timbers of the World*
(Marlborough, Wilts.: Crowood Press, 1999)
ISBN-10: 1861268475
ISBN-13: 978-1861268471

Flynn, James H., Jr, and Holder, Charles D. (eds.),
A Guide to Useful Woods of the World, 2nd edn.
(Madison, WI: Forest Products Society, 2001)
ISBN 1 892529 15 7

Hoadley, R. Bruce, *Identifying Wood: Accurate Results with Simple Tools*
(Newtown, CT: Taunton, 1990)
ISBN 0 942391 04 7

Hoadley, R. Bruce, *Understanding Wood: A Craftsman's Guide to Wood Technology* (Newtown, CT: Taunton, 2000)
ISBN 1 56158 358 8

O'Donnell, Michael, *Turning Green Wood*
(Lewes, East Sussex: GMC Publications, 2000)
ISBN 1 86108 089 1

Porter, Terry, *Wood: Identification & Use*
(Lewes, East Sussex: GMC Publications, 2004)
ISBN 1 86108 377 7

Raffan, Richard, *Turned-Bowl Design*
(Newtown, CT: Taunton, 1987)
ISBN 0 918804 82 5

Wood and How to Dry it: The Best of Fine Woodworking *Magazine*
(Newtown, CT: Taunton, 1986)
ISBN 0 918804 54 X

The Wood Database (October 2015) (www.wood-database.com)
ISBN-10: 098224603X
ISBN-13: 978-0982246030

Remember also that the Internet can be a great source of information regarding timbers, drying and seasoning, finishing and project ideas. There are many official sources of up-to-date information regarding the status of particular timbers, but here are three that are well worth keeping an eye on:

- International Union for the Conservation of Nature (IUCN) Red List of Threatened Species **www.iucnredlist.org**

- Convention on International Trade in Endangered Species (CITES) **www.checklist.cites.org**

- Forest Stewardship Council **www.fsc-uk.org**

Other useful websites
The Plant List
www.theplantlist.org

Catalogue of Life
www.catalogueoflife.org

For information on toxic woods
www.hse.gov.uk/pubns/wis30.pdf
www.ubeaut.com.au/badwood.htm
www.woodbin.com/ref/wood-toxicity-table/
www.uic.edu/sph/glakes/harts1/HARTS_library/woodchrt.txt
www.dmwoodworkers.org/images/NonImage/General/WoodToxicity.pdf
www.statelinewoodturners.com/Toxicwood_article.html

Acknowledgements

Thanks again to: Walter Hall, Alan Holtham, John Hunnex, John Jordan, Ray Key, Mike Mahoney, Bert Marsh and his family, Binh Pho, Terry Porter, Joey Richardson, Steven Russell, Neil Scobie and family, Chris Stott, Curt Theobald and Chris West for their much-valued assistance in supplying pictures and information, or for allowing examples of their work to be included.

I would like to thank the following people for helping me to obtain the relevant timbers for this book:

David Bates of Stiles & Bates
www.stilesandbates.co.uk

Kirk Boulton of Exotic Hardwoods
www.exotichardwoodsukltd.com

Dave Green of Turners Retreat
www.craft-supplies.co.uk

Peter Hemsley of The Toolpost
www.toolpost.co.uk

Simon Hope of Hope Woodturning
www.hopewoodturning.co.uk

David Mounstevens of Yandles & Sons Ltd
www.yandles.co.uk

Darrel Nish of Craft Supplies USA
www.woodturnerscatalog.com

Ken Southall of the International Wood Collectors Society
www.woodcollectors.org

Rob Wilson of Dalmann UK
www.dalmannuk.com

My thanks to Stephen Haynes, the book's editor. It was a pleasure working with him on the first edition of this book and I am very glad to have the privilege of his working with me on this edition. His diligence and patience have been greatly appreciated.

My grateful thanks to Sara Harper, Senior Project Editor, for her patience and ever-present smile, even when I was pushing my luck with deadlines, and for keeping everything on track.

Thanks to Chloë Alexander for her hard work in designing this book.

Photographic credits

All photographs in this book are by Anthony Bailey and Mark Baker, © GMC Publications Ltd 2004 and 2016, with the following exceptions: Mark Baker: pp. 6, 11, 12, 21; Walter Hall: p. 87 (top); Alan Holtham: pp. 20 (top centre), 21 (bottom left, bottom left/centre), 22 (bottom left and right), 24 (top right, top centre), 27 (top R), 29 (top) 30 (top L); John Hunnex: pp. 45 (bottom centre), 105; John Jordan: front cover (centre right), back cover, p. 20 (bottom centre), 31 (right), 33, 40 (bottom right); 45 (top), 66, 67 (bottom), 77 (top), 85, 103, 106, 107 (top); Ray Key: 49 (bottom), 54 (top), 57 (bottom right), 58, 71, 77, 81 (top), 95 (top), 115 (both); Raymond Llewellyn/Shutterstock: p. 9; Mike Mahoney: 39, 41 (bottom), 45 (bottom left); 79 (bottom), 99, 107 (bottom); Bert Marsh: pp. 55 (bottom), 62, 63, 65, 69, 70, 73, 75 (top), 89 (top), 97, 119, 120, 150 (red mallee), 177 (lilac); Binh Pho: p.41 (top); Joey Richardson: p.27 (bottom), 42 (bottom right), 87 (bottom); Steven Russell: p. 135 (pecan); Neil Scobie: p. 28 (top); Chris Stott: p.67 (top), 83 (left), 95 (bottom), 105 (top); Curt Theobald: front cover (centre left), 31 (top), 89 (bottom); Chris West: p.26 (top right).

About the author

Mark Baker has always been fascinated by timber. The ability to work with such a wonderful medium and to create something that will be admired is fantastic, despite the occasional frustrations that arise in the design and making process.

Mark loves exploring the different woods, shapes, surface enhancement and experimenting in his work and readily admits that not everything goes to plan, but comments that this is all part of the fun. His work is very much influenced by the ancient world and you can see elements of ancient Rome, Greece, Asia and the trade routes through the continents in his turnings.

On leaving school, Mark worked as a carpenter and joiner for five years. He then helped set up a training centre with a fully equipped woodworking workshop for autistic adults. He was an instructor there for eight years before going on to be a product manager for a well-known Sheffield-based tool manufacturer. From there he was head-hunted to become editor of *Woodturning* magazine and, in addition, he is also the Group editor of the magazine woodworking group, which includes the Woodworkers Institute website – Europe's largest woodworking website resource.

Mark demonstrates internationally and has also written the following books, all published by GMC:

Turned Toys
ISBN-13: 978-1-78494-065-2

Woodturning Projects: A Workshop Guide to Shapes
ISBN-13: 9781861083913

Woodturning: A Craftsman's Guide
ISBN-13: 9781861088499

Weekend Woodturning Projects: 12 Designs to Build Your Skills
ISBN-13: 9781861089229

Index of botanical names

Index of common names

To order a book, or to request a catalogue, contact:
GMC Publications Ltd
Castle Place, 166 High Street, Lewes, East Sussex, BN7 1XU, United Kingdom
Tel: +44 (0)1273 488005
www.gmcbooks.com